"The apostle Paul has always been a hero whom I loo[k?] [...] unrelenting faithfulness in the worst kinds of trials is a [...] and missionary. In the midst of suffering, hardship, an[d ...] [...]ment or his own friends and fellow workers, Paul remained steadfast, dynamic, and utterly devoted to Christ. This invaluable study of Paul's life from Rob Ventura and Jeremy Walker is a wonderful, powerful, soul-stirring examination of Paul's self-sacrifice and his unfaltering service to the church. It will both motivate and encourage you, especially if you're facing trials, opposition, or discouragement in your service for Christ."

—John MacArthur, *Pastor/Teacher of Grace Community Church in Sun Valley, California and President of The Master's College and Seminary*

"Rob Ventura and Jeremy Walker's *A Portrait of Paul* is biblically sound, pointedly practical, and sagaciously simple. In addition to an exposition of Colossians 1:24–2:5, they provide the reader with a host of citations from other pertinent texts of Scripture as well as judicious quotes from past and contemporary authors, all of which help to trace out the contours of Paul's life and ministry. Each chapter concludes with practical applications directed both to fellow pastors (or aspiring pastors) and also to fellow Christians. I heartily recommend this book to anyone who would seek to imitate Paul as Paul sought to imitate Christ."

—Robert R. Gonzales Jr., *Academic Dean and Professor of Biblical Studies, Reformed Baptist Seminary*

"The greatest need in churches today is for godly men to shepherd the flock of God. No church will rise any higher than the level of its spiritual leaders. Like priest, like people. To this end, Rob Ventura and Jeremy Walker have done an exceptional job in providing a model for pastoral ministry, drawn from the extraordinary example of the apostle Paul. This book is built upon careful exegesis, proper interpretation, penetrating insight, and challenging application. Herein is profiled the kind of minister every church so desperately needs and what every *true* minister should desire to become."

—Steven J. Lawson, *Senior Pastor of Christ Fellowship Baptist Church in Mobile, Alabama*

"In this dual-authored portrait of Paul as a minister of the gospel, Ventura and Walker have captured the very essence of ministry. On every page, we are forced to reflect upon the dimensions of apostolic ministry and urged to comply. Packed with exposition and application of the finest sort, these pages urge gospel-focused, Christ-centered, God-exalting, Spirit-empowered, self-denying ministry. I warmly recommend it."

—Derek W. H. Thomas, *John Richards Professor of Theology, Reformed Theological Seminary, Jackson, Mississippi*

"This work on the Christian ministry is a clarion call to true devotion and piety in the pastorate. The theology is pure and the language is as powerful as it is beautiful. I pray that every pastor and congregant might take up this book and read it. It will hold a place in my library beside Baxter's *Reformed Pastor*, Bridges's *Christian Ministry*, and Spurgeon's *Lectures*. I will refer to it often. It will serve as a great antidote against all that might cause my heart to stray from Christ's call."

—Paul Washer, *Director of HeartCry Missionary Society*

"What is *A Portrait of Paul: Identifying a True Minister of Christ*? It is, first, the effort of two young pastors to teach themselves and their churches what it means to be a true minister of Christ. It is, second, an exposition of Colossians 1:24–2:5 which attempts to understand how Paul's ministry gives them and their churches a paradigm of faithful ministry. It is, third, biblical exposition of Scripture in the best historic and Reformed tradition with careful exegesis, sound doctrine, popular appeal, and practical application. As such, it is a challenging book to read as Rob and Jeremy lay before us, for instance, the selflessness and suffering true ministry requires. It is, however, a good, useful, and profitable book to read. It can, and I hope it will, do much good!"

—Sam Waldron, *Academic Dean and Professor of Systematic Theology, Midwest Center for Theological Studies*

"When I first sensed God's call to the preaching ministry, I did a study of the life and ministry of the apostle Paul. And, oh, what a study that was! It opened my eyes to the difference between ministry in the New Testament and what is in vogue today. Rob Ventura and Jeremy Walker have now brought all of those truths that I saw into this one volume. I, therefore, commend this book to all who want to take God's call to the work of ministry seriously. For, in these pages, is the heart and experience of a true minister of the new covenant."

—Conrad Mbewe, *Pastor of Kabwata Baptist Church in Lusaka, Zambia*

"As the diverse churches of the world have demonstrated throughout history, there is no better place to turn, when confronted with the complexities of pastoral leadership, than the Scriptures. Each church in each generation must revisit this resource and view it anew through its particular historical, theological, cultural and political lens. The authors of *A Portrait of Paul* engage precisely in this task. With Colossians as their main laboratory, they probe the text and engage Paul in a conversation about pastoral ministry—its priorities, foundation, and potential—and a profile of pastoral mission and leadership emerges. All who read this book will discover an invitation to join this rich conversation and take away numerous fresh perspectives to challenge and shape their thinking."

—Philip H. Towner, *Dean of the Nida Institute for Biblical Scholarship at the American Bible Society*

"What Walker and Ventura have done in this splendid book is to return to the fountainhead of Christianity, to the apostle Paul with the authority the Lord Christ gave to him, his wisdom and compassion, and examine the apostle's relationship with one congregation, how he advised and exhorted them concerning the demands of discipleship and their relationship with fellow believers. Paul became Christ's servant and mouthpiece to them and he has left us with a timeless inspired example. He exhorted his readers more than once to be followers of him as he followed God. With a refreshing contemporary style, and with humble submission to the Scripture, these two ministers have given to us a role model for pastoral life. This is a very helpful book and a means of grace to me."

—Geoff Thomas, *Pastor of Alfred Place Baptist Church in Aberystwyth, Wales*

A Portrait of Paul

A Portrait of Paul

Identifying a True Minister of Christ

Rob Ventura and Jeremy Walker

Reformation Heritage Books
Grand Rapids, Michigan

A Portrait of Paul
©2010 by Rob Ventura and Jeremy Walker

Reformation Heritage Books
2965 Leonard St., NE
Grand Rapids, MI 49525
616–977–0889 / Fax 616–285–3246
orders@heritagebooks.org
www.heritagebooks.org

Printed in the United States of America
10 11 12 13 14 15/10 9 8 7 6 5 4 3 2 1

Library of Congress Cataloging-in-Publication Data

Ventura, Rob.
 A portrait of Paul : identifying a true minister of Christ / Rob Ventura and Jeremy Walker.
   p. cm.
 ISBN 978-1-60178-090-4
 1. Paul, the Apostle, Saint. I. Walker, Jeremy (Jeremy R.), 1975- II. Title. III. Title: Identifying a true minister of Christ.
 BS2506.3.V46 2010
 225.9'2—dc22
 ⧽ 6534 83686   2010032473

For additional Reformed literature, both new and used, request a free book list from Reformation Heritage Books at the above mailing or e-mail address.

CONTENTS

FOREWORD

Have you ever wondered what the gospel ministry should be like? Or what kind of minister your church should look for? If you are a minister, have you ever established in your own mind what the ideal and pathos of an apostolic pattern of ministry should look and feel like?

Other than our Lord Jesus Himself, there is no better representative in the Scriptures than the apostle Paul for visualizing the gospel ministry. In numerous letters, Paul makes himself and his ministry stunningly vulnerable. Repeatedly, he sets before us not only the origin, essence, and goal of his ministry, but also its joys, hardships, conflicts, and warnings. Paul allows us not only to view his daily work but also opens up his mind and soul in an amazing way.

In this gripping, well-written book, Rob Ventura and Jeremy Walker mine the riches of Paul, showing us the mind, heart, and life of a genuine minister who is on fire for the glory of God, the growth of believers, the establishment of Christ's church, and the salvation of the lost. No minister can read this book without being profoundly convicted of his shortcomings and deeply moved to aspire to more faithful ministry. No church member can read this book without acquiring a better understanding of what a minister should be and without being stirred up to pray for his pastor, or, in the case of a pulpit and pastoral vacancy, for finding the kind of pastor these pages so vividly display.

Having taught in pastoral ministry for twenty-five years at a seminary level, I have never read a book that so powerfully presents a Christ-centered model for biblical ministry as *A Portrait of Paul*. Books, seminaries, and experience all play an invaluable role in preparing a man for the ministry, but this book affirms, with John Newton, that "none but He who made the world can make a minister." After you read this book, you will understand Charles Spurgeon, who said, "Do not be a minister if you can help it," as well as Thomas Watson, who said, "The ministry is the most honorable employment in the world. Jesus Christ has graced this calling by His entering into it." You will also understand what my father said to me after I was called to the ministry: "To serve as a minister of Jesus Christ is a more important calling than living in the White House."

A Portrait of Paul is a great book that should serve as required reading in an introductory course on Christian ministry. Every minister should own a copy and read it. Laypeople should also read it to understand their pastor and ministry of all kinds in the church of Jesus Christ.

May God use this book in a mighty way to stir pastors and laypeople to fervency of heart for the church as the bride of Jesus Christ and for the amazing calling of pastoral ministry. Let us all pray daily for Word-based, God-fearing, Christ-exalting, sober-minded ministers to fill this needy earth with sound preaching, holy lives, and loving pastoral counsel—ministers whose very lives are transcripts of their sermons. This is the crying need of the universal church and of the world today.

—Joel R. Beeke

PREFACE

Rob Ventura

As a new pastor entering full-time ministry, I had been asking myself, "What kind of minister am I going to be?" and "What type of ministry do I want to pursue in the church where I labor?" While preaching a series of consecutive expository sermons from the book of Colossians 1:24 to 2:5, I found the main answers to my questions and thought that what I had learned from God's Word would be helpful to others. After seeking counsel from several trusted men, I was encouraged to write this book.

In studying this section of Colossians, I was utterly struck and extremely challenged by the life and labors of the apostle Paul and became convinced that he portrays an outstanding model for biblical ministry. For churches seeking men to fill their pulpits, he serves as an excellent example of the sort of man churches should pursue. For the gospel minister, he provides an excellent picture of what the man of God must strive to be by God's grace.

The Puritan Thomas Brooks once said, "Example is the most powerful rhetoric." I believe that he was right. My prayer is that God Almighty would be pleased to use this book to be a rich blessing and help to all who read it. May the Lord Jesus Christ, who is head of the church, be praised in all things.

Jeremy Walker

In the kindness of God, I was preaching through Colossians at a time when I was also asking some significant questions about my calling and sphere of ministry. As I dug deep into Paul's convictions expressed and exemplified in his dealings with the Colossians, I was taught, reproved, corrected, and instructed in righteousness. Studying through this passage in Colossians 1 and 2 helped to clarify and confirm my own convictions immeasurably.

In a sermon on Acts 13:49, entitled "Gospel Missions," the inimitable Charles Haddon Spurgeon sent out a call for apostolic men to go about their work in an apostolic style backed up by apostolic churches and under an apostolic influence of the Holy Spirit.[1] We might not agree with every nuance of Spurgeon's understanding, but surely this is the crying need of our day, certainly in the Western church. Paul models the kind of minister of God's grace in Christ that I wish to be, God enabling me. Paul's apostolic zeal, faith, love, endeavor, sacrifice, and purpose as preacher and pastor are sadly lacking in my own experience, and we have few consistently exemplary ministers today who hold up this standard.

I had no intention or expectation that this meditating and preaching process would bear fruit in the form of a book. When Rob first contacted me, he had been preaching through Colossians at a faster pace than I and had already begun to consider publishing something on this epistle. When he asked me to author the book with him, I tentatively agreed.

Unlike Paul, I fear that I cannot readily point to myself as a pattern of genuinely Christlike ministry. But I can point to Christ, and I can point to what there is of Christ in Paul. Insofar as we have been faithful to the text of God's Word, my sincere desire and hope is that those who read this volume with a Berean spirit (Acts 17:11) will agree that in the apostle Paul, a true minister of Jesus Christ, we see a man who can and should be emulated, imitating him as far as he also imitated Christ (1 Cor. 11:1).

---

1. "Gospel Missions" in *The New Park Street Pulpit*, 3 vols. (1892; repr., Grand Rapids: Baker, 1994), 2:177–84.

Acknowledgments

Rob Ventura

The old adage says, "Many hands make light work." This is certainly true concerning the book that you now hold in your hands. God in His good providence brought together a solid group of men to work with me on this project; I believe without them this book would not have been completed. I thank them all very much. I must mention three men first.

Jeremy Walker, my co-author. To be honest, Jeremy wrote the greater portion of this book. He took my material, cleaned it up, added much of his own material, wrote chapters of his own, and made this book what it is today. Brother, it has been a great blessing to work with you.

Jack Buckley, my co-pastor. Jack reviewed and corrected my initial rough drafts. I am very thankful, dear brother, for all of your help. Your contributions to this book on many different levels have played a huge part.

Rob Freire. Rob, your excellent editing of this project and insightful comments before it went over to the publisher have been fantastic. Thank you so much for all the time that you have spent to see this book come to completion.

There are two other men that I want to mention who are directly connected to this project. Dr. Robert Burrelli and Michael Ives read the final draft and made some wonderful suggestions. Thanks so much for all of your help.

I want to thank the very dear congregation that I am privileged to pastor in Rhode Island, Grace Community Baptist Church. You all make it a joy to serve you in the Lord. I pray that what has been written in this book would always be true of me, for your good and for the glory, praise, and honor of our risen Redeemer, Jesus.

I would also like to give a special thanks to Dr. Joel R. Beeke and the entire staff at Reformation Heritage Books. Working with you has been a real joy to my soul.

There are others who have been a significant help to me over the years, either on a personal or pastoral level, whom I want to mention. I thank you all very much as well: Jim Domm, Ron Abrahamsen, the congregation of Englewood Baptist Church (New Jersey), Sean Isaacs, Greg Nichols, Dr. Sam Waldron, Albert N. Martin, Dr. William R. Downing, James Dolezal, Alfred Ventura, Jeff Ventura, Ivone Salka, Greg Salka, Gus Duner, David Wolfe, and Alberto Ramirez.

Finally, there is my beloved family, my wife and three children. You all mean so much to me. I thank God for you and love you all very much.

I dedicate this book to the loving memory of Pastor Sherwood B. Becker, my former co-pastor, who went to glory April 19, 2009. How thankful I am to God that throughout his fifty-three years of pastoral ministry he remained a true minister of Jesus Christ.

Soli Deo Gloria

Jeremy Walker

I am grateful for Rob Ventura's drive and diligence, which have kept this project (and his fellow author) on the road where I might have dawdled and daydreamed. Rob had an idea, a team, and a deadline, and he drove them all like Jehu. Without Rob, you would not be reading this book now. Rob is a publisher's rose-tinted dream and a co-author's smiling nightmare.

I want most of all to express my thanks to God for the men who have been faithful examples and patient mentors to me as I have begun learning what it means to be a true-hearted undershepherd in the service of Jesus Christ, not least among whom is my father. Some of those men are long dead, but through books and memories they continue to speak. To those who remain: thank you, fathers and brothers. I trust that you know who you are; your investment in me I cannot repay.

My thanks are also due to my wife, who is a priceless encouragement and help to me in pursuing the ideals set out in this book.

Who now rejoice in my sufferings for you, and fill up that which is behind of the afflictions of Christ in my flesh for his body's sake, which is the church: whereof I am made a minister, according to the dispensation of God which is given to me for you, to fulfil the word of God; even the mystery which hath been hid from ages and from generations, but now is made manifest to his saints: to whom God would make known what is the riches of the glory of this mystery among the Gentiles; which is Christ in you, the hope of glory: whom we preach, warning every man, and teaching every man in all wisdom; that we may present every man perfect in Christ Jesus: whereunto I also labour, striving according to his working, which worketh in me mightily. For I would that ye knew what great conflict I have for you, and for them at Laodicea, and for as many as have not seen my face in the flesh; that their hearts might be comforted, being knit together in love, and unto all riches of the full assurance of understanding, to the acknowledgement of the mystery of God, and of the Father, and of Christ; in whom are hid all the treasures of wisdom and knowledge. And this I say, lest any man should beguile you with enticing words. For though I be absent in the flesh, yet am I with you in the spirit, joying and beholding your order, and the stedfastness of your faith in Christ.

— the Apostle Paul, Colossians 1:24–2:5

Would I describe a preacher, such as Paul,
Were he on earth, would hear, approve, and own—
Paul should himself direct me. I would trace
His master strokes, and draw from his design.
I would express him simple, grave, sincere;
In doctrine uncorrupt; in language plain,
And plain in manner; decent, solemn, chaste
And natural in gesture; much impressed
Himself, as conscious of his awful charge,
And anxious mainly that the flock he feeds
May feel it too; affectionate in look,
And tender in address, as well becomes
A messenger of grace to guilty men.

—William Cowper, *The Task*, book II, lines 395–407

INTRODUCTION

Finding faithful pastors is one of the most difficult tasks facing Christ's church. Any local church that conscientiously seeks to be biblical should understand the need to bring in and train up men that meet the biblical standard for ministers of the gospel. When the pastoral search begins, the applicant pool may appear to teem with possibilities. Annually, fresh crops of seminary graduates seek respectable assignments, and many of these young men abound with big plans, optimism, and energy. Occasionally, more experienced ministers become available, men who range from battle proven to battle broken. Who will be chosen? Which man is best for your church? Sorting through all the options and finally calling the right person takes considerable effort, sanctified discernment, and earnest prayer.

Is there an ideal pastor? There is one: His name is Jesus Christ. He sets the standard for all who would follow in His footsteps. But do not forget the interwoven and full-orbed perfections of the Lord Jesus: no one was gentler than He or consumed with such holy zeal. No one spoke with such tenderness to those in genuine need or with more bite to those who bitterly opposed the will of God. He was a true friend of sinners and a fierce enemy of hypocrites. He could call a child to Himself and embrace him; He could make a whip of cords and drive thugs from the temple of God. He was loved with profound attachment by His friends; He was hated with deep loathing by His enemies. At times thousands hung upon His words; He died a deserted and forsaken man.

Those who follow in the footsteps of a crucified Christ partake of His character, though always imperfectly. Would you want such a man to shepherd you?

Suppose someone were to suggest a man with a reputation for stirring up trouble, although he has seen many people converted. Wherever he goes, he seems to divide opinion. He is often run out of town before he seems to make much progress, sometimes causing riots and disturbances. Sometimes he is so quick to stir up antagonism that he cannot avoid a beating, and his body bears witness to the bruising he has borne. He would be ugly even without those scars and is a powerful, though not an overly polished, speaker. He is a regular troubler of the civil and religious authorities and has the jail record to prove it. He struggles with several chronic health conditions, sometimes being completely, albeit temporarily, debilitated by them. He is not always easy to work with, and some of his companions have gone their separate ways; in fact, some of those with whom he has worked are not even walking with Jesus any longer. He is in many respects a driven man, full of energy and with no appetite for the status quo, always unsettling things and people. When there is tension in his relationship with a church, he will write letters dealing with their faults and defending his own calling and reputation. Despite the fruits of his ministry, he has left no megachurches behind him, but rather small groups of faithful men and women.

If you instinctively back away from the idea of considering such a man as a pastor and preacher, consider this: you would be in danger of the great folly of rejecting the apostle Paul. You could hardly make a worse decision.

This raises fundamental questions: How do we recognize true ministers of Christ? How do we assess faithful pastoral labors? Far too often, our criteria are merely natural and often subjective. We look at the trappings. We seek corporate or even carnal measures of success. How many converts does he have? How big was his last congregation? Is he well liked by the media? What are his academic credentials? Is he respected across the religious spectrum? How many missionaries does his church support? How many conferences does he speak at? Is he a nice guy?

But we also must think beyond the pastoral search. Recognizing true ministers of Christ also applies when evaluating *existing* ministries. How many pulpits today are trampled down by intruders, by those who have run but were never sent by God (Jer. 23:21)? Or, how many ministers need serious personal reformation in order to conform to the biblical standard of ministry? What effects do such people have upon the churches they serve? Are they not a deadly blight upon the household of faith (2 Peter 2:12–17)?

Many churches endure substandard and even crippling ministries, as though God has nothing to say on the matter. However, God is far from silent. He sets forth His objective and essential qualifications for gospel ministers in His Word (1 Tim. 3:1–7; Titus 1:5–9; 1 Peter 5:1–4). Not content with that, God also fleshes out these credentials in the biblical portraits of faithful ministers— apostles and others. These men of God who meet the divine standard are a blessing to His people. Conversely, imposters are a curse to them.

So what does a true pastor look like? What constitutes a faithful ministry? How can we identify the life and labors of one called by God to serve in the church of Jesus Christ? To address these questions, we will turn to the first chapter of Paul's letter to the Colossians and focus on the end of that chapter, a section in which the apostle describes his pastoral relation to the people of God in Colosse.

In the church at Colosse, Jesus Christ's supremacy was being assaulted. Epaphras, one of the church's faithful and earnest ministers, had traveled the long road to Rome to consult with the imprisoned apostle about the false teaching that was beginning to seep into the church. He had described to Paul the situation in Colosse, the things that were being taught, and the effect that they were having. From his prison cell, the apostle wrote back to the church to provide an antidote for the false teaching to which they were being subjected. There is almost endless debate about the precise nature of "the Colossian heresy" and its particular elements. However, while the diagnosis may be difficult, the symptoms were apparent. One thing in particular is plain: the errorists of Colosse were undermining Christ's centrality and robbing Him of His supremacy.

These false teachers were very persuasive (Col. 2:4): they did not immediately deny Christ; rather, they set out to devalue and ultimately to dethrone Him. They did not absolutely refuse and reject the Lord, but rather undermined Him. Their heresy was not explosive, but erosive and corrosive. The saints in the church at Colosse were hearing this poisonous whisper: "Christ is not enough!"

The errorists were suggesting to the saints that there was something else, something different, something more that was required in order to enjoy all the fullness of salvation. Alongside of Christ, and therefore ultimately against Him, they were advocating philosophy and human tradition (Col. 2:8), religious ritual (v. 16), the mysticism of angelic worship (v. 18), the asceticism of a self-imposed religion (vv. 20–23)—in fact, just the kind of things that you will find promoted as the paths to peace with God in the "Spirituality and Religion" section of most major modern bookstores.

The apostle Paul would have none of this. He knew that all we need for life and salvation is bound up in the person and work of God's Son, the Lord Jesus Christ. For in Him alone "dwelleth all the fulness of the Godhead bodily. And ye are complete in him, which is the head of all principality and power"

(Col. 2:9–10). As the commentator Robert Hawker says, Paul "well knew, that the most effectual way, under God the Spirit's teaching, to establish the Church in *the faith once delivered unto the saints*, must be, in holding up to their view, the Person and glories of Jesus. And, it must be confessed, that he hath done it in this Epistle, most blessedly."[1]

Engaging the false teachers and defending against their assault on Christ and His church, Paul's solution is at once simple, brilliant, and comprehensive. He provides a rich and full exposition of Christ's person and work, weaving a stunning tapestry in which the present realities of redemption in Christ are set forth. In Colossians 1:15–22 he makes several bold assertions concerning the preeminence of the Lord Jesus, who is supreme in His person (v. 15a), in creation (vv. 15b–17), in the church (vv. 18–19), and in reconciliation (vv. 20–22). God's beloved Son is the head of the first and the new creations, and the one in whom God has brought all things into submission to Himself. In light of this, Paul argues that nothing needs to be or can be added to the Lord Jesus' completely sufficient person and work. Christ alone is to be trusted, loved, worshiped, and followed above all others as the one in whom all saving fullness is found and enjoyed.

Having laid this vital foundation, Paul must next dismantle the particular errors that are current among the Colossian Christians. Emphasizing that he is a minister of the very gospel by which they have been saved (Col. 1:23), he then opens his heart and gives them and us the servant perspective that governs his endeavors. He wants them to be able to recognize a true God-ordained ministry. He accomplishes this by describing his own life and labors. These would appear in sharp contrast with those of the errorists who were seeking to deceive them (Col. 2:4). Why should the Colossians listen to Paul and not to the self-appointed gurus? Because he was a true, God-appointed servant of Christ (Col. 1:1), and the others were not. But how were they to discern between a true man of God and a counterfeit? How were they to tell the genuine from the imposter, the shepherd from the thief or mere hireling (John 10:10, 13)?

In addressing these issues, Paul provides the church in Colosse with a mini-manual for ministry. He demonstrates that there is a full and precise correspondence between the plan of God for the church and the aim of a faithful servant of Christ: what God wills, the preacher sets out to accomplish. Colossians 1:24 through 2:5 is a distinct unit of thought in which the apostle discloses several

---

1. *The Poor Man's New Testament Commentary* (Birmingham, AL: Solid Ground Christian Books, n.d.), 3:36.

distinguishing marks that characterize a biblically faithful minister and ministry, and it is these distinctives that we will address in the chapters of this book.

We agree with R. C. Lucas, who says, "It was important for the Colossians, as it is for us, to have some standards by which to measure the claims people make for themselves, and by which true spiritual leadership may be known in the churches. The permanent value of this great passage is that it provides the church in every generation with just such a standard."[2]

Our humble prayer is that the Spirit of God will use this book to that great end. Our aim is to put in your hands a guide enabling you to understand and identify what a true minister of Christ looks like and how he lives and works. This book looks at the life and ministry of the apostle Paul, as set forth in Colossians 1:24 to 2:5, as a model and standard for the ministry of the Lord Christ. According to the Scriptures, spiritually healthy children of God should be part of a healthy local church and under the care of her undershepherds; this portrait of Paul will help you to make wise choices in every aspect of this vital matter. Here, churches looking for a pastor will find guidance in what a faithful man of God looks like. Christians looking for a church will find a tool by which they can assess the pastors of the flock in the light of God's Word, finding men to whom they can commit the care of their souls. Christians already in a church will be better equipped to pray for their pastors and will further understand what it really means to be shepherded by a man after God's own heart. Ministerial students pursuing the work of the ministry will see a picture of a man they should seek to imitate. Pastors and church planters—our brothers in this labor—will, like us, have to deal with sins and shortcomings but will also find here the model of a Christlike man, made competent by God's saving grace in Jesus for the work to which he was called, a man who stirs us up to pursue the high calling with which we have been called. We hope that by these means we might help to promote and encourage faithfulness to God in gospel ministry, encouraging and assisting men who seek to follow Paul, just as he also followed Christ (1 Cor. 11:1).

---

2. *The Message of Colossians and Philemon: Fullness and Freedom* (Downers Grove, IL: IVP, 1980), 67.

1 | THE JOY OF
PAUL'S MINISTRY

Who now rejoice in my sufferings . . .
— Colossians 1:24

Glory be to God for the furnace, the hammer, and the file. Heaven shall be all the fuller of bliss because we have been filled with anguish here below, and earth shall be better tilled because of our training in the school of adversity.[1]
— Charles Spurgeon

Most of us, most of the time, assume that suffering is a time of misery and grief. Few can testify in truth, "I now rejoice in my sufferings." And yet that is the sincere declaration of the apostle Paul. Joy, even in suffering, is a distinguishing mark of his character and ministry.

The nature of Paul's suffering

What are the sufferings to which Paul refers? They plainly include the sufferings connected with his imprisonment in Rome for preaching the gospel to the Gentiles. Twice Paul mentions his confinement in this letter: in Colossians 4:10 he refers to "Aristarchus my fellowprisoner," and later he calls upon the Colossians to remember his chains (4:18).

Paul is sitting bound in jail. Things are not looking good for him. No doubt he is uncertain about his future. And what does he say? He declares that even while experiencing this difficult trial, he now rejoices. His language tells us that his rejoicing was a present and ongoing experience, not in spite of his sufferings, but rather in them. The caged bird is singing! It would be one thing if Paul

---

1. Charles Spurgeon, "The Minister's Fainting Fits," in *Lectures to My Students* (Edinburgh: Banner of Truth, 2008), 191.

managed to rejoice at the onset of his troubles but then gradually sank into discouragement after having endured them for some time. That makes sense to us, and all too often reflects our own experience. But these are sufferings that are associated with Paul as a minister of Jesus Christ. It is not masochism ("I rejoice because I am suffering") or asceticism ("I rejoice in my self-imposed suffering") or stoicism ("I rejoice despite my sufferings"). It is a distinctively Christian response to what are, in this instance, distinctively Christian trials and tribulations: it is the joy of a gospel minister in the midst of the sufferings associated with his gospel ministry.

The life of a faithful minister involves suffering. False prophets often win the affection of men; truth speakers will incite evil speech from many. Our Lord warned His disciples, "Woe unto you, when all men shall speak well of you! for so did their fathers to the false prophets" (Luke 6:26). Paul's own call to ministry involved a declaration that he would suffer: "For I will shew him how great things he must suffer for my name's sake" (Acts 9:16). Again, before He died, Christ urged the disciples to "remember the word that I said unto you, The servant is not greater than his lord. If they have persecuted me, they will also persecute you; if they have kept my saying, they will keep yours also" (John 15:20). Paul himself warns Timothy that "all that will live godly in Christ Jesus shall suffer persecution" (2 Tim. 3:12).

Many of Paul's sufferings were in his body. Paul asked the Corinthians about the self-proclaimed "super-apostles" afflicting that church:

> Are they ministers of Christ? (I speak as a fool) I am more; in labours more abundant, in stripes above measure, in prisons more frequent, in deaths oft. Of the Jews five times received I forty stripes save one. Thrice was I beaten with rods, once was I stoned, thrice I suffered shipwreck, a night and a day I have been in the deep; in journeyings often, in perils of waters, in perils of robbers, in perils by mine own countrymen, in perils by the heathen, in perils in the city, in perils in the wilderness, in perils in the sea, in perils among false brethren; in weariness and painfulness, in watchings often, in hunger and thirst, in fastings often, in cold and nakedness. (2 Cor. 11:23–27)

At the same time, those Corinthian super-apostles spent much of their time insinuating and declaring all manner of falsehoods against the apostle, and Paul's own spiritual children were believing the lies (1 Cor. 4:15). His good was declared to be evil; his sacrifices were called expressions of his worthlessness; his gentleness was called weakness; his humility was called emptiness. He declared himself ready "very gladly [to] spend and be spent for you" and in the same breath delivered this sad testimony: "though the more abundantly I love you, the less I be loved" (2 Cor. 12:15). The Corinthians flung Paul's love and labors back in his face. There are few things that cause more agony for a minister of Christ than to pour out his soul on behalf of Christ's people, only to have his motives misinterpreted, all kinds of sin imputed to him, and his earnest entreaties and heartfelt efforts ignored, rejected, and even sometimes angrily despised and hurled back against him.

The apostle wrote to the Philippians of certain men who preached Christ from envy and strife as well as those who did so from goodwill. "The one," said Paul, "preach Christ of contention, not sincerely, supposing to add affliction to my bonds" (Phil. 1:15–16). While Paul's example of imprisonment for the sake of Jesus had encouraged some to boldness in their witness, some—and we are not sure of their exact identity—preached Christ from flawed motives, intending to undermine Paul's authority, trouble the church, unsettle Paul's soul, and generally aggravate his imprisonment in whatever ways they could. A spirit of faction dominates some who are preaching the Lord Jesus. And yet Paul rejoices and will rejoice that Christ is preached (Phil. 1:18).

Paul is troubled by the condition of the lost: "I say the truth in Christ, I lie not, my conscience also bearing me witness in the Holy Ghost, that I have great heaviness and continual sorrow in my heart. For I could wish that myself were accursed from Christ for my brethren, my kinsmen according to the flesh" (Rom. 9:1–3). This is the language of an abiding trial of soul in which he is constantly distressed by the spiritual condition of the great mass of his own nation. Even when Paul is necessarily opposed to foes of the gospel, he—like his Lord weeping over Jerusalem (Luke 13:34–35)—does so with tears: "For many walk, of whom I have told you often, and now tell you even weeping, that they are the enemies of the cross of Christ: whose end is destruction, whose God is their belly, and whose glory is in their shame, who mind earthly things" (Phil. 3:18–19). The lostness of the lost, including the present and future distresses of those who set themselves against the LORD and His Anointed (Ps. 2:2), cause the apostle genuine grief of soul.

In addition to the physical sufferings he endures, over and above the opposition he faces, loaded on top of the lies told about him, and added to his groaning over the lost, Paul writes of "that which cometh upon me daily, the care of all the churches" (2 Cor. 11:28). We must recognize here an underpinning reality. As an apostle, Paul had a right to be responsibly concerned for all the churches. This is not a right that extends to ministers today. To be certain, every Christian ought to have an abiding concern for the advance of Christ's kingdom in every place, but while there may be a similar duty of concern and prayer, there is no identical responsibility of leadership. A faithful pastor, under normal circumstances, ought to have his heart particularly engaged on behalf of the people over whom God has placed him and will know the burden of concern that weighs down his soul over the struggles, sins, trials, and difficulties that afflict the flock. Sitting under his ministry is a man wrestling with arrogance, lust, pride, anger, or bitterness. Also there is a woman who is grieving or proud or aggressive or gossiping or sometimes absent. This family is profoundly dysfunctional; these members are drifting away; those friends have not been seen for some time; that brother is sick; that sister is afflicted in soul; this falsehood has found a toehold in the congregation; this misunderstanding is dividing the brothers. How much care and prayer do these sorrows draw out of his soul? And yet, this is only his flock. He may and should be concerned at the rise of error on the broader scale. There may be brother ministers whose sorrows he shares and who share his sorrows. He may invest in the work of the kingdom on a broader scale through fraternals, conferences, preaching in other congregations, and the like. He may have a reputation for wisdom and find himself sought by others for counsel. And yet, for all that, he has no apostolic authority over multiple churches. He is answerable primarily for the health of the flock over which he has been appointed.

Now imagine that concern legitimately multiplied a hundred times. Imagine the tension between the profound joys and the profound distresses of a man answerable for so many congregations, the weariness of soul and the darkness of mind that sometimes would sweep across him. He is aware of packs of wolves circling many different flocks; he has responsibility to exhort and encourage other undershepherds; he receives letters and emissaries from various congregations bringing questions, bearing news, and seeking counsel. These things constantly demand his attention and lie upon his heart. Daily he feels the distracting anxiety of how things go in the churches for which he bears some responsibility, under God.

We might pause to ponder for a moment the heart of Christ. Here is one whose absolute concern is matched by absolute wisdom and power, who is never overburdened by the concern for all His redeemed that lies constantly upon His heart. He never ceases to pray for us with perfect insight and perfect awareness, offering up to His heavenly Father perfectly framed petitions for just those things that we need. Here is the great Shepherd of the sheep. While He is the confidence of all undershepherds, and they labor confident of His ability to bring all His sheep safely home (John 10:28–30), they—like Him—feel deeply the needs and concerns of the sheep.

Whether internal or external, whether on his own behalf or on behalf of others, the suffering of a servant of Christ is real and often brutal. However, the joy associated with such suffering is just as real and unusually sweet. When the apostles had been beaten and commanded not to speak in the name of Jesus, "they departed from the presence of the council, rejoicing that they were counted worthy to suffer shame for his name" (Acts 5:41). Peter also urged the saints that they "think it not strange concerning the fiery trial which is to try you, as though some strange thing happened unto you: but rejoice, inasmuch as ye are partakers of Christ's sufferings; that, when his glory shall be revealed, ye may be glad also with exceeding joy" (1 Peter 4:12–13). It is the distinctive character and circumstances of this suffering that enable Paul, the other apostles, and those who follow them to rejoice in those sufferings.

Paul's own response is grounded in a grasp of the truth, for doubtless the thought of Christ's glory and supremacy sustained him, together with a sense of his own gospel privileges and the honor of his ministry. It is grounded in humility, for there can be no rejoicing in the heart of a man who thinks he deserves far better than what he receives. It is grounded in a right recognition of the value of our sufferings, in the minister's identification with Christ Himself and in the purpose of the suffering that Christ has undergone and that he is experiencing. Neither is this statement from the apostle isolated. As we survey other Scriptures describing Paul's trials, we find that his rejoicing in the midst of difficulties was characteristic of his ministry.

The nature of Paul's joy

Consider what is recorded in Acts 16. It is midnight. Paul and his fellow laborer Silas are in a dark jail cell, their feet fastened in stocks. Earlier that day, they had been falsely accused of being great troublemakers and of teaching unlawful customs. They had been profoundly distressed by the activity and plight of a demon-possessed slave girl and had cast a spirit of divination out of her, thus depriving her masters of the profits they made through her fortune telling. Stirring up the crowd, the girl's wicked taskmasters incited the magistrates to convict and imprison the apostle and his companion. The judgment included a severe beating with rods: many stripes were laid on them before they were cast into the prison (Acts 16:23).

Paul and Silas sit unjustly condemned, their bodies bruised and bleeding. They are unable to move or to discover a position that will lessen the agony. They are locked in a foul prison alongside others who probably deserved to be there. If ever men had reason to resent such unjust treatment, they did. But as we peer through the bars on that night, what do we find? "And at midnight Paul and Silas prayed, and sang praises unto God: and the prisoners heard them" (Acts 16:25).

Paul did not succumb to the temptations presented by this trial. He did not doubt God or, worse, indict Him. He did not grumble. He was not planning a lawsuit against those who wronged him. Rather, we hear continual prayer being offered up to God. We hear hymns sung to their most worthy Lord, penetrating the cells of their fellow prisoners. Are these not expressions of true joy in the midst of brutal affliction? Says G. Campbell Morgan, "Any man can sing when the prison doors are open, and he is set free. The Christian's soul sings in prison."[2] The church father Tertullian is even blunter, asserting, "Nothing the limb feels in the stocks when the mind is in heaven."[3] Paul's response under these rigors tells us volumes about this man and bids us follow him as he also followed Christ (1 Cor. 11:1).

Or consider Paul's experience recorded in 2 Corinthians 12:7–10. Here we find Paul's disclosure of the thorn in his flesh:

> And lest I should be exalted above measure through the abundance of the revelations, there was given to me a thorn in the flesh, the messenger of Satan to buffet me, lest I should be exalted above measure. For this thing I besought the Lord thrice, that it might depart from me. And he said unto me, My grace is sufficient for thee: for my strength is made perfect in weakness. Most gladly therefore will I rather glory in my infirmities, that the power of Christ may rest upon me. Therefore I take pleasure in infirmities, in reproaches, in necessities, in persecutions, in distresses for Christ's sake: for when I am weak, then am I strong.

He described this particular grievance as "a messenger of Satan to buffet me." Portraying his trial in such terms, Paul was certainly not depicting some trifling inconvenience that was merely a nuisance to him but rather a source of profound distress. It is no wonder that the apostle pleaded with the Lord repeatedly that

---

2. Quoted in William MacDonald, *The Believer's Bible Commentary*, ed. Art Farstad (Nashville: Thomas Nelson, 1980), 1636.

3. Quoted in R. C. H. Lenski, *The Interpretation of the Acts of the Apostles* (Peabody, MA: Hendrickson Publishers, 2001), 672.

this thorn might depart from him. Using words found elsewhere in the context, Paul's various trials are further described as involving weakness, infirmities, reproaches, needs, persecutions, and distresses suffered for Christ's sake. Note also that Paul did not enjoy the suffering itself. Instead, he pleaded earnestly and repeatedly that the Lord would remove it from him.

But we ask again: what was Paul's disposition in the midst of this pummeling? We find a wholehearted trust in the sufficiency of God's grace and the manifestation of Christ's strength in Paul's weakness. In Charles Spurgeon's quaint language, we find Paul confident that Christ's ocean of grace is sufficient to fill the teaspoon of his human need (2 Cor. 12:9). We find Paul not mourning his lack of native strength but rather gladly boasting in his weakness because he knew that Christ would overrule that frailty with omnipotent power, that the apostle's weakness would provide a platform on which Jesus Christ would display His divine strength. We find Paul taking pleasure in his infirmities, not in the removing of them. The knowledge that when he is weak he is strong in Christ gives him great joy.

One might react strongly to the apostle: "Paul, have you lost your mind? You boast in your infirmities! You take pleasure in your needs! When you are weak, you are strong? What kind of nonsense is this?"

Yet, to use Paul's own words, he certainly is not mad but speaks "words of truth and soberness" (Acts 26:25). Is not the acknowledgment of weakness a prelude to seeking help? Is not the recognition of God's power, goodness, and faithfulness in Christ to His servants sufficient grounds to appeal for His mighty assistance in every good endeavor? Most assuredly, Paul is eminently sane!

Scripture gives us another example of this characteristic rejoicing in difficulty. Paul also wrote the letter to the Philippians from prison, and there we read: "Yea, and if I be offered upon the sacrifice and service of your faith, I joy, and rejoice with you all. For the same cause also do ye joy, and rejoice with me" (Phil. 2:17–18).

Paul has been pleading for true unity in the context of church life, a unity that will manifest itself in a biblical like-mindedness, self-sacrificing love, and a lowliness of mind that esteems others better than oneself. Our Lord Jesus Christ supremely exemplified such a mind. Though He is fully God, He is also fully man, yet without sin. If such a glorious person could take on the form of a bondservant and humble Himself, being obedient even to the extent of suffering His horrific death on the cross, how much more ought His creatures to walk in humble and universal obedience? With this standard, Paul implores his readers to obey God, to work out their own salvation with fear and trembling.

And he gives them reason to expect success, because God would be working in the believers both to will and to do for His good pleasure (Phil. 2:12–13). As an effective teacher, Paul then provides concrete examples. Complaining and disputing are not to be heard in any of their activities (Phil. 2:14). Rather, they are to sustain a tenacious hold on God's Word, which is to be the touchstone of all that they do (Phil. 2:16).

Such ongoing faithfulness to the Scriptures would be proof positive that Paul's labors among them were in fact successful. They would demonstrate that the sufferings he was enduring were not in vain but were being honored by God and used by Him to establish maturing believers who were healthy, functioning members of a local church.

How did Paul regard these trials that he endured as a true servant of Christ? Did they cause him to lose heart? Did his unrelenting difficulties and the prospect of execution pound him down to the point of hopeless discouragement? Did they squeeze bitter complaints or resentment from his lips? No, for as we see in Philippians 2:17, though the apostle was, as it were, being poured out as a drink offering on behalf of those to whom he ministered, he was glad and rejoiced in the midst of extremities that would have broken many a man.

We see from these examples that Paul's rejoicing in suffering was no unusual thing for him. Because Paul knew that God is sovereign, that He ordains each of his trials and works all things together for his good, Paul was joyful under duress (Rom. 8:28). This was a notable characteristic of his ministry.

We must ask again how Paul approached these trials. His rejoicing was neither a product of irrational optimism nor humanistic psychology. He did not play mind games with himself or others in some delusional denial of reality. He underwent his trials—pain and all—with his eyes wide open. In each situation, he sought Christ's aid, pouring out his heart in prayer. He kept in view the truths of God's greatness and His sufficiency to overrule seemingly bleak circumstances to His ultimate glory. He had confidence that Christ's grace and strength would carry him through and above his weakness, and, therefore, he was able to rejoice. The examples we have considered bear this out. It is not mere positive thinking ("This is not as bad as I think; I can get through this on my own") that Paul exhibits and that the Scriptures set before us for emulation. It is biblical thinking ("I am weak. God is almighty and faithful, always true to His Word; I will therefore appeal to Him through Christ, my all-sufficient mediator, for help").

Paul's abiding joy was not contingent upon his circumstances. Rather, it was bound up in the God of all grace who saved him (Phil. 4:10–14; Rom. 15:13). Paul's joy was supernatural, produced in him by the Holy Spirit (Gal. 5:22).

FELLOW CHRISTIAN

What kind of man do you want as an undershepherd? The apostle was a man whose thoughts and emotions were anchored in Christ and His truth. He knew himself—who and what he was—and he knew his God. This provided the foundation for a stable joy even in the face of profoundly painful circumstances of body and soul.

When you consider a man to minister God's Word to you, look for one who embraces Paul's attitude toward suffering for Christ's sake, even if he does not measure up to Paul either in the degree of his suffering or in the excellence of his response. Let him not be a man whose mission in life is the avoidance of suffering. He cannot be a faithful minister if he will sacrifice anything and everything to avoid pains and persecutions from within and without the professing church, from burdens and grief in his own soul.

Let him be a man filled with stable joy rooted in the person and work of his Savior. By this, of course, we do not mean a man with a forced grin fixed on his face, persuaded that the number of teeth he shows is a register of his happiness. We do not mean a pulpit clown or a man with a talent for one-liners or even possessed of a rich and ripe sense of humor (though we hope he has that). This is not about the constitution of a man, but the conviction of a man. A man may have a constitutional inclination to mirth and happiness and still demonstrate an aversion to or an absence of Christian joy. The faithful minister must be one whose joy is the joy of serving Christ and His church in fair weather or foul.

As you reflect on his character and qualifications, ask whether the object of your interest glories in tribulations, knowing that tribulation produces perseverance, and perseverance, character, and character, hope (Rom. 5:3–4). Does he rejoice in his sufferings, knowing that God always has his best in view, trusting that God will sustain him (1 Cor. 10:13)? Does he trust in God at all times, pouring out his heart before Him, confident that God is his refuge (Ps. 62:8)?

Ask him how he responds to trials and distresses. Observe those responses, if you can. Is he a whiner and complainer? When the going gets tough, a minister like Paul looks to the Lord, from whom comes his help, saying with the psalmist, "It is good for me that I have been afflicted; that I might learn thy statutes" (Ps. 119:71). He does not gripe with Cain, "My punishment is greater than I can bear" (Gen. 4:13).

What of your present pastor? Is he trying to be such a man? If he is seeking to be faithful to Christ and His flock, you might not be able to pray him out of suffering, but you can certainly ask God to give him a humble spirit and an uplifted heart in that suffering. You should ask whether you may be the cause of some of his grief and trials. Do not make it your job in life to provide scope for his greater sanctification: "Obey them that have the rule over you, and submit yourselves: for they watch for your souls, as they that must give account, that they may do it with joy, and not with grief: for that is unprofitable for you" (Heb. 13:17). If he finds pain elsewhere, let your conduct and attitude be the ground of joy, that—even should there be legitimate difference between you—you respond in a thoroughly Christian spirit.

FELLOW PASTOR   Are you ready to suffer? We do not ask you to invite or pursue suffering, but to remember that everyone who desires to live godly in Christ Jesus will suffer persecution (2 Tim. 3:12). If we are faithful, suffering will come.

If you set out to be, and increasingly become, a man who lives godly in Christ Jesus, then persecution will be yours. Like Paul, you may face false accusations, rejections, and resistance from within and without the church. You may face opposition from civil and religious authorities. You may even find yourself threatened physically, with those threats at times carried into actions.

In addition, there will be profound burdens of soul that you will feel. The more you love your people, the more their pains and grief will become yours. The more you love them, the more their sins and struggles will trouble you. The more you love them, the more you will pray for them and visit them. The more you love them, the more constrained you will be to address those sins and struggles graciously and tenderly, though firmly and plainly. You will see men and women who hear the gospel over and over again and who seem to grow more careless, whose soul-damning indifference will cause you agonies in your own spirit.

The more you love Christ, the more zealous you will be for His glory, the more concerned you will be for His honor. You will be grieved when false teaching besmirches Him and when true saints wander from Him. You will be distressed when He is unloved and disregarded; you will be moved to tears and to holy indignation when His truth is denied, His worship tainted, His church assaulted, and His person dishonored.

You will, if you love Christ and His people, feel and pray and respond and act for the glory of the Savior's name and the health of His body, the church. And you may well have it all flung back in your face.

There will be those who love to have the preeminence who will not receive you and who will hang upon the hook of their resistance to you a hundred reasons to ignore you. There will be those who will despise your youth, whether or not you give them reason to do so. For others, the problem may be that you are too old and therefore behind the times. There will be men who think that they deserve greater prominence, or who have wives seeking prominence for their husbands, regardless of their graces and gifts, and perhaps even as an avenue for their own domineering spirit. There will be those persuaded that they are called to lead who show no inclination to serve. There will be those who are angered by every attempt to call them individually, or the church corporately, to repentance and reformation, who will resist every charge to consider their ways and turn their feet back to God's testimonies (Ps. 119:59).

You will find hurting sheep so maddened by pain and worry and grief that they barely know themselves, sheep who will buck and kick the moment you press your fingers into their wool. Your probing shepherd's fingers may find old wounds that were never washed and cleaned, old breaks that never properly set, diseases and afflictions and infections that have been allowed to fester over years by neglectful, even if well-intentioned, pastors. Others will bear the scars of false teaching and cruelty. You will determine to deal with those things, and you may be surprised and horrified when a sheep snarls and even bites.

You will seek by all means to advance the cause of truth and call the church of Christ back to the old paths, the good way where there is rest for the soul (Jer. 6:16). You will find good men and women so entrenched in tradition or so molded by worldly principles that they will resist you with all their might. For such, all change is to be shunned, and they have no intention of being stirred from their slumber, even if the body grows cold and the mind numb and the soul careless and the world is being lost.

Do not say, "It will never happen to me." Remember the sad experience of Jonathan Edwards, that great preacher and theologian. Under God he had been blessed with laboring at the forefront of genuine revivals of religion. He served the church to which he ministered faithfully and lovingly for twenty-three years, and God had used him as the means of great blessing to many (three-quarters of the membership had been admitted by Edwards). There came a point when Edwards took a stand on a matter of principle. The fundamental issue was Edwards's refusal to allow to the Lord's Table professing Christians whose lives fell short of their profession. The eventual outcome was the separation of Edwards and the church and the removal of the pastor and his family to the remote outpost of Stockbridge. There Edwards put his talents to use in what was, by the standards of the time, a far less worthy sphere of service in which he faced intense opposition.[4]

Are you ready for such a life, brother? By all means, it is not always like this, but this—in part or in whole—will be the portion of every man who seeks to shepherd a church with faithfulness and love. Again, we read the testimonies of the past, and sometimes we imagine that men greatly used by God sailed serenely through life, without, above, or unaware of the abuses flung against them. That is an utterly false perspective. There is a Christlike pattern, a through-suffering-to-glory trajectory, which every faithful child of God undergoes. There is no crown without a cross, and—far from being exempt from such a principle—the minister of Christ is often called to show these things in himself first.

That is the reality of the suffering a faithful elder must be prepared to face. But the joy is equally real and overwhelmingly excellent.

How much joy do we find in the midst of difficulty? Are there periods when, though sorrowful, we are always rejoicing (2 Cor. 6:10)? Can we say—if not now perfectly, at least with increasing understanding and conviction—with Paul in Romans 8:18 that we "reckon that the sufferings of this present time are not worthy to be compared with the glory which shall be revealed in us"? Paul could say to the believers in Thessalonica, "And ye became followers of us, and of the Lord, having received the word in much affliction, with joy of the Holy Ghost" (1 Thess. 1:6). Can you say this to your flock too?

These are matters that should drive us to search our hearts. We must face these questions before the Lord, asking Him to try us and know our ways (Ps. 139:23–24). Paul knew that his best life was not now, but rather is the life to come. Thus he could confidently say, "For which cause we faint not; but though our outward man perish, yet the inward man is renewed day by day. For our light affliction, which is but for a moment, worketh for us a far more exceeding and eternal weight of glory" (2 Cor. 4:16–17). Paul knew that "if we suffer, we shall also reign with him" (2 Tim. 2:12); suffering with Him leads to our being glorified together with Him (Rom. 8:17). With this expectation he could say in Philippians 4:4, "Rejoice in the Lord always: and again I say, Rejoice."

The joy of the faithful pastor is centered in Christ. If the Master is preached, exalted, known, and glorified, then the servant is more than content—he rejoices. If your joy is grounded in your own reputation, then it will rise and—mainly—fall with your honor in the world, and your honor will never amount to much

---

4. See chapters 16–21 of Iain H. Murray, *Jonathan Edwards: A New Biography* (Edinburgh: Banner of Truth, 1987) for more detail on this period of Edwards's life.

if you are faithful to your Lord. If it is tied to the apparent prosperity of your ministry, it may prove changeable as the sea and can even be snatched away entirely in an instant. If it has its roots in circumstance, it will crumble when you most need to manifest that joy for Christ's glory.

We will suffer, but when we do we must turn to Christ Jesus and make our complaints known to Him. Our sovereign God is possessed of enough wisdom and power to turn our most desperate needs and our direst straits into occasions for our sanctification and the church's blessing and—above all—Christ's glory. Is Christ weaker now than He was in the days of the apostles? Is He less loving or less gracious?

We do not need then to whip ourselves up or even to be always gazing for the silver linings to the darkest clouds. We are not promised that we will see those things, but we know that they must be there, even when hidden from our eyes. We are weak, but Christ is strong and faithful to the end. We can rejoice in knowing Him and doing His will, even when all things seem against us, driving us to despair. His ear is open to our cry; His eye is set upon His people; His heart is entirely for us; His own hand will bring Him—and us—the victory.

May the Lord give those of us who are ministers of Christ much grace to embrace this perspective from the heart.

2 | THE FOCUS OF PAUL'S MINISTRY

Who now rejoice in my sufferings for you . . .
— Colossians 1:24

The people are not for the minister, but the minister is for the people; and he is to lose himself in their service and for their benefit.[1]
— William M. Taylor

Paul's ministerial joy did not exist in a vacuum. It had a specific context and a definite direction. It was not the selfish joy of self-gratification. Rather, being patterned after Christ and governed by Paul's desire for the good of others, his joy ran counter to the world and its appetites.

The problem of selfishness

Selfishness is caring unduly or supremely for oneself, fixing the eye on one's own comforts or advantage. Selfishness says, "It's all about me." The selfish person subordinates other people's aspirations and needs to his own. He must have things his way. It is not that such a man is perpetually disagreeable; rather, he becomes that way when the pursuit of someone else's agenda runs across or against his own.

Our world is full of selfishness. Wherever we turn, people boldly assert themselves in pursuit of their own wants, preferences, and rights. Perhaps never before has a generation in the Western world been so characterized by the "me first" mentality, plagued with the conviction that the will of the individual reigns supreme and therefore always looking out for number one. This selfish attitude,

---

1. William M. Taylor, *The Ministry of the Word* (Harrisonburg, VA: Sprinkle Publications, 2003), 12.

prevalent throughout our culture, is one of the bitter fruits of our fallen condition apart from God's grace in Christ.

Selfishness is an ugly sin wherever it is found and should have no home in the church of Christ. When it is found in gospel ministers it is unusually repugnant, being utterly out of place. Yet the church has always been plagued with ministers who care more for their own ease and comfort than for that of their flocks. Christ Jesus warns of the one who is "an hireling, and not the shepherd, whose own the sheep are not, [who] seeth the wolf coming, and leaveth the sheep, and fleeth: and the wolf catcheth them, and scattereth the sheep. The hireling fleeth, because he is an hireling, and careth not for the sheep" (John 10:12–13). Such a man is more concerned for his own safety than for the safety of Christ's sheep.

The selfish minister, in neglecting the selfless servant spirit of a true pastor, subverts the gospel itself. His underlying attitude to life paints an inaccurate picture of the very nature of Christianity. The self-absorbed minister portrays something that is not even Christian and is a shame to the Lord he professes.

The principle of selflessness

The example and teachings of our Lord Jesus Christ stand in sharp contrast to all selfish attitudes. When the disciples were arguing about who should have the preeminence, "Jesus called them unto him, and said, Ye know that the princes of the Gentiles exercise dominion over them, and they that are great exercise authority upon them. But it shall not be so among you: but whosoever will be great among you, let him be your minister; and whosoever will be chief among you, let him be your servant: even as the Son of man came not to be ministered unto, but to minister, and to give his life a ransom for many (Matt. 20:25–28; cf. Mark 10:45).

When our Lord was about to die, He took the towel and the basin, and—assuming the place of the servant—He washed the feet of His disciples. He did not miss His opportunity:

> So after he had washed their feet, and had taken his garments, and was set down again, he said unto them, Know ye what I have done to you? Ye call me Master and Lord: and ye say well; for so I am. If I then, your Lord and Master, have washed your feet; ye also ought to wash one another's feet. For I have given you an example, that ye should do as I have done to you. Verily, verily, I say unto you, The servant is not greater than his lord; neither he that is sent greater than he that sent him. If ye know these things, happy are ye if ye do them. (John 13:12–17)

The Bible repeatedly shows us that Jesus came not to do His own will, but the will of the Father who sent Him (John 6:38). The Christ did not please Himself (Rom. 15:3), but took upon Himself poverty—in every sense—in order that others might become rich (2 Cor. 8:9). Grounded in His own example, the Lord Jesus constantly and consistently prescribes self-sacrifice, self-denial, and service from evangelical motives—that is, springing out of gospel realities and driven by a gospel dynamic—for all those who would be true followers of Him. He declares, "Whosoever will come after me, let him deny himself, and take up his cross, and follow me. For whosoever will save his life shall lose it; but whosoever shall lose his life for my sake and the gospel's, the same shall save it" (Mark 8:34–35). True disciples of Christ are to be characterized by self-denial rather than self-assertion, by sacrificial obedience rather than self-centeredness. Self-assertion, self-determination, and self-actualization are the world's obsession.

Paul—a true servant of Christ Jesus—was neither a contradiction to his office nor to the faith he professed. It is natural to ask why he told his Colossian readers that he rejoiced in his sufferings. Was he some masochistic fellow with a martyr complex? Did he simply thrive on the excitement of living his life on the edge, a ministerial adrenaline junkie who got his buzz from "extreme pastoring"?

Not remotely. Rather, Paul draws attention to one of the key reasons he viewed his trials with joy. He says in Colossians 1:24, "[I] now rejoice in my sufferings for you." Literally, he says that his sufferings were "on behalf of you all." Paul's ministry was sacrificial, focused on others rather than on himself. The trials he endured were for the benefit of the Colossian believers.

As we will see more plainly when we look at the hardships of Paul's ministry, the apostle is not for one moment trespassing on Christ's role as a mediator. Indeed, before writing these words, Paul had risen to extraordinary heights of holy eloquence in declaring that Christ alone is the Redeemer, so he is hardly now claiming any redemptive function in his own suffering. There is no implication that Paul is making a contribution to Christ's cross work, the once-for-all and completely sufficient atonement accomplished by the death of the Lord Jesus. Nevertheless, Paul unashamedly states that the sufferings in which he rejoices are those experienced on behalf of Christ's body, which is the church.

To grasp Paul's meaning in verse 24, it is vital that we understand at least something of the nature of Christ's church: it is not a building in which people gather, or a bare association of likeminded friends, or a mere religious club. The church is a body, the community of God's redeemed people. It is entered through union with its head, Jesus Christ, a union accomplished in regeneration and established by faith alone (Col. 1:18). No one becomes part of the church simply by being around the body, but each individual becomes a member by being joined to its head. Sinners, who once were cut off from God, being antagonistic toward Him in thought and deed, have been brought into subjection by the mighty Savior and reconciled to God (Col. 1:21–24). Having been regenerated by the power of Christ's Spirit (Col. 2:11–13), they become living stones in a new temple made without hands, purchased by His sacrificial death and held together by the crimson cement of Christ's blood.

Unless we understand something of the vital union that exists between the Head of the church and His body, we will never appreciate the depths of Paul's affection for the church and his willingness to suffer for her. Neither will we ever be able to emulate the apostolic spirit. We will consider this more closely in the next chapter, but, for now, recognize that while most people are driven almost entirely by self-interest, Paul was motivated by something entirely different. Self-interest was certainly one of the driving forces behind the false teachers in Colosse who—for their own advantage—cheated the people with deceptive doctrines (Col. 2:8, 18). However, there is an implicit contrast between Paul's labors and the errorists'. He sets forth the marks of genuine and counterfeit ministers and ministries. He would have the Colossian believers know that the false teachers operated out of selfish motives. It should have been evident to every child of God in Colosse and beyond, from Paul's words and deeds, that Paul had selfless aims. The apostle demonstrated to the Colossian believers that he was a true minister of Christ: he sought their immediate and eternal good and not merely a following—not what was theirs, but they themselves (2 Cor. 12:14).

The practice of selflessness

Selflessness was Paul's characteristic attitude—a self-denying, Christ-obeying, church-serving demeanor lay at the heart of his labors. This emphasis is evident throughout Paul's epistles. Surveying the New Testament record, we find in him a consistent and Christlike example of deep and selfless concern for everyone he served. It is worth our while to consider the composite sketch of Paul's focus on others, as he demonstrates and teaches what it means to work "for you"—that is, for the church of Jesus Christ.

Paul's prayers were marked by and overflowing with thanksgiving and concern for the church of Jesus Christ.

> First, I thank my God through Jesus Christ for you all, that your faith is spoken of throughout the whole world. For God is my witness, whom I serve with my spirit in the gospel of his Son, that without ceasing I make mention of you always in my prayers; making request, if by any means now at length I might have a prosperous journey by the will of God to come unto you. (Rom. 1:8–10)

> We give thanks to God and the Father of our Lord Jesus Christ, praying always for you. (Col. 1:3) [2]

Paul was not ashamed to express his love openly for the people for whom Christ had died.

> For out of much affliction and anguish of heart I wrote unto you with many tears; not that ye should be grieved, but that ye might know the love which I have more abundantly unto you. (2 Cor. 2:4)

> For I would that ye knew what great conflict I have for you, and for them at Laodicea, and for as many as have not seen my face in the flesh. (Col. 2:1)

Paul was willing to endure the sufferings inflicted on him for the sake of the church.

> And whether we be afflicted, it is for your consolation and salvation, which is effectual in the enduring of the same sufferings which we also suffer: or whether we be comforted, it is for your consolation and salvation. (2 Cor. 1:6)

> For this cause I Paul, the prisoner of Jesus Christ for you Gentiles, if ye have heard of the dispensation of the grace of God which is given me to you-ward.... Wherefore I desire that ye faint not at my tribulations for you, which is your glory. (Eph. 3:1–2, 13)

Paul was willing to deny himself, making whatever sacrifices were necessary for the people of God.

> For though I be free from all men, yet have I made myself servant unto all, that I might gain the more. And unto the Jews I became as a Jew, that I might gain the Jews; to them that are under the law, as under the law, that I might gain them that are under the law; to them that are without

---

2. See also Ephesians 1:16; Philippians 1:4; Colossians 1:9; 1 Thessalonians 1:2; 2 Thessalonians 1:3, 11; 2 Thessalonians 2:13; Philemon 1:4.

law, as without law, (being not without law to God, but under the law to Christ,) that I might gain them that are without law. To the weak became I as weak, that I might gain the weak: I am made all things to all men, that I might by all means save some. And this I do for the gospel's sake, that I might be partaker thereof with you. (1 Cor. 9:19–23)

Even as I please all men in all things, not seeking mine own profit, but the profit of many, that they may be saved. (1 Cor. 10:33)

Paul's life and labors were conscientiously directed toward the children of God: his gifts, graces, and blessings were perceived in the context of the church and invested in it.

And whether we be afflicted, it is for your consolation and salvation, which is effectual in the enduring of the same sufferings which we also suffer: or whether we be comforted, it is for your consolation and salvation. (2 Cor. 1:6)

So being affectionately desirous of you, we were willing to have imparted unto you, not the gospel of God only, but also our own souls, because ye were dear unto us. (1 Thess. 2:8)[3]

One of Paul's highest concerns was the present and ultimate salvation of the people of God.

For what is our hope, or joy, or crown of rejoicing? Are not even ye in the presence of our Lord Jesus Christ at his coming? For ye are our glory and joy.... Therefore, brethren, we were comforted over you in all our affliction and distress by your faith: for now we live, if ye stand fast in the Lord. For what thanks can we render to God again for you, for all the joy wherewith we joy for your sakes before our God. (1 Thess. 2:19–20; 3:7–9)

Therefore I endure all things for the elect's sakes, that they may also obtain the salvation which is in Christ Jesus with eternal glory. (2 Tim. 2:10)

Some of Paul's deepest desires and longings were prompted by the state of Jesus Christ's church.

For I am jealous over you with godly jealousy: for I have espoused you to one husband, that I may present you as a chaste virgin to Christ. (2 Cor. 11:2)

Are they Hebrews? so am I. Are they Israelites? so am I. Are they the seed of Abraham? so am I. Are they ministers of Christ? (I speak as a

---

3. See also 2 Corinthians 5:13.

fool) I am more; in labours more abundant, in stripes above measure, in prisons more frequent, in deaths oft. Of the Jews five times received I forty stripes save one. Thrice was I beaten with rods, once was I stoned, thrice I suffered shipwreck, a night and a day I have been in the deep; in journeyings often, in perils of waters, in perils of robbers, in perils by mine own countrymen, in perils by the heathen, in perils in the city, in perils in the wilderness, in perils in the sea, in perils among false brethren; in weariness and painfulness, in watchings often, in hunger and thirst, in fastings often, in cold and nakedness. Beside those things that are without, that which cometh upon me daily, the care of all the churches. (2 Cor. 11:22–28)[4]

Paul felt and acted like a godly parent toward the church of Jesus Christ.

My little children, of whom I travail in birth again until Christ be formed in you. (Gal. 4:19)

But we were gentle among you, even as a nurse cherisheth her children: so being affectionately desirous of you, we were willing to have imparted unto you, not the gospel of God only, but also our own souls, because ye were dear unto us. For ye remember, brethren, our labour and travail: for labouring night and day, because we would not be chargeable unto any of you, we preached unto you the gospel of God. Ye are witnesses, and God also, how holily and justly and unblameably we behaved ourselves among you that believe: as ye know how we exhorted and comforted and charged every one of you, as a father doth his children, that ye would walk worthy of God, who hath called you unto his kingdom and glory. (1 Thess. 2:7–12)

Paul's closest and most commended companions were of the same mind and heart.

But I trust in the Lord Jesus to send Timotheus shortly unto you, that I also may be of good comfort, when I know your state. For I have no man likeminded, who will naturally care for your state.... For [Epaphroditus] longed after you all, and was full of heaviness, because that ye had heard that he had been sick. (Phil. 2:19–20, 26)

Epaphras, who is one of you, a servant of Christ, saluteth you, always labouring fervently for you in prayers, that ye may stand perfect and complete in all the will of God. For I bear him record, that he hath a great zeal for you, and them that are in Laodicea, and them in Hierapolis. (Col. 4:12–13)[5]

---

4. See also Romans 1:11–12; Galatians 4:11; 1 Thessalonians 2:19–20.
5. See also 2 Corinthians 8:16.

Paul modeled an attitude that should characterize every believer.

> [Love]…doth not behave itself unseemly, seeketh not her own, is not easily provoked, thinketh no evil. (1 Cor. 13:5)

> Let nothing be done through strife or vainglory; but in lowliness of mind let each esteem other better than themselves. Look not every man on his own things, but every man also on the things of others. (Phil. 2:3–4)

These various passages reveal Paul's selfless service for the church of the Lord Jesus Christ. In a world in which "all seek their own" (Phil. 2:21), Paul was a man who continually sought to fulfill the second table of the law: he loved his neighbor as himself (Matt. 22:39), and, as he had opportunity, he did good to all, especially to those who were of the household of faith (Gal. 6:10). Perhaps nowhere does the breadth and depth of Paul's pastoral heart manifest itself as clearly as it does in his parting words to the elders of Ephesus, recorded in Acts 20:17–38:

> And from Miletus he sent to Ephesus, and called the elders of the church. And when they were come to him, he said unto them, Ye know, from the first day that I came into Asia, after what manner I have been with you at all seasons, serving the Lord with all humility of mind, and with many tears, and temptations, which befell me by the lying in wait of the Jews: and how I kept back nothing that was profitable unto you, but have shewed you, and have taught you publicly, and from house to house, testifying both to the Jews, and also to the Greeks, repentance toward God, and faith toward our Lord Jesus Christ. And now, behold, I go bound in the spirit unto Jerusalem, not knowing the things that shall befall me there: save that the Holy Ghost witnesseth in every city, saying that bonds and afflictions abide me. But none of these things move me, neither count I my life dear unto myself, so that I might finish my course with joy, and the ministry, which I have received of the Lord Jesus, to testify the gospel of the grace of God. And now, behold, I know that ye all, among whom I have gone preaching the kingdom of God, shall see my face no more. Wherefore I take you to record this day, that I am pure from the blood of all men. For I have not shunned to declare unto you all the counsel of God. Take heed therefore unto yourselves, and to all the flock, over the which the Holy Ghost hath made you overseers, to feed the church of God, which he hath purchased with his own blood. For I know this, that after my departing shall grievous wolves enter in among you, not sparing the flock. Also of your own selves shall men arise, speaking perverse things, to draw away disciples after them. Therefore watch, and remember, that by the space of three years I ceased not to

warn every one night and day with tears. And now, brethren, I commend you to God, and to the word of his grace, which is able to build you up, and to give you an inheritance among all them which are sanctified. I have coveted no man's silver, or gold, or apparel. Yea, ye yourselves know, that these hands have ministered unto my necessities, and to them that were with me. I have shewed you all things, how that so labouring ye ought to support the weak, and to remember the words of the Lord Jesus, how he said, It is more blessed to give than to receive. And when he had thus spoken, he kneeled down, and prayed with them all. And they all wept sore, and fell on Paul's neck, and kissed him, sorrowing most of all for the words which he spake, that they should see his face no more. And they accompanied him unto the ship.

You can feel the deep-seated passion of Paul's heart as you read these words. Here is a man sacrificial in love, selfless in service, earnest in labor, honest in dealing, conscientious in duty, sober in warning, fierce in defense, faithful in prayer, fixed upon Jesus, pouring himself out as a drink offering on the sacrifice and service of the faith of the church (Phil. 2:17).

We can note in passing that there is a sweet encouragement in these words from Acts 20 for Christ's true servants. The faithful labors of a faithful man often are—and ought to be—rewarded (even in this life) with the affectionate love of faithful believers. It is frequently true that a faithful man of God enjoys the heartfelt affection of those whom he serves, as Paul did the affection of the Ephesian elders. Such reciprocal love only heightens a man's readiness to serve the body of Christ.

However, fundamentally we are seeing what it means to be a gospel minister. Richard Baxter urges that "the whole of our ministry must be carried on in a tender love to our people. We must let them see that nothing pleaseth us but what profiteth them; and that what doeth them good doth us good; and that nothing troubleth us more than their hurt."[6]

There was nothing accidental in such a life of service, nor was it Paul's native constitution to have such an attitude. By nature, the apostle was a blasphemer, a persecutor, and a violently insolent man (1 Tim. 1:13). He reminds the Galatians of his aggression, arrogance, and unholy zeal, and of the great change that occurred in him: "For ye have heard of my conversation in time past in the Jews' religion, how that beyond measure I persecuted the church of God, and wasted it: and profited in the Jews' religion above many my equals in mine own nation, being

---

6. Richard Baxter, *The Reformed Pastor* (Edinburgh: Banner of Truth, 1974), 117.

more exceedingly zealous of the traditions of my fathers. But when it pleased God, who separated me from my mother's womb, and called me by his grace, to reveal his Son in me, that I might preach him among the heathen..." (Gal. 1:13–16).

However, when he was confronted and captured by a gracious Christ, Paul was completely changed. He lived no longer for himself. Self had been dethroned, and he walked now in the cross-bearing path of the crucified Redeemer: "I am crucified with Christ: nevertheless I live; yet not I, but Christ liveth in me: and the life which I now live in the flesh I live by the faith of the Son of God, who loved me, and gave himself for me" (Gal. 2:20). As a redeemed man, the willing service of Christ's body—the church—became consciously and deliberately the tenor of Paul's ministry. Selfishness had vacated his soul, and love to God in Christ, with all who belong to Him, had taken up residence. Thomas Manton describes this contrast: "Self-love prompteth us merely to seek our own things, but charity [love] seeketh the profit of others. It doth not drive on a self-seeking trade, or mind these things which make for our own advantage, but the welfare of others, and is as sensible and zealous for other men's good as of its own."[7]

As we observe the life and ministry of the apostle, we should be overwhelmed by Paul's fundamental perception of himself rooted in the realities of his redemption: "For we preach not ourselves, but Christ Jesus the Lord; and ourselves your servants for Jesus' sake" (2 Cor. 4:5). This was his understanding of himself: a slave of the church for the sake of her dying and risen Lord. That qualifier—"for Jesus' sake"—is vital. This is what keeps the minister from craven fear and playing to the crowd. The "for you" is governed by the "for Him."

As the servant of the Lord, a preacher is simply bringing to bear Christ's rule in Christ's church. It is this faithfulness to Christ that keeps a pastor faithful to Christ's flock. He has the true needs of the sheep in mind, not necessarily their felt wants. This enables him to speak necessary truth in love, even when it is painful. It keeps him from giving up on the people he serves when they ignore his counsels, reject his words, and despise his person. He knows that "all scripture is given by inspiration of God, and is profitable for doctrine, for reproof, for correction, for instruction in righteousness: that the man of God may be perfect, thoroughly furnished unto all good works" (2 Tim. 3:16–17). He is not ashamed to employ the tools God has given him in the full range of their effective usefulness, though initially the cutting, filing, and sanding down of the child of God may be—for him and for his pastor—a painful experience. The

---

7. Thomas Manton, *Complete Works* (Birmingham, AL: Solid Ground Christian Books, 2008), 18:310.

faithful gospel minister is so determined to do good to the church of Christ that he is willing to be despised by the people he serves in order to do them that good. So Paul could say that he "will very gladly spend and be spent for you; though the more abundantly I love you, the less I be loved" (2 Cor. 12:15).

This selfless love and concern will sustain service even in the face of resistance and unwillingness to receive it. Even though sheep do not have sharp teeth and claws, undershepherds may feel them butt with hard heads at times. The behavior of imperfect believers, still wrestling with remaining sin, does not change the fact that they are Christ's blood-bought flock, united by living faith to their head, Jesus, as members of His body. The pastor is responsible to go on seeking the good of Christ's sheep, even if they are not immediately happy in being so shepherded. It is love for the Head of the church that keeps love for her members alive and works itself out in selfless service. It is the gospel minster's recognition that he himself was loved when he was utterly unlovely, when sin not only remained in him but reigned in him, that keeps him loving and serving the relatively unlovely who have—like him—been loved and saved by Christ.

Nothing but the grace of God in Christ at work in a pastor and preacher's heart can breed this sacrificial and serving love for the church and keep it alive. It was the indwelling Spirit and the constant supply of God's grace in Christ that enabled Paul to maintain a selfless attitude toward the church when—considered as a whole or in its local expressions—she was ignorant of his love, careless of it, and even at times resentful of its heartfelt expressions. This is something that does not come naturally to selfish men but is supernaturally worked by the Spirit of God in the hearts of His servants. Such faithful servants pursue it in their prayers, repenting of its absence and pleading for its increasing presence. It is the Spirit of God who lusts against the flesh, one manifestation of which is selfish ambition: it is by living and walking in the Spirit that selflessness is cultivated (Gal. 5:16–26).

Paul himself relies on the very thing that he prays for the Colossians—a filling with the knowledge of God's will in all wisdom and spiritual understanding, that they might have a walk worthy of the Lord, fully pleasing Him, being fruitful in every good work and increasing in the knowledge of God, strengthened with all might, according to His glorious power, for all patience and longsuffering with joy (Col. 1:9–11).

With the imprint of Christ's life and love pressed upon his soul, Paul did not set out in the ministry seeking what he could get from other people. Rather, he approached it asking the question, "How can I best serve others?" Though the Lord would lead him through many heavy trials, in the midst of them all the apostle was enabled to seek the spiritual prosperity of others. It was the knowledge that his Christlike sufferings were serving the church that brought joy to Paul's soul. There was a grand purpose that outweighed everything else— the salvation and sanctification of those to whom he ministered, for the glory of their Savior. He could greatly rejoice as he saw the image of Christ displayed in ever sharper focus in the lives of His people.

FELLOW CHRISTIAN

A true pastor is a man committed to the well-being of Christ's church, even if the well-being of the church must come at his own expense. If you are considering a man to be your pastor, take an opportunity to consider the degree of selflessness that he demonstrates. Look at the way he treats his wife and his children, his friends and his neighbors. Is he a "me first" man, or does he serve Christ, then others, and only then consider himself? Is he a man who will willingly serve the sheep, even if it brings harm and criticism upon him? Will he love you and others enough to say the hard things when they need to be said for the good of those under his pastoral care?

But you must also ask yourself, "Am I willing to be served by a physician of souls who will be faithful not only in feeding me with good food but also in prescribing necessary medicine for the health of my soul—medicine that may not always taste good even while it does good?" Are you willing to be pastored by a man who loves you enough to tell you things that may not always be pleasant to hear? Will you love him and receive his admonitions under those circumstances? There is no value in lauding the idea of a faithful minister if you reject his faithful dealings with you. He must be committed to employing all of Scripture in all its functions, and you must be committed to receiving it insofar as he remains faithful to his Savior and yours, humbly following the doctrines and dictates of Scripture.

We urge you to pray for your pastors, that they might know and feel in ever deeper degree the privilege and honor of serving Christ's church as bondservants of Jesus and, therefore, bondservants of the body for the sake of the Head. The gospel minister must be a man into whose heart the cross has been driven. There is nothing more contrary to self than this, but he is particularly exhorted to such a life. He—in company with every other true child of God—has taken up his cross in order to walk in the steps of the Master. Will you pray for him, that he might know the joy that comes from all kinds of suffering for the glory of Christ and the good of the church?

Remember also that such an attitude and such activity is not limited to the elders of a local church. It is urged upon every child of God. One of the greatest encouragements that your pastors can know is to see you also embracing a selfless, serving life, working with them for the blessing of your brothers and sisters in the family of God. Are you seeking to be the kind of man or woman that Paul exhorted the members of the church to be? Is the mind that was in Christ Jesus (Phil. 2:5–8) manifest in your life? Do you esteem others better than yourself? Are you looking out for their interests as well as your own (Phil. 2:3–4)? There is little that will urge a faithful man on to greater self-denial than a self-denying spirit among the people of God.

FELLOW PASTOR

We must ask ourselves hard and pointed questions: Why do I do what I do? What motivates me? Why do I pray, prepare, preach, write, speak, work, visit? On what principle is my life organized?

Are your efforts "for me" or "for you"—that is, are you truly working for the church for which Christ gave His life? Self is a powerful idol and can bear a great deal in the hope of being exalted at last. It is even willing to give every appearance of humility in order that it might be lifted up. Here our selfish hearts lie grievously exposed: they can wear the mask of service in pursuit of a throne of honor. How often and how readily are we repenting of the great selfishness that so quickly creeps into the work that we do and hinders us from the work that we ought to be doing?

Remember, too, that suffering for the sake of Christ's church is not a romantic theory. It is a gritty reality concerning the people to whom we minister week by week whose idiosyncrasies are as contrary to us as ours are to them, whose sins and shortcomings grate upon us personally and pastorally, whose lack of responsiveness and sometimes outright resistance to truth make us often ready to throw up our hands and conclude that there is no way that we can be sufficient for these things. Consider those people. Let their faces come before the eyes of your mind, their lives play out for a few moments on the screen of your imagination. We are called to shepherd the flock of Christ. Over those images in your head, can you write the words "for you"?

We will never be able to ground our ministries in that "for you" until all our being and doing is grounded first in "for Him," recognizing the scriptural reality of the body of Christ. To serve the members is to serve the Head; to dress the stones of the temple is to glorify the one who indwells the temple. The church is His body, the blood-purchased, blood-sanctified, deeply beloved bride of Jesus Christ. Consequently, we are to serve that church—in its concrete local expressions of real, sinful, saved people.

We must closely examine our own hearts and discern our own likeness to Jesus. He came not to be served, but to serve, and to give His life as a ransom for many (Matt. 20:28). We cannot atone for our people nor are we called to do so, but we are to work out a life of cross-centered service for the sake of their immortal souls. That means preaching a crucified Christ from the pulpit, but it also means following a crucified Christ out of it. Are we, when out of the pulpit, evidently a follower of the crucified Jesus whom we proclaim in it? Do our people—Christ's people—know of our love and concern for them? Have we told them? Have we showed them? Are we ashamed openly to express our love for the people for whom Christ has died? If they cannot always see it, what does our heavenly Father see? Are our prayers marked by and overflowing with thanksgiving and concern for the church of Jesus Christ? Are we willing to endure the sufferings inflicted on us for the sake of the church? Are we willing to deny ourselves and make ourselves available to them? Will we make whatever sacrifices are necessary for the people of God? Are our labors conscientiously directed toward the children of God—our gifts, graces, and blessings perceived in the context of and invested in the church? Is one of our highest concerns the present and ultimate salvation of the people of God? Are some of our deepest desires and longings prompted by the state of the church? Do we feel and act like godly parents toward the church of Jesus Christ? Are our closest companions of the same mind and heart, prompting us to such an attitude and activity? Do we imitate Paul as he imitated Christ?

Paul commands us as Christians, "Let no man seek his own, but every man another's [well-being]" (1 Cor. 10:24). Are we who lead in the church being exemplary in this area? Are we leading in service, modeling the mind that was in Christ as an example to the flock? Walter Chantry reminds us, "'Self–centred Christian' is a term of impossible contradiction. A self-serving minister is one of the most loathsome sights in all the world. When the Great Shepherd calls a man to preach the gospel and shepherd his flocks, he issues a call to double denial of self."[8] How loathsome a sight is your heart?

Are you willing to be faithful? Are you ready to cry out to Christ—who loved you and gave Himself for you—for an insistent and persistent care and

---

8. Walter Chantry, *The Shadow of the Cross: Studies in Self–Denial* (Edinburgh: Banner of Truth, 1981), 57.

concern for His people? Are you willing to love abundantly, though the more you love the less you are loved? Are you ready to serve God's people with what they need, more than with what they sometimes want?

How do inherently selfish sinners like us cultivate this disposition? We must go back to the crucified Savior. Such a self-denying, church-oriented focus comes only from a heart that spends much time at the cross, remembering all that Jesus has done for us.

3 | THE HARDSHIPS OF PAUL'S MINISTRY

*Who now rejoice in my sufferings for you, and fill up
that which is behind of the afflictions of Christ in my
flesh for his body's sake, which is the church . . .*

— COLOSSIANS 1:24–25

*Though millions of precious saints have shed their blood for Christ, whose souls are
now crying under the altar,* How long, Lord, how long! *yet there are many more
coming on behind in the same path of persecution, and much Christian blood must
yet be shed, before the mystery of God be finished; and notwithstanding this lucid
interval, the clouds seem to be returning again after the rain. Thus you see to what
grievous sufferings the merciful God hath sometimes called his dearest people.*[1]

— JOHN FLAVEL

Have you known any martyrs? Church history overflows with examples of sterling
Christians who have given their lives for the sake of Christ. One of Western
Protestantism's most enduring and effective works of literature is Foxe's *Book of
Martyrs*, a compilation of histories of Christians suffering in the service of Jesus.
Modern times have supplied us with more names, including some that have—
in the eyes of some Christians—already become almost glamorous at a slight
distance, such as those of Jim Elliot or John and Betty Stam. However, while
many in the modern West know the stories, few of us have known any martyrs.
Few of us have holes in our lives, gaps in the ranks of friends or families, created
by our loved one's death in the service of King Jesus. In some parts of the world,
death at the hands of the enemies of Christ's kingdom is all too common.

It was our privilege to know two of Christ's martyrs. Since 1999 Pastor Arif
Khan and his wife Kathleen (Kathy to her friends) had faithfully labored in

---

1. John Flavel, "Preparations for Sufferings, or The Best Work in the Worst Times" in
Works, 6 vols. (Edinburgh: Banner of Truth, 1968), 6:9.

Islamabad, Pakistan, where Pastor Arif had planted a church. In August 2007, three people—a disaffected ex-member of the church, his wife, and a gunman from an aggressively Islamic region—made their way by deceit into the Khans' home and shot our friends dead.[2]

Our friends. The believers. The martyrs.

Why were they there? What had carried them from the comfortable confines of the United States, away from friends and family, children and grandchildren? Why leave their home church? Why stay in Pakistan when reaction to American foreign policy and activity made their existence there increasingly dangerous? Why remain in the face of threats to their lives? Why teach and live so as to seal their testimonies with their life's blood?

How do you reach this point? Not necessarily the point of martyrdom, but the point of willing and entire consecration, of being sold out for the one living and true God, ready to give all that you are and have for His sake and for His cause?

What would the Khans have said? At least part of their answer—a great part of their answer—would have been for the sake of Jesus Christ's body, the church. They had a consuming desire to see the church built up so that through those who have been redeemed the manifold wisdom of God would be known to others (Eph. 3:10). They saw the importance of spreading the gospel to a lost world. This man and woman "loved not their lives unto the death" (Rev. 12:11). One of their own pastors said of Arif Khan, "He was a marked man. He talked of dying for Christ as though it was having a mole removed."[3]

It is not often that we meet people who are willing to spend their energy and even give their lives for the sake of seeing the church of the Lord Jesus Christ established and strengthened. This was the mind of the Khans; it was also the mind of the apostle Paul.

Paul gave his all for the people of God. He loved them at great personal cost. As he writes his letter, Paul tells the Colossians that he rejoices even in his prison sufferings because of his love for them. Now he specifically points to the nature and purpose of those sufferings, saying, "I…fill up that which is behind of the afflictions of Christ in my flesh for his body's sake, which is the church" (Col. 1:24). What does he mean, and what must we understand?

---

2. See Daniel Bergner, "The Believers," *The New York Times Magazine*, December 30, 2007, http://www.nytimes.com/2007/12/30/magazine/30khans-t.html for more information about the Khans (accessed June 28, 2010).

3. Ibid.

Confusion?

Paul's language of suffering for the sake of the church has given rise to many controversial and contradictory interpretations. It may be, as several commentators have noted, the most debated verse in the entire letter. It has been much abused, and some have interpreted it in ways that promote unorthodoxy or superstition. Three main perspectives have dominated the understanding of this passage.[4]

First is the atoning interpretation. Some have suggested that Paul is making a contribution to the work of Christ Jesus in dying as a substitute for His people—Jesus' vicarious, redemptive suffering. The implication is that the saints need to add to Jesus' work on the cross because it is somehow incomplete.

A second view, the eschatological interpretation, is that Paul refers to the full measure of the sufferings that the entire church must go through before Jesus returns. Those who hold to this view understand Paul's words here as a fulfillment of such passages as Daniel 7:21–22 and 12:1. In the New Testament, passages such as Matthew 24:4–14 and Mark 13:9–20 are brought to bear. Some interpreters believe these and other passages have the sense of a given measure of suffering that must be completed before Christ comes in glory. They suggest that the suffering of those associated with the Messiah will quicken the coming of the end of this age and will usher in the age to come.

The third possibility is the mystical or spiritual interpretation. In this understanding, Paul is referring to Jesus' active sympathy with His people in their afflictions, so that what His people endure, Christ endures as well. This idea is grounded in the identification of Christ with His people, which Paul profoundly appreciated (Acts 9:4–5). It is possible to suggest in this regard that Paul is undergoing in his own body those physical sufferings that were aimed at Jesus by His enemies but which—because the Lord Himself is not physically present to bear them—are falling upon His people: there is a sense in which he is putting himself in the way of the blows directed at Jesus.[5]

Clarification

So what does Paul mean? First, we must consider the words of the sentence itself. The word that has to do with "filling up" appears only here in Scripture.

---

4. See, for example, Richard R. Melick, *Philippians, Colossians and Philemon* in *New American Commentary* (Nashville, TN: Broadman Press, 1991), 32:238–40.

5. A more detailed and technical overview can be found in Peter O'Brien, *Colossians and Philemon* (Colombia: Nelson, 1982), 77–81; or in Douglas Moo, *The Letters to the Colossians and to Philemon* (Grand Rapids: Eerdmans, 2008), 151–53.

It carries the idea of completing something for someone else. The present tense of the verb and the immediate context in which it is used tell us that this was something that Paul was continually doing. When Paul speaks of something "behind of the afflictions of Christ," the language suggests something lacking, that which still exists or is left over.

Then there is the word *afflictions*. This word speaks of oppression, tribulation, trouble, or persecution. It is, however, crucial that this word is never used in the Bible to refer to the sufferings that Jesus underwent on the cross for our sins.

Second, we must put this declaration in the context of the whole Colossian letter. The whole point of the letter so far has been to establish Christ's supremacy as the saving and sovereign head of His people (contrast Paul's self-owned label in verse 25 of "minister," not mediator or redeemer).

So, in Colossians 1:14, Paul speaks of Jesus as the one "in whom we have redemption through his blood, even the forgiveness of sins." The present possession of redemption and forgiveness is based upon the precious blood of our Savior, and not the sacrificial work of any sinner, even one who was an eminent apostle.

Paul says again with reference to Jesus, "It pleased the Father that in him should all fulness dwell; and, having made peace through the blood of his cross, by him to reconcile all things unto himself; by him, I say, whether they be things in earth, or things in heaven. And you, that were sometime alienated and enemies in your mind by wicked works, yet now hath he reconciled in the body of his flesh through death, to present you holy and unblameable and unreproveable in his sight" (Col. 1:19–22).

There is nothing lacking in the Lord Jesus Christ, either in His person or in His work. All saving fullness dwells in Him, and He is the means by which the Father reconciles men to Himself. Specifically, the terms of that peace He secured are written in the blood that Jesus shed on the cross for His people. It is the bloody death of Jesus alone that saves.

In these words there is neither room nor need for any other but Christ. If all fullness dwells in Him, what shall fallen mankind add to Him or His work? If it has pleased the Father to reconcile people to Himself solely by means of the crucified Christ, how can any suggest that Christ is in any way insufficient, especially after His glorious resurrection vindicated all that was said about Him (Rom. 1:4; 4:25)? If peace was already secured through the blood of Christ upon the cross, once for all (Eph. 2:13–14), what place is there for any other grounds of peace?

Indeed, Paul will not let this theme lie: "And you, being dead in your sins and the uncircumcision of your flesh, hath he quickened together with him, having forgiven you all trespasses; blotting out the handwriting of ordinances that was against us, which was contrary to us, and took it out of the way, nailing it to his cross" (Col. 2:13–14).

To take the perfection of Christ and His work and to say that people somehow must add further to it completely misunderstands and undermines the profound nature of what God has accomplished through His incarnate Son. It fails to take account of the complete inability of anyone to please God, let alone save himself, apart from the glorious Jesus.

Would it not be both foolish and blasphemous to seek to insert human effort, positively or negatively, into the divine plan of a gracious salvation? Did Christ not say, "It is finished" (John 19:30)? Paul would surely be the world's most incompetent debater if he were now to state something that runs directly or even tangentially counter to all that he has just established. He is a wiser man than that.

Third, we must also take into account the comprehensive and consistent testimony of Scripture. The plain teaching of the Word of God is that Christ alone accomplished all that was required for the salvation of His people when He suffered once and for all in their place at Golgotha (see, for example, Isaiah 53:4–6 or Hebrews 1:3; 10:14). There is no deficiency of any sort in Christ's sacrificial death, and to suggest otherwise opens the door to a host of other empty possibilities, including the notion of works of supererogation (the idea that unusually holy people have a surplus of merit that others can benefit from), the veneration of Mary the mother of Christ, and the concept of penance for sins.

It is already clear that the atoning interpretation is entirely incorrect. Christ's sacrifice for sin was in no way deficient. The sufferings that Paul underwent had no saving merit: the apostle did not contribute in any way whatsoever in redeeming the people of God. Jesus Christ alone has suffered once for sins, the just for the unjust, that He might bring us to God (1 Peter 3:18). Our Bibles make plain that it is Christ alone, through His saving sufferings, who brings us into a right relationship with God the Father.

However, there are other lines of thought in Scripture that we must take into account when working out what Paul does mean. In 1 Corinthians 12:12 Paul states that the saints are many members of one body, the head of which is Christ. The same unity of identity is plain in Matthew 25:34–40, where the works done for Christ's people are considered as done to Christ Himself (or not, vv. 41–46). This involves unity of mission. In Acts 13:47 Paul appropriates language that Isaiah uses of the Lord Jesus to assume the same gospel role in setting forth the Christ: "For so hath the Lord commanded us, saying, I have set thee to be a light of the Gentiles, that thou shouldest be for salvation unto the ends of the earth." This further implies unity of suffering, and Paul had this ground into his consciousness from the beginning of his ministry: "And he fell to the earth, and heard a voice saying unto him, Saul, Saul, why persecutest thou me? And he said, Who art thou, Lord? And the Lord said, I am Jesus whom thou persecutest: it is hard for thee to kick against the pricks.... For I will shew him how great things he must suffer for my name's sake" (Acts 9:4–5, 16).

In summary, the sufferings of the body of Christ—the church—are the sufferings of Christ Himself (1 Cor. 1:5; 1 Peter 4:13), not in a redemptive, but nevertheless in a real, sense.

How, then, do we understand Paul's plain declaration that he is in the process of filling up what is lacking in the afflictions of Christ, contributing to the completion of something that has yet to be completed? It is plain that Christ's saving sufferings are completed and done, but, while God is judicially satisfied, Christ's enemies are not satisfied in any sense. Their hatred is not exhausted, so they vent their loathing of the Head on the members of His body, just as Christ said they would: "And ye shall be hated of all men for my name's sake: but he that endureth to the end shall be saved.... It is enough for the disciple that he be as his master, and the servant as his lord. If they have called the master of the house Beelzebub, how much more shall they call them of his household?" (Matt. 10:22, 25).

And again:

> If the world hate you, ye know that it hated me before it hated you. If ye were of the world, the world would love his own: but because ye are not of the world, but I have chosen you out of the world, therefore the world hateth you. Remember the word that I said unto you, The servant is not greater than his lord. If they have persecuted me, they will also persecute you; if they have kept my saying, they will keep yours also. But all these things will they do unto you for my name's sake, because they know not him that sent me. (John 15:18–21)

Christ is no longer atoning, but He is still assaulted by His enemies, and they carry out that assault by attacking His servants on the earth. William Hendriksen says,

> We should bear in mind that although Christ by means of the afflictions which he endured rendered complete satisfaction to God, so that Paul is able to glory in nothing but the cross (Gal. 6:14), the enemies of Christ were not satisfied! They hated Jesus with insatiable hatred, and wanted to add to his afflictions. But since he is no longer physically

present on earth, their arrows, which are meant especially for him, strike his followers. It is in that sense that all true believers are in his stead supplying what, as the enemies see it, is lacking in the afflictions which Jesus endured. Christ's afflictions overflow toward us.[6]

John MacArthur agrees: "Paul was receiving the persecution that was intended for Christ. Jesus, having ascended to Heaven, was out of their reach. But because His enemies had not filled up all the injuries they wanted to inflict on Him, they turned their hatred on those who preached the gospel. It was in that sense that Paul filled up what was lacking in Christ's afflictions."[7]

We should also remember Revelation 12, where the enraged dragon wages war against the rest of the woman's offspring because the ruling Child has defeated him and is now out of his reach. A similar sense is given by our Lord in Mark 13:9–20, where there are suggestions of a finite degree and appointed period of such afflictions, the completion of which will usher in the last judgment. It may be, then, that Paul is also conscious that his sufferings as a servant are bringing that measure closer to its completion and so ushering in the great and terrible day of the Lord.

We deduce from the language and from the immediate and the wider context that while there is probably an eschatological edge in Paul's thinking, his focus is on the mystical union that exists between Christ and His people. The apostle's sufferings are ministerial sufferings as a man of God, not mediatorial sufferings rivaling or contributing to those of the sinless Son of God. The only thing that can be considered in any way lacking in the sufferings of Christ is the ongoing afflictions that God's people experience on Christ's behalf in our flesh (Col. 1:24) at the hands of evil men. Such men have to settle for persecuting the Lord's people, because the physical person of Christ is out of their reach. Paul suffered as a servant and ambassador of Christ at the hands of evil men because of his allegiance to Jesus. As wicked men sought to kill our Lord (John 8:40), so they seek to kill His followers. The world has an abiding enmity against Christ that He is not here personally to receive, and it is expressed in the opposition and persecution of Christ's people—especially of His faithful ministers. Our Lord told us emphatically that we would bear such persecutions: "These things have I spoken unto you, that ye should not be offended. They shall put you out of the synagogues: yea, the time cometh, that whosoever killeth you will think that he

---

6. William Hendriksen, *Colossians* in *New Testament Commentary: Philippians, Colossians and Philemon* (Edinburgh: Banner of Truth, 1962), 87.

7. John McArthur, *Colossians and Philemon* (Chicago: Moody Publishers, 1996), 76.

doeth God service. And these things will they do unto you, because they have not known the Father, nor me. But these things have I told you, that when the time shall come, ye may remember that I told you of them. And these things I said not unto you at the beginning, because I was with you" (John 16:1–4).

Paul delights in the privilege and dignity of association with Christ in afflictions. Such sufferings contain in themselves the blessing of fellowship with Him. Remember Daniel's three faithful friends in Babylon when they refused to bow down and worship the idol that Nebuchadnezzar had erected. They were determined to honor God, whether or not He saved their lives, and they went to the fiery furnace expecting to die. It was only once they were cast into the flames that a fourth figure was found with them in the literal fire of Nebuchadnezzar's wrath, the form of whom was "like the Son of God" (Dan. 3:25). One martyr of old is said to have wrestled with a lack of assurance when facing death at the stake. Determined nevertheless to honor Christ, he went to his death with his heart unquiet. It was when the flames were lit around him that he knew a restored sense of the presence of Jesus. As the fire burned higher he cried aloud with joy: "Now He comes! Now He comes!" When Paul had been persecuting the Christians, Christ was not absent (Acts 9:5). Christ Himself feels the neglect of and assaults upon His people (Matt. 25:41–45).

However, in saying all this about Paul's vertical relationship to Christ, we must not imagine that he has lost track of his horizontal relationships to other believers. The apostle is conscious not only of his relationship to the Head but also to the other members of the body.

Clarity: for the church

As we have already seen, Paul's suffering does not occur in a vacuum—it does not take place in isolation from others. Furthermore, the apostle is selfless in his suffering. Paul's sufferings as a servant of Jesus are "for his body's sake, which is the church." Paul here fills out what it means to suffer "for you"—it is the identity of the "you" that merits this suffering. Here again we see Paul's shepherd's heart surfacing. Not only are the sufferings experienced in connection with Christ Himself, but they are also experienced for the sake of Christ's body, in the establishment and edification of true churches.

Why is Paul writing from a Roman prison? Because, as Christ's apostle to the Gentiles, his testimony in Jerusalem so incensed the crowd that he was arrested for his own protection. His ministry and the sufferings associated with it are for the sake of the Gentiles, among whom are the Colossians and most of the readers of the book that you are holding. Out of those sufferings flow rich comfort and consolation to the church (2 Cor. 1:8–11) and exhortation and example to others (2 Tim. 3:10–12; 1 Cor. 11:1). The commentator Matthew Poole suggests that Paul effectively says, "Christ in his rank suffered what was necessary for my redemption; now I, in my turn, (by his gift, Phil. 1:29), undergo what afflictions are useful for his glory. He purchased salvation by his cross, I advance his kingdom and cause by my combats."[8]

Paul's readiness to suffer for the sake of others and his awareness of the potential effect of such sufferings remind us of the bold declaration made by the Reformation martyr, Hugh Latimer. Along with his younger friend and fellow minister, Nicholas Ridley, he stood fastened to a stake. As flames were kindled around the feet of the two men, Latimer leaned across to encourage his friend with these words: "Be of good cheer, Master Ridley, and play the man; we shall this day light such a candle, by God's grace, in England as I trust shall never be put out."[9] Here is the same joyful confidence in sufferings—even to death—with a view to the blessing of Christ's body. By these means and in this spirit the true gospel advances (Phil. 1:12; 2 Tim. 2:10).

Douglas Moo states it this way:

> Because Paul's apostolic ministry is an "extension" of Christ's work in the world, Paul identifies his own sufferings very closely with Christ's. These sufferings have no redemptive benefit for the church, but they are the inevitable accompaniment of Paul's "commission" to proclaim the end-time revelation of God's mystery (vv. 25–27). It is in this way that Paul's sufferings are "on behalf of" the church, including the Colossian Christians. And, of course, as a prisoner for the gospel, Paul is suffering for them even as he writes. As members of the fellowship of those raised with Christ and forming therefore part of Paul's body, we also are the beneficiaries of Paul's suffering.[10]

He who once persecuted the church (1 Cor. 15:9) is now being persecuted for the church. He who cared little for the church now devotes himself to her, whether he lives or dies. There is a Christlike tenor and fervor to Paul's life. Since

---

8. Matthew Poole, *A Commentary on the Holy Bible*, 3 vols. (Edinburgh: Banner of Truth, 1963), 3:712.

9. A good place to learn more of Hugh Latimer and Nicholas Ridley, together with John Hooper, Rowland Taylor, and John Bradford—all martyred for Christ—is J. C. Ryle, *Five English Reformers* (Edinburgh: Banner of Truth, 1981).

10. Douglas Moo, *The Letters to the Colossians and Philemon* (Grand Rapids: Eerdmans), 152–53.

his conversion, the enemies of the church have become his enemies, and he is doing all he can to secure the welfare of the church in the face of assaults upon her, enduring all things for the sake of the elect (2 Tim. 2:10). Every blow that is aimed at the church he is willing to take. All her hardships he is willing to bear. Paul, by God's grace, is ready to absorb the hostility of the world against Christ and His people for the sake of those people and for the glory of Christ.

Paul's willingness is grounded in his sense of vocation. He has been commissioned a servant of the church of Jesus Christ by God Himself, as we will see in the next chapter. He was no self-appointed authority, but rather a God-appointed minister. Paul—like his Lord—did not view himself as one who should be served, but saw himself as a servant of others. It is this that made him willing to stand with and for the church of His Savior in the face of all the opposition and abuses being hurled at her. There was a holy resignation in his attachment to the church, a disposition of readiness to suffer for her sake, that surfaces throughout his writing. Paul plainly states this:

> But we have this treasure in earthen vessels, that the excellency of the power may be of God, and not of us. We are troubled on every side, yet not distressed; we are perplexed, but not in despair; persecuted, but not forsaken; cast down, but not destroyed; always bearing about in the body the dying of the Lord Jesus, that the life also of Jesus might be made manifest in our body. For we which live are alway delivered unto death for Jesus' sake, that the life also of Jesus might be made manifest in our mortal flesh. So then death worketh in us, but life in you. (2 Cor. 4:7–12)

Paul knew why he did what he did, why he lived as he lived, and why he was ready to die as he died. Arif and Kathy Khan knew it also. Countless martyrs—many of whom will never be known by any but the Lord whom they loved and perhaps a few of those whom they served—have known it. Faithful men and women—and faithful pastors through the ages—who were persecuted and oppressed and marginalized and sidelined and dismissed have known it. Are you willing to suffer? On what basis? "For his body's sake, which is the church."

FELLOW CHRISTIAN How do you feel about the church of Jesus Christ? What do you think of her? What is your commitment to her? The apostle John makes love for one's brothers a non-negotiable characteristic of a true Christian (1 John 3:14). A faithful pastor will willingly suffer for the sake of Christ's body: is it not becoming for every child of God to entertain the same attitude toward the bride of Christ?

The call to suffer for the sake of other saints may have particular resonance for a gospel minister, but it has broad application to every member of the body (see 1 Corinthians 12). Indeed, when Paul was stoned at Antioch and left for dead, he was able in due course to remind those believers who had gathered around his apparently lifeless body that "we must through much tribulation enter into the kingdom of God" (Acts 14:22; cf. 2 Tim. 3:12).

Let us not be so afraid of Christ's afflictions that we rob Him of His honor and ourselves of the blessings of suffering for His name. Paul saw this as a privilege, not to be pursued masochistically as some twisted badge of honor, but something to be borne as a gift given: "For unto you it is given in the behalf of Christ, not only to believe on him, but also to suffer for his sake" (Phil. 1:29–30). Do you run from the fires of persecution, forgetting that Christ is walking in them to bless you with His presence in a way that you have not yet known (Dan. 3)?

Do not lose sight of the dire warning in these verses to all who lay their hand upon the apple of Christ's eye. Christ takes notice of all the assaults committed against His members on the earth, and He will return to judge all those who have not turned to Him for mercy. There will be many with fists, boots, batons, sticks, rocks, and guns raised against the church when Jesus returns. There will be many with mouths open to spew violence and aggression toward the people of God. They will see Jesus coming in His glory, and they will hear, in effect, what Paul heard: "I am Jesus whom thou persecutest" (Acts 9:5). Those who have stood against Christ and against His people without repentance will be exposed, declared cursed, and cast away into everlasting punishment (Matt. 25:41–46). The souls of those under the altar, men and women slain for the Word of God and the testimony which they held, who have been crying out to God for justice and judgment, will know the peace of God's divine vengeance against His and their enemies (Rev. 6:9–11). Justice will be done when the righteous Judge appears (2 Tim. 4:8).

Therefore, stand with and pray for your pastors. Recognize their calling, and support and encourage them in it. When Paul was afflicted, he could tell his brothers in Thessalonica, "We were comforted over you in all our affliction and distress by your faith" (1 Thess. 3:7). Your faith, your standing fast, will be their great encouragement and a sweet motive to hold fast themselves. Your prayers to God on their behalf will hold them up when they have no strength left in themselves, enabling them to be faithful to your souls.

| **FELLOW PASTOR** | If you serve Christ faithfully, you will suffer. You might not be called to spill your blood as a testament to the One who loved you and gave Himself for you, but you will invest your |

days, your years, your tears, your sweat, your labor. You may never preach to more than fifty people; speak at conferences; write an article, review, blog post, or book; or sit on any important committees. Your sufferings may be emotional and spiritual and mental agonies rather than physical pains. You may yet find your mind and body collapsing under the strain of serving Christ and His church. Toward the end of what was known as the Downgrade Controversy, a battle fought over the intrusion of liberalism into the churches of the day, Charles Spurgeon was counting the cost of his adherence to the truth. In March 1891, a preacher from his Pastors' College called E. H. Ellis left for Australia. Spurgeon bade him farewell with these words: "Good bye, Ellis; you will never see me again, this fight is killing me."[11] You may not compare yourself to Spurgeon in his accomplishments under God, but you may feel, like him, that your fight is killing you. You may labor week in, week out, and feel that you inch forward and slide back. You may live longing for an outpouring of God's Spirit on you and your ministry and the people whom you serve that you will never see. You may be in a country where your Savior is virulently hated, and people attack you with swords; you may be in a country where your Redeemer is arrogantly despised, and people attack you with words. You may live under threat of your life, or no one may care whether you live or die. You may be ignored; you may be rejected; you may be loathed. You will scratch and struggle and strive. There will be mountains you wish to conquer and hills you can barely climb. You will long to see feeble saints assured, and you will watch them struggle to their graves with the light of the gospel seeming barely to reach them. You will long to see the arrogant Christian humbled, the lazy made diligent, the lonely drawn in, the old fruitful, the young vigorous, the careless engaged, the fearful bold, the miserable joyful, the downcast lifted up. You will rejoice over your every small gain and be disappointed at your little progress. And you will keep going.

You will often be unappreciated by the people you serve; they will wonder what you do with your time to such little effect. You will ask the same question of yourself. Your faith may be shaken and then be established; your hope may waver and then be made strong; your love may grow cold before it burns hot. You may be ready to resign on many Mondays, and you will stand to preach again every

---

11. Charles Spurgeon, *Autobiography* (Pasadena, TX: Pilgrim Publications, 1992), 3:152.

Lord's Day and every other day that God gives you strength and opportunity. You will see the enemies coming, and you will cry from the walls. You will watch their approach, and you will plant your feet in the gates. You will feel isolated, and you will nevertheless stand in the gap. You will observe error and preach truth. You will watch for the wolves and feed the sheep. You will, like your great model, "seek that which was lost, and bring again that which was driven away, and will bind up that which was broken, and will strengthen that which was sick" (Ezek. 34:16). You will see men and women whom you love bruised and broken and battered by the assaults of the world, the flesh, and the devil. You will have weeping women and miserable men turn to you in their darkest hours and ask you for reasons and look to you for words of hope. You will see the hosts of hell and all the expressions of satanic malice the world can conjure flung against the church of Jesus Christ. And you will put your soul, your strength, your mind, your heart, your very body, between them and the church. And one day it will kill you, whether swiftly or slowly, and you will lie with your strength spent in the battle, and you will cross the river to your reward.

Why will you do it? Why do you do it? Because the church is the body of Christ, and every member is precious to Him.

If you see and embrace what it means for the church to be the body of Christ, you will rejoice in those very sufferings, because they are for the sake of His body, which is the church. How can we avoid those afflictions if we walk in the footsteps of the Redeemer? Will we sacrifice faithfulness and the joy of it in order to be spared suffering?

Like the apostle, we must reckon with the union between Christ and His people, recognize the antagonism still directed toward the Head and His body, and not sit by and let it happen. Paul stood strong as a good soldier of Jesus Christ, and we must pray and work at the same. He called on his fellow believers to act like men: "Watch ye, stand fast in the faith, quit you like men, be strong" (1 Cor. 16:13). The fight is to the death, but Christ has promised that the gates of Hades will not prevail against His church (Matt. 16:18).

Let us not be foolish: Christ's enemies are still attacking the church, and will until the end comes. Are you willing to stand valiantly with and for her? You do not know what will come—loss of reputation, opposition from within or without the professing church, physical persecutions—but will you defend those who have been committed to your care?

As we stand between the people of God and the enemies of God, many good things will come. The body of Christ, the church, will find an example of principled courage and holy rejoicing in bearing witness for the Lord. If we follow Paul, we will pass on this disposition to others living in the midst of a crooked and perverse generation (Phil. 2:15). Paul pressed upon the church in Philippi the good effects of his suffering: "But I would ye should understand, brethren, that the things which happened unto me have fallen out rather unto the furtherance of the gospel; so that my bonds in Christ are manifest in all the palace, and in all other places; and many of the brethren in the Lord, waxing confident by my bonds, are much more bold to speak the word without fear" (Phil. 1:12–14).

It will be a source of comfort to the body of Christ in times of trouble. Paul said to the church in Corinth, "And whether we be afflicted, it is for your consolation and salvation, which is effectual in the enduring of the same sufferings which we also suffer: or whether we be comforted, it is for your consolation and salvation" (2 Cor. 1:6).

Suffering will bring you through fire and water and out to a place of rich fulfillment (Ps. 66:12). It will secure the blessing of seeing the church of Christ complete and perfect in the day of Christ: "For what is our hope, or joy, or crown of rejoicing? Are not even ye in the presence of our Lord Jesus Christ at his coming? For ye are our glory and joy" (1 Thess. 2:19–20).

It will serve the glory of the Head of the body, the church, on the day when He declares in its ultimate sense, "Behold, I and the children whom the LORD hath given me are for signs and for wonders in Israel from the LORD of hosts, which dwelleth in mount Zion" (Isa. 8:18).

Paul loved God's people in every true church and had their greatest good constantly in mind. He rejoiced in his sufferings because he knew the good that would accrue to others by means of them. He sought their good above his own. He suffered with joy for the sake of Christ's body, which is the church. Only with God's help may we do the same.

4 | THE ORIGIN OF PAUL'S MINISTRY

...the church: whereof I am made a minister, according to the dispensation of God which is given to me for you... — Colossians 1:24–25

You can never safely look upon the ministry as a profession, the entrance to which is spontaneous and subject to choice. It is a dispensation, an "Oikonomia," a law of the household of God; rising above the mere acknowledgement of duty, to an experience of the constraining love of Christ; to an appreciation of the infinite value of the Gospel, which we have been taught by his own Spirit and power, and the joy and hope of which we have truly and clearly received.[1] — Stephen H. Tyng

Paul never ceased to marvel at the new creation worked in the hearts of God's elect: "If any man be in Christ, he is a new creature: old things are passed away; behold, all things are become new" (2 Cor. 5:17). That "behold" captures at least something of the wonder of the Damascus road where Saul of Tarsus, the arrogant, insolent, blaspheming persecutor, was confronted and captured by the risen Christ, at first overwhelmed with and then overjoyed by His glory. This turn of events was almost unbelievable to the disciples, who once feared the mention of Paul's name (Acts 9:26). Christ Jesus had made this man a Christian. But beyond that, He had made him a minister. The instinct of Paul's renewed heart was to ask, "Lord, what do you want me to do?" The answer, as Paul later recalled it, was clear and categorical:

> But rise, and stand upon thy feet: for I have appeared unto thee for this purpose, to make thee a minister and a witness both of these things

1. Stephen H. Tyng, *The Christian Pastor: The Office and Duty of the Gospel Minister* (Birmingham, AL: Solid Ground Christian Books, 2006), 28–29.

which thou hast seen, and of those things in the which I will appear unto thee; delivering thee from the people, and from the Gentiles, unto whom now I send thee, to open their eyes, and to turn them from darkness to light, and from the power of Satan unto God, that they may receive forgiveness of sins, and inheritance among them which are sanctified by faith that is in me. (Acts 26:16–18)

This encounter left the apostle with a profound sense of his identity and calling, a grace-soaked notion of who he was as a man and what he was as a minister. But Paul's self-awareness was not the same as arrogant self-esteem or pompous, self-assured pride. After all, Paul had become a humble man, always marveling that "unto me, who am less than the least of all saints, is this grace given, that I should preach among the Gentiles the unsearchable riches of Christ" (Eph. 3:8).

But Paul also knew that he was a privileged man. He was secure in God's calling, knowing himself to be an apostle of Jesus Christ (Col. 1:1), recognizing that he was a servant together with other gospel laborers (Col. 1:7), but also made meek as one who had received a particular mercy: "And last of all he was seen of me also, as of one born out of due time. For I am the least of the apostles, that am not meet to be called an apostle, because I persecuted the church of God. But by the grace of God I am what I am: and his grace which was bestowed upon me was not in vain" (1 Cor. 15:8–10). In this, Paul is a truly Christlike man. He sees his life as one of obedience and service, even to the extent that he identifies himself in terms of his relationship to the church, its glorious Head, and blessed members.

While Paul describes himself in his relationship to the Colossians, what he is to them is also true of his relationship to the whole apostolic church as Christ's servant to the Gentiles. Never did the church have another servant such as Paul. He expressed this sense of his calling in writing to the church at Corinth: "For we preach not ourselves, but Christ Jesus the Lord; and ourselves your servants for Jesus' sake.... For all things are for your sakes, that the abundant grace might through the thanksgiving of many redound to the glory of God" (2 Cor. 4:5, 15).

Paul is also modeling what his fellow servants must be in a particular church or in their relationship to any number of churches, for every overseer is a servant of God and a steward in His house (Titus 1:7). For example, Epaphras—who is probably one of the Colossian pastors—is a man of Pauline spirit, a faithful minister of Christ on behalf of the church he serves (Col. 1:7). You do not have to be an apostle to have an apostolic spirit and aim in ministry. As Paul will go on to declare in Colossians 1:28, "We preach" Christ. Every faithful minister preaches Jesus like the apostle. Today's gospel ministers can still learn their character, relationships, obligations, and expectations from the apostle:

"Brethren, be followers together of me, and mark them which walk so as ye have us for an ensample" (Phil. 3:17).

The servant of the church

When Paul speaks of becoming a minister or servant of God's gospel, according to the stewardship from God that was given to him, a sense of wonder at God's grace in Christ conditions the apostle. He who had been a monster was "made a minister" (Col. 1:25). The persecutor is now the preacher and pastor; the one who made the church suffer now suffers for the church. It is as if Paul said, "Come and share in the marvel of this—that I myself have been made a servant of the church of Jesus."

Observe, first, *the calling*. Paul was not a volunteer for this task. His desire for and delight in this labor were not the product of nature. He is willing because God has made him willing. He is not self-appointed, for the sense is of an outside agency operating upon him. He may be contrasting himself at this point with the false teachers, men who—a little like the so-called super-apostles afflicting the church at Corinth, coming with their self-penned letters of recommendation (2 Cor. 3:1)—had no authority other than their own sense of importance and deluded notions of position and worth. The clear implication is that God's irresistible grace had been at work. God had formed Paul for the task, and salvation full and free now fired him with the passion for God's glory that characterized his life.

But we can also see here *the role* to which the apostle was called. He became a minister, a working servant. He was a leader but not a lord. While he walked the earth, the Lord Christ needed to warn His disciples as they argued about which of them could be considered the greatest: "And he said unto them, The kings of the Gentiles exercise lordship over them; and they that exercise authority upon them are called benefactors. But ye shall not be so: but he that is greatest among you, let him be as the younger; and he that is chief, as he that doth serve. For whether is greater, he that sitteth at meat, or he that serveth? is not he that sitteth at meat? but I am among you as he that serveth" (Luke 22:25–27).

Peter never forgot his Lord's rebuke and communicated its sense later in his life as a servant of Jesus Christ: "Feed the flock of God which is among you, taking the oversight thereof, not by constraint, but willingly; not for filthy lucre, but of a ready mind; neither as being lords over God's heritage, but being ensamples to the flock. And when the chief Shepherd shall appear, ye shall receive a crown of glory that fadeth not away" (1 Peter 5:2–4).

As we have seen before, Christ reverses the expectations of the world, and this is a lesson that Paul, like Peter, learned well. His greatness lies in service, just as Christ's did. The true man of God leads by serving. He is called not to domination but to ministration. He rises by falling. The way up is down. This is a paradox that the world simply cannot grasp, and it is an attitude that ought to distinguish God's true servants. Paul's sense of self is not one of mindless self-effacement, as if he must become the doormat of the world. Rather, he is—like his Master—a servant of all (Mark 10:45). He is called not first to honor, but to labor; he is sent not for applause from men, but for activity on behalf of men. His is the glorious privilege of stooping to serve, the high and dignified calling of hard and humble work.

The stewardship from God

Paul now highlights the governing awareness that lies behind his conception of himself and the service he undertakes. His ministry is "according to the dispensation of God which is given to me for you" (Col. 1:25). Paul is an enlisted man, called into service by God Himself. He is speaking of himself as much as of anyone else when he says to Timothy, "No man that warreth entangleth himself with the affairs of this life; that he may please him who hath chosen him to be a soldier" (2 Tim. 2:4).

As someone so commissioned, Paul works on God's terms and is governed by God's will; his desire is to please God. He is a servant of the church because he is a steward of God: his authority derives from God, and he is ultimately accountable to God. He is to act in accordance with God's plan and purpose and is answerable to God for those acts. We see Paul's sense of this, for example, in 1 Corinthians 4: "Let a man so account of us, as of the ministers of Christ, and stewards of the mysteries of God. Moreover it is required in stewards, that a man be found faithful. But with me it is a very small thing that I should be judged of you, or of man's judgment: yea, I judge not mine own self. For I know nothing by myself; yet am I not hereby justified: but he that judgeth me is the Lord" (1 Cor. 4:1–4).

A similar awareness of duty, a sense of holy obligation, comes through strongly later in that letter: "For though I preach the gospel, I have nothing to glory of: for necessity is laid upon me; yea, woe is unto me, if I preach not the gospel! For if I do this thing willingly, I have a reward: but if against my will, a dispensation of the gospel is committed unto me. What is my reward then? Verily that, when I preach the gospel, I may make the gospel of Christ without charge, that I abuse not my power in the gospel" (1 Cor. 9:16–18).

The word translated *dispensation* is derived from two other words, and— while there may be a sense of working within God's overarching administration or sovereign plan (cf. Eph. 1:10; 3:2, 9)—it probably carries the primary idea of the stewardship, management, arrangement, or direction of a household. The word was commonly used in Paul's day to describe one who watched out for the interest or cared for the property of someone else. It is like the position that Joseph held in Potiphar's house:

> And Joseph found grace in his sight, and he served him: and he made him overseer over his house, and all that he had he put into his hand. And it came to pass from the time that he had made him overseer in his house, and over all that he had, that the LORD blessed the Egyptian's house for Joseph's sake; and the blessing of the LORD was upon all that he had in the house, and in the field. And he left all that he had in Joseph's hand; and he knew not ought he had, save the bread which he did eat. And Joseph was a goodly person, and well favoured. (Gen. 39:4–6)

In other words, Paul is telling us here that he—according to God's plan and purpose for his life—was made a household manager, a steward, with the divine intention that he should handle and supervise God's affairs in the house of God, the church (1 Tim. 3:5, 15), in accordance with the direction that he received from Christ through His Word and Spirit. He is, in a sense, a trustee, the supervisor of God's business in God's house, administering God's "spiritual treasures" on God's behalf.[2]

Paul's service of the church of Jesus Christ was appointed for him and entrusted to his care in accordance with God's gracious and sovereign will. The Lord God has a plan, and for the fulfillment of that plan He appointed the apostle Paul to an office, the parameters and terms of service of which were set by God. Paul had high privileges and a sacred trust, and he was not free to act outside of them or contrary to them. He was a household servant: the house was the church, and the head of the house the Lord Himself—Christ (Heb. 3:6). Paul's labors for the church must therefore be accomplished in accordance with the stewardship that God gave him, not dictated by his own agenda. Jean Daillé explains:

> For the steward, or dispenser, has power not to do any thing of his own head, and after his own fancy, but only to dispense what the master has given him, and precisely in such a manner as he has described to him. If he takes upon himself to do more, he exceeds the bounds of his

---

2. William Hendriksen, *Colossians* in *New Testament Commentary: Philippians, Colossians and Philemon* (Edinburgh: Banner of Truth, 1932), 88.

commission; and all that he does or says beyond them is void and of no force, nor does it oblige any one of the household to obey it.[3]

The Lord Christ was Paul's Savior and Master, and the apostle knew himself to be a custodian of God's truth. This awareness of his place rises constantly to the surface in his letters:

> For if I do this thing willingly, I have a reward: but if against my will, a dispensation of the gospel is committed unto me. (1 Cor. 9:17)

> For this cause I Paul, the prisoner of Jesus Christ for you Gentiles, if ye have heard of the dispensation of the grace of God which is given me to you-ward. (Eph. 3:1–2)

> But contrariwise, when they saw that the gospel of the uncircumcision was committed unto me. (Gal. 2:7)

> According to the glorious gospel of the blessed God, which was committed to my trust. (1 Tim. 1:11)[4]

These verses make it plain that all authority—in the church as much as anywhere else—is subject to God's authority. A minister's authority in Christ's church derives from Christ and is exercised on behalf of Christ; for its exercise, he will be answerable to Christ. Paul communicates this awareness of his calling in speaking to the Ephesian elders:

> And when they were come to him, he said unto them, Ye know, from the first day that I came into Asia, after what manner I have been with you at all seasons, serving the Lord with all humility of mind, and with many tears, and temptations, which befell me by the lying in wait of the Jews: and how I kept back nothing that was profitable unto you, but have shewed you, and have taught you publickly, and from house to house, testifying both to the Jews, and also to the Greeks, repentance toward God, and faith toward our Lord Jesus Christ. (Acts 20:18–21)

In other circumstances he has to be more robust. When confronting the Galatian heresy, Paul challenges the believers in this way: "For do I now persuade men, or God? or do I seek to please men? for if I yet pleased men, I should not be the servant of Christ. But I certify you, brethren, that the gospel which was preached

---

3. Jean Daillé, *The Epistle to the Colossians* in *An Exposition of the Epistles of Saint Paul to the Philippians and* Colossians (Stoke-on-Trent, UK: Tentmaker Publications, 2008), 72.

4. See also Romans 15:15–16; 2 Corinthians 5:18–19; and Titus 1:1–3.

of me is not after man. For I neither received it of man, neither was I taught it, but by the revelation of Jesus Christ" (Gal. 1:10–12).

The minister is not a free agent or loose cannon. It is not his own will or whim that governs him. It is not even the will or whim of a particular church that directs him. It is God's gospel that he preaches, and he is free to preach no other. It is the will and purpose of Almighty God that guides his life and dominates his awareness of who he is and what he must do. He labors under a present sense—often a weighty sense—of his stewardship from God, and he serves the church in accordance with that stewardship, discharging his responsibility to the body of Christ as one standing before God Himself: "But as we were allowed of God to be put in trust with the gospel, even so we speak; not as pleasing men, but God, which trieth our hearts" (1 Thess. 2:4). It is this that conditions Paul; it is his primary attachment and his governing concern. His ministry, message, and methods are all subject to God.

The church needs such men still, and they are still being given to and for the church. We must pay close attention to the fact that the stewardship that Paul has been given terminates on the church. This is God's design and purpose: He gives gospel ministers to the church for her good.

If a man called by God is rightly to have his mind on heavenly things, then his feet ought to be firmly planted on the ground, in the center of the church of our Lord. His primary obligation to God secures the good of the church, because it is "for you"—for the body of Christ—that this stewardship is given to the apostle. Notice, then, that the church is not only at the forefront of a pastor's mind, but it is at the forefront of God's mind when He gives a pastor to the church. The risen Christ has the temporal and eternal well-being of His church in His heart when He sends those whom He has appointed to shepherd her:

> And he gave some, apostles; and some, prophets; and some, evangelists; and some, pastors and teachers; for the perfecting of the saints, for the work of the ministry, for the edifying of the body of Christ: till we all come in the unity of the faith, and of the knowledge of the Son of God, unto a perfect man, unto the measure of the stature of the fulness of Christ: that we henceforth be no more children, tossed to and fro, and carried about with every wind of doctrine, by the sleight of men, and cunning craftiness, whereby they lie in wait to deceive; but speaking the truth in love, may grow up into him in all things, which is the head, even Christ: from whom the whole body fitly joined together and compacted by that which every joint supplieth, according to the effectual working in the measure of every part, maketh increase of the body unto the edifying of itself in love. (Eph. 4:11–16)

Paul is not ministering in isolation. Though an apostle, he is not simply a minister at large, but a minister given to and for the church of Christ: she is the object of all his efforts, the center of his concerns. All his labors have reference to the church in accordance with the stewardship that he has from God. He does not go beyond the bounds of his authority in writing the way he does to the Colossian church (even though Colossians 2:1 suggests that he has never met most of the people personally), for God has given him to and for her as an apostle, just as God still gives ministers to and for His individual churches.

Do you see how this liberates the godly minister to be the pastor that a church needs rather than the one that she simply wants? In the professing church of Christ there are those who are not truly saved, and that will be revealed in what they do and in what they fail to do, how they operate and what they expect. They will have an agenda that is often explicitly contrary to the will of God, whether or not that agenda is ever made public. This will be manifest in many ways. The famous Welsh preacher, Christmas Evans, once vividly described what he imagined Satan would look like if he came to church:

> The way in which a man hears the Gospel is an index to the state of his heart and the nature of his affections and desires. If we were to suppose that Satan came into the congregation, what kind of hearer would he be? He is the inveterate enemy of all truth, righteousness and godliness; and the sanctification of the soul, devotion, and spiritual affections in the worshippers of the house of God vex [annoy] him sorely [greatly]. If one day, then, in human form he took his place amongst the hearers of the everlasting Gospel, we may fancy that, in order to hinder and annoy as much as possible, he would take his seat in a conspicuous place, either under the pulpit or in front of the gallery, before the eyes of all. Then he would pull ugly faces and close his eyes, and appear as if asleep. He would most anxiously guard against giving the slightest indication of being touched by what was said. Not a trace of conviction, submission, peace and joy should on any account ever appear. He would scowl and knit his brows and shake his head, and show every disapproval of the Gospel he hears, as if he would change every man in the place into the same devilish disposition. Such, I say, would be the deportment of the arch-enemy as a hearer of the Word of God. But have we not seen many that have the name of Christ upon them an exact picture of this?[5]

5. Quoted in Owen Jones, *Some of the Great Preachers of Wales* (Stoke-on-Trent, UK: Tentmaker Publications, 1995), 179.

How many pastors have preached with such glaring, glowering, growling faces before them? How does a faithful man hold to his course under such circumstances and preach the gospel simply and earnestly? Only through a binding sense of his stewardship before God.

There are also true sheep who are still learning, saved sinners who are sinners still. They may embrace the idea of a faithful ministry in principle, but they do not always enjoy it in practice, especially when it comes close to home. Their ignorance and arrogance can lead—even unwittingly—to their working at cross-purposes to the Scriptures, and sometimes a violent eruption follows. It is the pastors who often bear the brunt of such eruptions. Particular applications of the truth, either in public or in private, that cut across the desires of a true Christian, can call forth a goat-like response even from a sheep. Some pastors regularly hear vague assertions like, "You should leave application for the Holy Spirit." This is often shorthand for, "How dare you say that to me, or at least to a church with me in the congregation!" or, "That is not a part of the truth that I ever want you to press on my conscience again!" It is not unknown for even true believers to resemble that Satan figure described by Evans, seated front and center, huffing and puffing and slamming down their Bibles in exasperation as the minister—though a sinner himself and with many flaws of his own—sets out to press home needful but unwanted truth to their souls, seeking by the application of the gospel ruler to make straight some warped part of their life.

Some adopt a passive-aggressive approach, their eyes glazing over with what becomes an all too familiar stare into the middle distance, as the truth applied is allowed simply to wash over and past them. When such "hearers" switch back on, they blithely continue exactly the same sinful or unfruitful patterns of behavior as before.

How does a faithful pastor overcome such opposition and continue to give the true sheep what they need rather than what—perhaps in their worst moments if not their best—they want? Only through a robust sense of his responsibility to God.

This sense of a stewardship from God, a divine mandate, secures for the church a pastor's affections, concerns, labors, graces, and gifts. It keeps him faithful, earnest, honest, and loving when he might be fearful, casual, evasive, and cool. The church can rejoice in that, and a minister must recognize it. All he has and is has been given by God for the sake of the church: he must, in accordance with the stewardship given, pour himself out into and on behalf of Christ's redeemed people, for it is with regard to the church—for her good—that he is called and commissioned.

| FELLOW
| CHRISTIAN

Recognize and rejoice in God's kindness to us, His purchased possession! Not only has He redeemed us by His own blood, but He keeps us as the apple of His eye and has given and keeps giving faithful men to shepherd the flock. He gave Paul to the Gentiles, to the Colossians, and to us—to the whole church. We must still receive the apostle's care and teaching and the teaching and care of those men subsequently appointed by God and laboring—with God, with Paul—to the same ends.

How do you think of your pastor? We are often tempted to separate people from our understanding of providence. That is, we are happy to account things and events as under God's control but to complain about the people with whom we come into contact. Have you considered, then, that the Lord has given that particular man "for you"? Presuming that he is faithful as called, he is not an accident, happy or otherwise, but a specific gift of God. He has been appointed by God, commissioned for his task, recognized by a church as such, granted graces and gifts for the good of the body. With all his imperfections and idiosyncrasies—and how many he will have!—he yet remains the servant of the Lord for you. How do you think of him and pray for him? Do you give thanks for him? Do you pray for his sanctification? Do you ask the Lord that he might see from Scripture more of what it means to shepherd the flock of which God has made him an overseer? If you do not, will you from this moment on?

How do you relate to him? Remember the earnest counsel of the writer to the Hebrews: "Obey them that have the rule over you, and submit yourselves: for they watch for your souls, as they that must give account, that they may do it with joy, and not with grief: for that is unprofitable for you" (Heb. 13:17; cf. 1 Thess. 5:12–13). Are you conscious of this responsibility? Are you a sheep of Christ who brings joy to your shepherd's heart? Do you cultivate a righteously humble attitude in your dealings with him, recognizing him as God's particular instrument for your sanctification?

If the local church of which you are a part needs her own pastor, you can be sure that you are praying in accordance with the mind of God when you ask for a faithful undershepherd. The Lord Jesus gives gifts to His church, and His heart is wide open toward her. He has her present and eternal well-being always on His heart. You do not ask for something contrary to God's will, but for something He delights to give. Come with hopeful confidence before Him, day by day, and ask Him for the man after His own heart who will—without fear or favor—serve Him among you and do your souls everlasting good by his faithful shepherding.

Do not forget the wider church in this. One of the crying needs of the day in which we live—a day of white fields and few laborers—is for the Lord of the harvest to thrust out workers into His harvest (Matt. 9:38). Are you praying that prayer? You have a specific mandate to do so. We also urge any young men who are reading this volume to pause at this point: Have you carefully considered the possibility that you may be part of the answer to the prayers of the church, and to your own prayers, in this regard? Do not divorce the end of Matthew 9 from the beginning of Matthew 10. At the end of Matthew 9 Jesus Christ commands His disciples to pray for harvesters sent from God. The very next thing we see is those same disciples equipped and sent out to the lost sheep of the house of Israel to preach the good news.

Brothers, we would not have you go without being sent, but we would have you willing and ready to go if the Lord sends you. Consider carefully—in the probing examination of your own heart, in consultation with other faithful men from the present and the past, and in the context of a faithful local church— whether or not you are one to whom the Lord Christ is giving graces and gifts for the sake of His church.

Perhaps you read some of these things, and—with the best will in the world—you are forced to acknowledge that your present pastor is not such a man. Perhaps your pastor is not even a man! Or perhaps he has run without being sent. Perhaps he is not truly converted. Perhaps he serves himself and not others. In responding to such painful circumstances, do not forget that you are still God's child, and you have a Great Shepherd who cares for your soul. We do not counsel you necessarily to remain where you are or to depart. We cannot make that decision for you. However, we urge you to act towards such a man with Christian love and candor and to do him all the good you can by your words, deeds, and prayers. He may be a hireling, or even a thief. Do not forget that even these trials are by the appointment of God and that He works all things together for good to those who love Him (Rom. 8:28) and can bring good out of the evil that men intend and do (Gen. 50:20), even when we cannot understand how. Who knows but that by these means God will draw out and cultivate graces in you that might otherwise never have come to light? Could you be the means of instructing or even winning over such a man by your prayers and example? Neither should you lose sight of the end of all things: those who watch for souls—those who hold this high and holy office, however they discharge it— will give an account to the Great Shepherd of the sheep. God Himself will deal with faithless shepherds. Some may yet be saved through fire (1 Cor. 3:12–15). Furthermore, there is a terrible end reserved for those who abuse and tear at the flock of the living God: such wolf-like would-be shepherds will be accountable to God Himself, and He is the righteous Judge of all the earth, who always does right (Gen. 18:25).

All that said, remember that you too have a stewardship. Whoever and whatever you are, if you are a member of the body of Jesus Christ, then you are equipped by His Holy Spirit to serve Him in His church (1 Cor. 12:4), possessing "gifts differing according to the grace that is given to us" (Rom. 12:6). You too are a disciple of the One who came not to be served, but to serve. Even "those members of the body, which seem to be more feeble, are necessary" (1 Cor. 12:22). God has Himself composed the body and has done so with consummate skill and wisdom: "For we are his workmanship, created in Christ Jesus unto good works, which God hath before ordained that we should walk in them" (Eph. 2:10). Do not despise your place in the body. There is no one in the house of God who is not a servant, though some have greater prominence than others. Every vessel in the house of God is made for honor, although each has its own sphere and function. You do not have an apostolic sphere, and you may not have a formal pastoral role, but you have grace and gifts granted by God for the glory of His eternal name and the good of your fellow members in the body. With the guidance and under the care of those appointed for the shepherding of the flock, join in employing those capacities given for the extension of Christ's kingdom and the honor of Jesus at the day of His return.

FELLOW PASTOR

When you consider your identity and your calling, go back to the root of the matter. What were you by nature? Were you a black-hearted wretch, sold under sin, running after all manner of iniquity as a thirsty man pursues a cool drink, seeking always to quench the burning desires of your sinful appetites and lusts? Were you a religious bigot, a Pharisee of the Pharisees, full of self and self-righteousness, proud that you were not like other men? Were you utterly ignorant of God's truth, wandering for many years without a thought of Him? Were you a well-instructed sinner, knowing much about God without truly knowing God and transgressing against the very light you were given? How wretched, vile, and guilty we have been, and how much foulness we often find remaining in our hearts.

What have you become by grace? A child of God—a blood-bought, blood-washed, blood-earnest Christian! That black heart has been made clean, and the reigning power of sin forever broken. That mere religion has been shredded, and in its place the Holy Spirit has given you a real relationship with the living

God, grounded in the life, death, and resurrection of the Savior. That ignorance has been taken away, and in its place is a true and growing knowledge of God Almighty. That instruction that once was a skeletal cage of lifeless bones has become a vehicle by which you know and serve the God of your salvation. You are redeemed, and more—enlisted to serve your God and His church by preaching the gospel of Jesus Christ. Not only a Christian, but a preacher!

Friend, do you ever pause to wonder that to you, who are less than the least of all the saints, this grace was given, that in some way you should preach among the Gentiles (or, indeed, the Jews) the unsearchable riches of Christ (Eph. 3:8)? You should! It should be the source of your constant joy and wonder that not only has God called you to Himself but sent you out from Himself to turn others like you from darkness to light. Do not lose this sense of grateful wonder, for it will dignify all that you do as an act of thankful obedience and joyful service to the Christ who loved you and gave Himself for you.

These things will keep you humble, not arrogant; they will make you secure rather than severe; they will never contribute to pride but give you stability and confidence in pouring yourself out for the church of the risen Jesus. They will give you a servant disposition.

Remember, too, that as a servant you are called to be blameless as a faithful steward in God's own house (Titus 1:7). When you are recognized by a local church as a gospel minister, that church is recognizing that you are commissioned by God for the work of ministry. You are their servant because you are God's steward.

That means that your duty is to be carried out on God's terms, in accordance with His will. You are not to construct your own ideas of what the church needs and discharge them as you see fit. You are constrained by your very identity to be what God knows the church needs: how and what you preach; how you pastor and with what words and spirit; your commitment to God's truth for the beginning and ongoing life of a church and every member of that body; her goals, her aims, her health, her progress. All these things are fundamentally governed by God. This is why Paul communicates so earnestly with young Timothy. Fearful of any delay, he writes in order "that thou mayest know how thou oughtest to behave thyself in the house of God, which is the church of the living God, the pillar and ground of the truth" (1 Tim. 3:15).

Later on he urges his fellow laborer in these words:

> Let no man despise thy youth; but be thou an example of the believers, in
> word, in conversation, in charity, in spirit, in faith, in purity. Till I come,
> give attendance to reading, to exhortation, to doctrine. Neglect not the
> gift that is in thee, which was given thee by prophecy, with the laying on

of the hands of the presbytery. Meditate upon these things; give thyself wholly to them; that thy profiting may appear to all. Take heed unto thyself, and unto the doctrine; continue in them: for in doing this thou shalt both save thyself, and them that hear thee. (1 Tim. 4:12–16)

We are free men in Christ, but not free agents. We have a calling to discharge, and we will be answerable to the God who enlisted us for the manner in which we have conducted ourselves and performed our duty.

Let us therefore be zealous to carry out our tasks with the utmost diligence, being found faithful (1 Cor. 4:2). The Lord's steward acts knowing that his Lord sees all that he does and cheerfully sets out to do his Master's will just as it was given to him. Always he relies upon the Word of God illuminated by the Spirit of God to discern the will of the Lord, and that alone is what he sets out to accomplish, without addition, subtraction, or deviation. Let us work within the bounds of our calling and commission and not expose ourselves either to the censure of God or the resistance of good men by overreaching ourselves: "Who then is a faithful and wise servant, whom his lord hath made ruler over his household, to give them meat in due season? Blessed is that servant, whom his lord when he cometh shall find so doing. Verily I say unto you, that he shall make him ruler over all his goods" (Matt. 24:45–47).

Without laziness or apathy, let us accept the charges given to us, conscious of their weightiness with God. When John Brown of Haddington wrote to a newly ordained student of his, he gave the following counsel: "I know the vanity of your heart, and that you will feel mortified that your congregation is very small, in comparison with those of your brethren around you; but assure yourself on the word of an old man, that when you come to give an account of them to the Lord Christ, at his judgment-seat, you will think you have had enough."[6]

Are you so serving as to be ready to give that account?

However, this sense of stewardship is not a matter of obligation only. It also frees you to be the man God has called and sent you to be. You are not and do not need to be governed by what the church wants, or thinks she wants. God willing, you serve in a faithful church of sheep hungry to know and do the will of God. But even then, you will find many who—for various reasons—are governed too often by their own wills and interested more often in their own ways than in

---

6. James Hay and Henry Belfrage, *Memoir of the Rev. Alexander Waugh* (Edinburgh: William Oliphant and Son, 1839), 64–65, quoted by Mark Dever, *What Is a Healthy Church?* (Wheaton, IL: Crossway, 2007), 37. Similar counsel has been attributed to Spurgeon also and probably to many other wise pastors.

the will and way of the Lord. There will be many who, in some area or other of life are—ignorantly or otherwise—swayed more or less by rationalism, traditionalism, pragmatism, or fatalism than by the Word of God, constructing and working out their own flawed agenda in the life of the church. They will have varying degrees of influence, authority, and power, and you—serving with a Christlike spirit, but conscious of your call and responsibility—will be able calmly and deliberately to advance God's agenda for the present and eternal blessing of His people. Sometimes there will be battles to fight, tensions to resolve, pushy people to face down, rocky business meetings to negotiate, angry reactions to sermons to handle, explosions in or after pastoral visits to manage. In all this, a sense that you are a steward of the house of God, commissioned by the Head of the household for the discharge of His good and perfect will, will make you circumspect yet bold, wise yet faithful, gentle yet determined, humble yet definite, in pursuing the ends for which Christ has given you to His church.

You are a servant of Christ's gospel for Christ's church. Joyfully recognize, receive, and realize your calling and duty as modeled by Paul. He could say, "Be ye followers of me, even as I also am of Christ" (1 Cor. 11:1). Let us labor by God's grace to embrace and fulfill our stewardship from God, that we might hear our Master say in that day, "Well done, thou good and faithful servant…enter thou into the joy of thy lord" (Matt. 25:21, 23).

5 | THE ESSENCE OF PAUL'S MINISTRY

...to fulfil the word of God; even the mystery which hath been hid from ages and from generations, but now is made manifest to his saints: to whom God would make known what is the riches of the glory of this mystery among the Gentiles; which is Christ in you, the hope of glory. — COLOSSIANS 1:25–27

A new way of "doing" church is emerging. In this radical paradigm shift, exposition is being replaced with entertainment, preaching with performances, doctrine with drama, and theology with theatrics. The pulpit, once the focal point of the church, is now being overshadowed by a variety of church-growth techniques, everything from trendy worship styles to glitzy presentations and vaudeville-like pageantries. In seeking to capture the upper hand in church growth, a new wave of pastors is reinventing church and repackaging the gospel into a product to be sold to "consumers."[1] — STEVEN LAWSON

What overarching and all-encompassing elements mark the ministry of a true man of God?

We have considered in previous chapters the *messenger* of God, the person and role of the minister of the gospel. As we continue to look at Paul and learn from the apostle's example, we need now to identify his *message* and the *means* of getting that message across. If we were to attempt to summarize the vital details and scope of his work, what would be included? What characterized his labors? What were the essential elements of his efforts? What does it mean to be a preacher of the Word? What was at the heart of his message? How did he carry out his task? We begin to answer those questions by considering the design and description of Paul's gospel labors.

---

1. Steve Lawson, *Famine in the Land* (Chicago: Moody Publishers, 2003), 25.

The design

Having been given a sacred stewardship from God, Paul now says to the Colossians that his assignment was "to fulfil the word of God" (Col. 1:25). This is the heart of his commission. In what sense did Paul fulfil the Word of God? This word *fulfil* can have several different senses in Scripture and is a rich concept. The root idea is to fill up or carry something out completely. It can also mean to make something fully known. All these uses are found in the Bible.[2]

How do we weave these strands together so as to gain a coherent understanding of Paul's declaration to these Colossian Christians? What does Paul want them and us to grasp as being of the essence of his stewardship with regard to them and to the church at large?

It may help us to answer these questions if we remember the commission that Paul received from the Lord Jesus Christ Himself. Paul recounted that experience before King Agrippa, as recorded in Acts 26:12–20:

> Whereupon as I went to Damascus with authority and commission from the chief priests, at midday, O king, I saw in the way a light from heaven, above the brightness of the sun, shining round about me and them which journeyed with me. And when we were all fallen to the earth, I heard a voice speaking unto me, and saying in the Hebrew tongue, Saul, Saul, why persecutest thou me? it is hard for thee to kick against the pricks. And I said, Who art thou, Lord? And he said, I am Jesus whom thou persecutest. But rise, and stand upon thy feet: for I have appeared unto thee for this purpose, to make thee a minister and a witness both of these things which thou hast seen, and of those things in the which I will appear unto thee; delivering thee from the people, and from the Gentiles, unto whom now I send thee, to open their eyes, and to turn them from darkness to light, and from the power of Satan unto God, that they may receive forgiveness of sins, and inheritance among them which are sanctified by faith that is in me. Whereupon, O king Agrippa, I was not disobedient unto the heavenly vision: but shewed first unto them of Damascus, and at Jerusalem, and throughout all the coasts of Judaea, and then to the Gentiles, that they should repent and turn to God, and do works meet for repentance.

That this clear directive burned itself into Paul's consciousness is clear from the repetitions and echoes of it that recur throughout his writing. For example, he has already used similar phrasing in speaking of the Colossians' salvation in

---

2. See Matthew 13:48; Romans 15:19; Acts 12:25.

Colossians 1:12–14. On at least three other occasions in Luke's record of the work of Christ through His apostles the same note is sounded:

> But the Lord said unto him, Go thy way: for he is a chosen vessel unto me, to bear my name before the Gentiles, and kings, and the children of Israel. (Acts 9:15)

> And thence sailed to Antioch, from whence they had been recommended to the grace of God for the work which they fulfilled. And when they were come, and had gathered the church together, they rehearsed all that God had done with them, and how he had opened the door of faith unto the Gentiles. And there they abode long time with the disciples. (Acts 14:26–28)

> And it came to pass, that, when I was come again to Jerusalem, even while I prayed in the temple, I was in a trance; and saw him saying unto me, Make haste, and get thee quickly out of Jerusalem: for they will not receive thy testimony concerning me. And I said, Lord, they know that I imprisoned and beat in every synagogue them that believed on thee: and when the blood of thy martyr Stephen was shed, I also was standing by, and consenting unto his death, and kept the raiment of them that slew him. And he said unto me, Depart: for I will send thee far hence unto the Gentiles. (Acts 22:17–21)

Clearly, the commission of Christ to the apostle was a decisive declaration in God's plan of redemption and in Paul's experience of his place in that plan. We come across this concept repeatedly in his thinking and feeling:

> That I should be the minister of Jesus Christ to the Gentiles, ministering the gospel of God, that the offering up of the Gentiles might be acceptable, being sanctified by the Holy Ghost. (Rom. 15:16)

> But when it pleased God, who separated me from my mother's womb, and called me by his grace, to reveal his Son in me, that I might preach him among the heathen; immediately I conferred not with flesh and blood… but contrariwise, when they saw that the gospel of the uncircumcision was committed unto me, as the gospel of the circumcision was unto Peter…that we should go unto the heathen. (Gal. 1:15–16; 2:7, 9)

> For there is one God, and one mediator between God and men, the man Christ Jesus; who gave himself a ransom for all, to be testified in due time. Whereunto I am ordained a preacher, and an apostle, (I speak the truth in Christ, and lie not;) a teacher of the Gentiles in faith and verity. (1 Tim. 2:5–7)

So when Paul speaks of fulfilling the Word of God, it is almost certain that his mission to the Gentiles plays a major part in his thinking. Paul is vindicating and validating the gospel as God's provision for sinners, as God's means of bringing the Gentiles into His kingdom in accordance with His plan and purpose. There is a sense of geographical extension, of the spread of the gospel through all the nations of the world. However, perhaps more prominent is a sense of spiritual intensity, of penetrating and effective divine power (cf. Romans 15:17–19). The dynamic and successful progress of the gospel is in view. Paul is called to lay it out in its entirety, to give full development to its design, to give full scope to its saving purpose.

Paul had been given a great stewardship from God, and he declared God's truth as fully and freely as he knew how, as God's means of calling the Gentiles to Himself and incorporating them together with saved Jews into the new covenant people of God. John Eadie comments:

> He carried out its design—held it up as the balm of the world—proclaimed it without distinction of blood or race. He did not narrow its purpose, or confine it to a limited sphere of influence; but, as the apostle of the Gentiles, he opened for it a sweep and circuit adapted to its magnificence of aim, and its universality of fitness and sufficiency. He carried it beyond the frontiers of Judea, lifted it above the walls of the synagogue, and held it up to the nations.... As an instrument of human regeneration, he brought it to perfection.[3]

In other words, Paul let it fly! The apostle to the Gentiles gave free reign to the gospel extensively and intensively, determined that—in accordance with his own stewardship and calling—it should reach as far and as deep as God designed and that it should fulfill its purpose of bringing in the nations.

The description

When Paul speaks of this fulfilling of the Word of God, he identifies that Word as "a mystery." When most people hear the word *mystery*, they think of a particular kind of story. Depending on your cultural awareness, it may involve Sherlock Holmes, Hercule Poirot, Scooby Doo, or some potboiler toward the lower end of the literary spectrum involving some shadowy figure known only as the Hooded Claw. The general notion is of some convoluted secret (often a crime)

---

3. John Eadie, *A Commentary on the Greek Text of Paul's Letter to the Colossians* (Birmingham, AL: Solid Ground Christian Books, 2005), 94–95.

shrouded in confusion and needing to be uncovered by the careful application of reason. Often there are clues and hints sown through the narrative, the plot thickening throughout and the suspense building until the missing piece of the puzzle finally falls into place. We are waiting to have revealed that of which we were unaware from the beginning.

The biblical concept has some similarities—for example, the idea of something being eventually revealed to us—but is at once simpler and far richer. In the Bible, a mystery is a truth known only by divine revelation. H. P. Liddon explains:

> What is the meaning of the word "mystery" in the New Testament? It is used to describe not a fancy, not a contradiction, not an impossibility, but always a truth, yet a truth which has been or which is more or less hidden. A mystery is a truth, a fact. The word is never applied to anything else or less; never to a fancy, never to an impossibility, never to a recognized contradiction, never to any shadowy sort of unreality. But it is a partially hidden fact or truth.[4]

We find some of the Old Testament background to this idea of a mystery in Daniel 2:19–30. Nebuchadnezzar had a fearful dream of a great image, a statue of sorts. He would tell no one what he had seen but demanded that his wise men tell him both the dream and its interpretation on pain of death. Daniel and his companions fell under this imperial edict but asked for and were given time to pray, seeking mercies from the God of heaven concerning the secret.

> Then was the secret revealed unto Daniel in a night vision. Then Daniel blessed the God of heaven. Daniel answered and said, Blessed be the name of God for ever and ever: for wisdom and might are his: and he changeth the times and the seasons: he removeth kings, and setteth up kings: he giveth wisdom unto the wise, and knowledge to them that know understanding: he revealeth the deep and secret things: he knoweth what is in the darkness, and the light dwelleth with him. I thank thee, and praise thee, O thou God of my fathers, who hast given me wisdom and might, and hast made known unto me now what we desired of thee: for thou hast now made known unto us the king's matter. (Dan. 2:19–23)

Daniel told King Nebuchadnezzar about the image in his dream and about the stone cut out without hands that struck and broke the image before becoming a great mountain and filling all the earth. He ascribed the knowledge of things to come that had been given to Nebuchadnezzar, as well as the understanding given

---

4. H. P. Liddon, *Penny Pulpit*, no. 1152, in *Sermon Bible*: Bible Explorer 4.0. CD-ROM.

to himself as a prophet, directly to God: "As for thee, O king, thy thoughts came into thy mind upon thy bed, what should come to pass hereafter: and he that revealeth secrets maketh known to thee what shall come to pass. But as for me, this secret is not revealed to me for any wisdom that I have more than any living, but for their sakes that shall make known the interpretation to the king, and that thou mightest know the thoughts of thy heart" (Dan. 2:29–30).

There is a secret that is made known to Daniel by God, who alone can reveal the dream and its meaning to men. However, Daniel's experience helps us not only to define *mystery* generically but also identifies the content of the specific mystery that Paul is addressing. Daniel explains to Nebuchadnezzar that he has envisioned empires piled one on top of each other, all ultimately destroyed by the indestructible kingdom that God will establish over all the earth. You might say, "Well, that's obvious." But is it? Is it not obvious only with hindsight illuminated by the divine explanation? Would you have jumped to those conclusions about future history if you had had such a dream? No, it required God to make it known through Daniel. There is something here of what Peter says:

> Of which salvation the prophets have enquired and searched diligently, who prophesied of the grace that should come unto you: searching what, or what manner of time the Spirit of Christ which was in them did signify, when it testified beforehand the sufferings of Christ, and the glory that should follow. Unto whom it was revealed, that not unto themselves, but unto us they did minister the things, which are now reported unto you by them that have preached the gospel unto you with the Holy Ghost sent down from heaven; which things the angels desire to look into. (1 Peter 1:10–12)

The New Testament uses the same language for the same idea. Our Lord uses the idea in Mark 4:11. Paul speaks of the glorification of the saints as a mystery in 1 Corinthians 15:51—you would never have guessed it, let alone dared to believe it, unless God had said it. In 1 Corinthians 2:7–10 we read,

> But we speak the wisdom of God in a mystery, even the hidden wisdom, which God ordained before the world unto our glory: which none of the princes of this world knew: for had they known it, they would not have crucified the Lord of glory. But as it is written, Eye hath not seen, nor ear heard, neither have entered into the heart of man, the things which God hath prepared for them that love him. But God hath revealed them unto us by his Spirit: for the Spirit searcheth all things, yea, the deep things of God. (1 Cor. 2:7–10)

Paul uses the word again when writing to the Romans: "Now to him that is of power to stablish you according to my gospel, and the preaching of Jesus Christ, according to the revelation of the mystery, which was kept secret since the world began, but now is made manifest, and by the scriptures of the prophets, according to the commandment of the everlasting God, made known to all nations for the obedience of faith: to God only wise, be glory through Jesus Christ for ever. Amen" (Rom. 16:25–27).

In both these instances, the context and content show us decisive divine action and definite divine truth brought to light in Christ and in the coming of the gospel to the nations of the world—the very mystery that God was pleased to begin making known through Daniel and other prophets. As we would expect (given what Paul says in this letter to the Colossians), the mission to the Gentiles is in plain view, as we've already seen in Acts 26:16–18.

The Word of God has to do with this mystery—the mystery of Jesus Christ: "And without controversy great is the mystery of godliness: God was manifest in the flesh, justified in the Spirit, seen of angels, preached unto the Gentiles, believed on in the world, received up into glory" (1 Tim. 3:16). It is the good news of God reconciling sinners to Himself in His Son, Jesus Christ. It declares the glorious nature and the great extent of that work of redemption. And this is something that man cannot know—is not capable of knowing—unless God reveals it to him: "The secret things belong unto the LORD our God: but those things which are revealed belong unto us and to our children for ever, that we may do all the words of this law" (Deut. 29:29).

Pause to compare God's knowledge with man's ignorance. No spiritual truth can be rightly known apart from God: "But the natural man receiveth not the things of the Spirit of God: for they are foolishness unto him: neither can he know them, because they are spiritually discerned" (1 Cor. 2:14). Men are so quick to subject the Scripture to their fallen reason, forgetting or ignoring that they are to subject their fallen reason to the Scriptures of God. Any religious or moral system—including perversions of true Christianity—that is built on man's reason rather than God's revelation is on rotten foundations indeed, but men do not even realize that they are blinded by sin. God must not only tell us the truth but enable us to perceive it: you can tell a blind man that the sun is shining, but he still needs eyes in order to behold it for himself. The problem lies not with the sun, but with the eyes of the one who is blind.

Perhaps some are setting out to crack the gospel nut with the hammer of man's reason, and it will not yield. It is preached and explained, and men say, "It doesn't make sense." What they mean is, "I don't understand." God replies, "How could you, without Me?' For my thoughts are not your thoughts, neither are your ways my ways, saith the LORD. For as the heavens are higher than the earth, so are my ways higher than your ways, and my thoughts than your thoughts. But as it is written, Eye hath not seen, nor ear heard, neither have entered into the heart of man, the things which God hath prepared for them that love him'" (Isa. 55:8–9; 1 Cor. 2:9). The good news begs human comprehension. It cannot be grasped until it is accepted as God makes it known to us. God's mercy would never be known unless He revealed it to us; this is God's grace in Christ: He has planned it, accomplished it, declared it, and applied it.

The Bible is God's revelation of His truth concerning salvation through faith in His Son, Jesus Christ. This was the mystery proclaimed as Paul fulfilled the Word of God. His message was God's revealed truth, and he goes on to explain it in a few brief words.

The mystery concealed

Paul tells us that the mystery with which he has to do—the truth of the nature and scope of God's good news to sinners—was hidden from ages and generations. That is, prior to its revelation by God, the nature and extent of God's kingdom established by Jesus Christ was not known by men. Daniel's words were *not* obvious; they were richly suggestive but not fully descriptive.

The Hebrew people had vague and restricted notions of both the essence and scope of the gospel. Many saw the kingdom as a thing of this world, an earthly dominion. Our Lord fought against this carnal conception (e.g., John 6:15). Even His disciples were profoundly confused for a long time, being still bewildered by what would happen at the time of His ascension: "When they therefore were come together, they asked of him, saying, Lord, wilt thou at this time restore again the kingdom to Israel?" (Acts 1:6). Furthermore, while there were indications of blessing for the Gentiles (such as Isaiah 49:6), most Jews—even believing ones—imagined that the way Gentiles might be saved was by becoming Jews (consider Paul's arguments with regard to the Galatian churches or Peter's problems recorded in Acts 10 and Galatians 2:11–21).

And what of the Gentiles themselves? With a few glorious exceptions indicative of the later spread of truth, they were without God and without hope (Eph. 2:11–12). Psalm 147:19–20 is plain: "He sheweth his word unto Jacob, his statutes and his judgments unto Israel. He hath not dealt so with any nation: and as for his judgments, they have not known them. Praise ye the LORD."

They did not know God's Word (cf. Rom. 2:14 and 3:1–2). They were sitting in darkness: they would not and could not know God until God brought them to Himself.

The mystery revealed

"But now…." What mercy is wrapped up in that emphatic phrase!

Perhaps we have become so accustomed to the light that we have lost our sense of wonder at having it. We were under the power of darkness; had we lived in the times of the hiding of the truth, it is almost certain that we would not have known the light. Praise Almighty God, the merciful Lord, that we live in the gospel age and that we are those to whom the good news is being preached with power.

It may even be that Paul is deliberately reclaiming the word *mystery* for the church in Colosse. There are indications that the false teachers troubling the Colossian church loved the idea of mystery as the world defines it but were using it to divert the people of God from the truth. They spoke about the mysteries of God and the inner secrets of religion in language similar to that of false teachers in our own day. Much popular religious error is obsessed with secrets or even "the secret," with things hidden, with "mysteries" to which the ignorant are now being initiated by those enlightened ones who have gone before. But Paul's point is that these are no longer hidden truths for a select few but things that have been made known for all to see. All that is needed for man's good and for his salvation has now been clearly revealed through God's holy Word. There is nothing left in darkness that we need for our salvation.

Here is *a dramatic appearance* indeed, a pivotal point in redemptive history. In contrast with whose former days, what was before hidden has now been brought to light, made visible to men in the new covenant in Christ Jesus.

Paul also makes plain that this is *a divine disclosure*. These things were not discovered accidentally or by means of human effort. Because they were beyond human wisdom, God showed them openly, made them manifest by divine power. It was God's sovereign will and His determined counsel and desire to make known this mystery to His people. The Lord, in His free and unmerited grace, has uncovered the truth. This was contrary to human plans and expectations: many Jews did not see it and most did not want it, and the Gentiles, for the most part, did not even know what they were missing. When Peter was challenged concerning God's mercy to the Gentile household of Cornelius, he replied, "What was I, that I could withstand God?" (Acts 11:17).

There is also here *a delightful privilege*. We should sense Paul's excitement. His language is intended to convey delight that this fact has been made known to the saints of God—all the redeemed of the Lord. It is a glorious thing to be made possessors of these things, not just in the intellect but by saving experience, not only through words to our ears but by life to our souls.

Furthermore, we should recognize that the revelation of God's plan was also its fulfillment. Christ accomplished God's purpose of salvation, and in doing so He made it known, bringing it to light. God set forth Christ as a propitiation on the cross (Rom. 3:25): He was prominently set forth that He might be seen, and He is still seen in the preaching of the gospel and the life of the church, which is His body.

Moreover, God's plan of salvation goes on being fulfilled. This is not a reality available only to those initiated into the higher echelons of knowledge, but it is the joy and delight of every true child of God who has come into possession of Christ. This is revelation by *participation* as well as *instruction*—not only do we know the truth, but we enter into it!

Christian friend, have you paused to wonder that God intended that you should come to know this gospel mystery by saving experience? God willed from all eternity purposed that you—in company with all the saints—should be made to know, in the fullest sense, these gospel realities. God did not intend for you to know merely the scraps and crumbs of gospel privilege but its majestic excellence, not its pennies and trinkets but its jewel-encrusted gold.

Paul says that all the saints have been shown "what is the riches of the glory of this mystery among the Gentiles." This gospel mystery is magnificent in every way. Paul does some linguistic gymnastics to try to communicate the intensity of the glory he has in view. He is searching for an adequate expression for the shining forth of God's character, the blaze of divine light in the gospel, the lavish blessings obtained in Jesus Christ (cf. Col. 2:2–3). There is something that is bright, substantial, and permanent—as well as abundant—about this mystery. *Glory* is the word Paul often uses for the being of Christ and the situation of those who are in Him, and here he bends language to emphasize the riches of the glory.

But we also see here the sphere in which that glory is displayed: "among the Gentiles." At this separation of time, space, and culture, it is difficult for most of us to grasp the significance of this declaration. When God spoke to men His revelation was usually made to His covenant people of old, namely Israel. These were the people called by His name and given great religious privileges unlike any other people on the face of the earth, "to whom pertaineth the adoption, and the glory, and the covenants, and the giving of the law, and the service of God, and the promises" (Rom. 9:4). But here Paul says that God in His love and mercy willed to make known the riches of the glory of the mystery to the Gentiles. With reference to this amazing act of God, F. B. Meyer exclaims, "that He should dwell in the heart of a child of Abraham was deemed a marvelous act of condescension, but that He should find a home in the heart of a Gentile was incredible."[5]

Never—never before the good news came in Christ—have we seen numbers of the Gentile community called out by God for Himself. But now here is God willing that those who had been viewed by the Jewish people as pagans fit only for the fires of hell should be brought to heaven, God determining to make those who were once spiritually bankrupt to be rich with all the riches found in His only Son. The Messiah in and among the Jewish people we could expect, but the Messiah in and among Gentiles as a redeemed society of saints is a new wonder of grace: William Hendriksen observes that here is "Christ in all his glorious riches actually dwelling through his Spirit in the hearts and lives of Gentiles."[6]

Paul is emphasizing that salvation is no longer just for one people. God has established a new community and society, a spiritual nation made up not just of Jews or only of Gentiles, but of both groups as Christians on an equal footing in Jesus. Believers "have put on the new man, which is renewed in knowledge after the image of him that created him: where there is neither Greek nor Jew, circumcision nor uncircumcision, Barbarian, Scythian, bond nor free: but Christ is all, and in all" (Col. 3:10–11). There are no more barriers. There is not one plan for the Hebrews and one plan for the nations, but one Messiah for both. They have become one man in Christ, one church redeemed by His blood.

Paul develops this theme in his letter to the Ephesians:

> Wherefore remember, that ye being in time past Gentiles in the flesh, who are called Uncircumcision by that which is called the Circumcision in the flesh made by hands; that at that time ye were without Christ, being aliens from the commonwealth of Israel, and strangers from the covenants of promise, having no hope, and without God in the world: but now in Christ Jesus ye who sometimes were far off are made nigh by the blood of Christ. For he is our peace, who hath made both one, and hath broken down the middle wall of partition between us; having abolished in his flesh the enmity, even the law of commandments contained in ordinances; for to make in himself of twain one new man, so making

---

5. F. B. Meyer, *The Secret of Guidance* (New York: Fleming H. Revell Company, 1896), 34.
6. William Hendriksen, *Colossians* in *New Testament Commentary: Philippians, Colossians and Philemon* (Edinburgh: Banner of Truth, 1932), 89.

peace; and that he might reconcile both unto God in one body by the cross, having slain the enmity thereby. (Eph. 2:11–16)

He expands this idea later in the epistle:

> For this cause I Paul, the prisoner of Jesus Christ for you Gentiles, if ye have heard of the dispensation of the grace of God which is given me to you-ward: how that by revelation he made known unto me the mystery; (as I wrote afore in few words, whereby, when ye read, ye may understand my knowledge in the mystery of Christ) which in other ages was not made known unto the sons of men, as it is now revealed unto his holy apostles and prophets by the Spirit; that the Gentiles should be fellowheirs, and of the same body, and partakers of his promise in Christ by the gospel: whereof I was made a minister, according to the gift of the grace of God given unto me by the effectual working of his power. Unto me, who am less than the least of all saints, is this grace given, that I should preach among the Gentiles the unsearchable riches of Christ; and to make all men see what is the fellowship of the mystery, which from the beginning of the world hath been hid in God, who created all things by Jesus Christ: to the intent that now unto the principalities and powers in heavenly places might be known by the church the manifold wisdom of God, according to the eternal purpose which he purposed in Christ Jesus our Lord: in whom we have boldness and access with confidence by the faith of him. (Eph. 3:1–12)

What a glorious gospel message has been committed to Paul's stewardship! This is the message he preached. Here is salvation for those who were far off. Here is reconciliation between Jews and Gentiles and between God and man. Here is one man in Christ before God, one gathering of the people of God from all nationalities. These great and glorious truths cost Paul dearly as he proclaimed them, and yet proclaim them he did, in the face of the hardships meted out by enemies of the gospel.

Note that this is not God's "Plan B." God has not failed with the Jews, and He is not now attempting to make the best of a bad job by reaching out to the previously ignored Gentiles. Rather, this is God's eternal purpose being worked out, the mystery made fully known. When God revealed Himself to Abraham, He spoke of the foreshadowing of this reality: "Now the LORD had said unto Abram, Get thee out of thy country, and from thy kindred, and from thy father's house, unto a land that I will shew thee: and I will make of thee a great nation, and I will bless thee, and make thy name great; and thou shalt be a blessing: and I will bless them that bless thee, and curse him that curseth thee: and in thee shall all families of the earth be blessed" (Gen. 12:1–3). Later, God assured Abraham that "in thy seed shall all the nations of the earth be blessed; because thou hast obeyed my voice" (Gen. 22:18).

In the second psalm, God speaks to His Messiah: "Ask of me, and I shall give thee the heathen for thine inheritance, and the uttermost parts of the earth for thy possession" (v. 8). Isaiah 11:10 provides an example of this theme, which the prophet constantly brings to light: "And in that day there shall be a root of Jesse, which shall stand for an ensign of the people; to it shall the Gentiles seek: and his rest shall be glorious." The prophet Hosea is also given glimpses of this glorious reality: "Yet the number of the children of Israel shall be as the sand of the sea, which cannot be measured nor numbered; and it shall come to pass, that in the place where it was said unto them, Ye are not my people, there it shall be said unto them, Ye are the sons of the living God" (Hos. 1:10). And again, "And I will sow her unto me in the earth; and I will have mercy upon her that had not obtained mercy; and I will say to them which were not my people, Thou art my people; and they shall say, Thou art my God" (Hos. 2:23).

The great mystery that God had willed to make known to the Gentiles was not some afterthought in the divine mind. Rather, it was God's design from the beginning for the glory of His eternal name, spoken of repeatedly by God though overlooked continually by men and, in Christ, unveiled in all its majestic fullness and with all its magnificent implications.

God's purpose was always that this richly glorious mystery should be declared in all its saving fullness among the nations. Here is the wonder of this mystery: "It is a light thing that thou shouldest be my servant to raise up the tribes of Jacob, and to restore the preserved of Israel: I will also give thee for a light to the Gentiles, that thou mayest be my salvation unto the end of the earth" (Isa. 49:6).

In Romans 15:8–12, the apostle claims glory for God in Christ in view of the advance of the gospel through the nations:

> Now I say that Jesus Christ was a minister of the circumcision for the truth of God, to confirm the promises made unto the fathers: and that the Gentiles might glorify God for his mercy; as it is written, For this cause I will confess to thee among the Gentiles, and sing unto thy name. And again he saith, Rejoice, ye Gentiles, with his people. And again, Praise the Lord, all ye Gentiles; and laud him, all ye people. And again, Esaias saith, There shall be a root of Jesse, and he that shall rise to reign over the Gentiles; in him shall the Gentiles trust.

By comparison, Jewish ceremonialism—which was one aspect of the mishmash of errors in Colosse—consisted in weak and beggarly elements (Gal. 4:9), which cannot compare with the riches of the gospel glories. Light has come to the

Gentiles, hope has come to the hopeless, those far off are being brought near, glory is being manifest among many who had no entitlement to know and enjoy it.

The mystery explained

What, then, are the riches of the glory of the mystery among the Gentiles? Paul brings us at last to his definition. He has deferred it so far, building the tension. Here is the core and climax of the gospel mystery: "Christ in you, the hope of glory." To use John Bunyan's imagery in *The Holy War*, Emmanuel has taken up residence in Mansoul. The triumphant Messiah dwells in His people— individually and corporately—and in doing so assures them of glory with Him.

Is Paul getting theologically confused here? Is it not the Holy Spirit who indwells us (1 Cor. 6:19)? Yes, but He is the Spirit of Christ; the Spirit is the promised Comforter (John 14:16–17), the one by whom Jesus will be with His people (vv. 19–28). This is not to dismiss the Spirit from His proper role, but rather to show Christ in His. Paul calls us away from all but Christ, for it is He who by His Spirit personally takes up residence within His elect people. This is no mere notion, no philosophical speculation (Col. 2:8), but a living reality, a complete Savior who removes the need for anything more, anything less, and anything else.

This is the riches of the glory of the mystery: Christ in His saving fullness, in all His reconciling triumph, as the glorified Messiah. Christ Himself—not just His blessings or His gifts—is in us. He reigns within, enthroned in the heart, filling us, supplying us, changing us, working upon us. His people are His body, and He as her risen head pours life into them and maintains it within them. It is the objective and subjective experience of every Colossian Christian and every saint that Christ is "in you." He is not merely among His people but has taken up permanent residence in every heart individually: He is the glory of the new covenant temple built of living stones (1 Peter 2:4–10).

And, further, the reality of Christ in you is "the hope of glory," the pledge of glory to come: it is the anchor of the promise of heaven. The unfailing experience of new life brings the unshakeable promise of eternal life (2 Cor. 5:1–5). Remember Paul's testimony to the Ephesians concerning Christ:

> In whom also we have obtained an inheritance, being predestinated according to the purpose of him who worketh all things after the counsel of his own will: that we should be to the praise of his glory, who first trusted in Christ. In whom ye also trusted, after that ye heard the word of truth, the gospel of your salvation: in whom also after that

ye believed, ye were sealed with that holy Spirit of promise, which is the earnest of our inheritance until the redemption of the purchased possession, unto the praise of his glory. (Eph. 1:11–14)

If Christ is in you, you cannot perish. He will not lose you. If He did, He would lose more than you, for how could He then say, "Behold I and the children which God hath given me" (Heb. 2:13)?

The whole body of Christ—Jew and Gentile believers, without distinction or exception—will reach the Promised Land, the new heaven and earth:

> But ye are not in the flesh, but in the Spirit, if so be that the Spirit of God dwell in you. Now if any man have not the Spirit of Christ, he is none of his. And if Christ be in you, the body is dead because of sin; but the Spirit is life because of righteousness. But if the Spirit of him that raised up Jesus from the dead dwell in you, he that raised up Christ from the dead shall also quicken your mortal bodies by his Spirit that dwelleth in you. (Rom. 8:9–11)

The indwelling of Christ guarantees our expectation of heavenly bliss. This indwelling and its sure consequence are the riches of the glory of the gospel mystery: "When Christ, who is our life, shall appear, then shall ye also appear with him in glory" (Col. 3:4).

When George Whitefield preached near the city of Bristol, he took the Word of God to the area of Kingswood. In this wretched place lived coal miners, almost bestial in their behavior. These men and women, moral, spiritual, and often physical wrecks, dwelt in little more than holes in the ground. They gathered to hear Whitefield preach Jesus to them, and the first signs of the work of the Spirit in the hearts of the Kingswood colliers were the white lines made by contrite tears running through the grime on their faces. Later, Charles Wesley wrote a hymn for these despised saints. "Christ in you" means that we can all sing it still, for it is our song too.

You simple souls that stray
Far from the path of peace,
That lonely, unfrequented way
To life and happiness,
How long will you your folly love,
And throng the downward road,
And hate the wisdom from above,
And mock the sons of God?

Madness and misery
You count our lives beneath;
And nothing great or good can see,
Or glorious, in our death!
As born to suffer and to grieve,
Beneath your feet we lie;
And utterly condemned we live,
And unlamented die.

So wretched and obscure,
The men whom ye despise,
So foolish, impotent, and poor,
Above your scorn we rise:
We, through the Holy Ghost,
Can witness better things;
For He whose blood is all our boast
Hath made us priests and kings.

Riches unsearchable
In Jesu's love we know;
and pleasures, springing from the well
Of life, our souls o'erflow;
The Spirit we receive
Of wisdom, grace, and power;
And always sorrowful we live,
Rejoicing evermore.

Angels our servants are,
And keep in all our ways,
And in their watchful hands they bear
The sacred souls of grace;
Unto that heavenly bliss
They all our steps attend;
And God Himself our Father is,
And Jesus is our friend.

With Him we walk in white,
We in His image shine,
Our robes are robes of glorious light,
Our righteousness divine;
On all the kings of earth
With pity we look down,
And claim, in virtue of our birth,
A never-fading crown.

‖ **FELLOW CHRISTIAN** Consider the privilege and glory of the saints of God. You have come to know, by a revelation involving participation, the mystery of the gospel. God speaks to you in the gospel, draws you and others in from without, in accordance with the glorious riches of His gospel in Christ Jesus.

Will you not seek preachers who will make this known in its glorious fullness, as God helps them? Why would you want a man who will tickle your ears with empty fancies when you might hear a man who would make known the mystery of God, the revelation of God's own self to needy sinners and hungry saints—"Christ in you, the hope of glory"?

God has revealed what He intends to be known. The gospel is not too high, too complex, too bizarre to be understood. It is great, glorious, and gracious. It is by this gospel that God saves sinners of all sorts, showing us our misery and His mercy and majesty. Reason cannot subdue this gospel—cannot exhaust it, cannot encompass it. Find a man whose reason is subject to revelation and who feels no need to embellish the perfect gospel. Find a man who is himself consumed with the Christ of the gospel and who has no desire other than to make Him known. This is what it means to preach the Word of God faithfully to others. Seek out a man who is persuaded that there is no hope of glory apart from Jesus. Do not listen to those who would preach some other hope apart from or alongside the

Lord Christ, for it is not true. Pay no heed to those who elevate human effort, religion, ritual, reason, other spirits and guides, or anything or anyone else.

Neither should you forget to pray for your pastors who are seeking to be faithful. Paul encouraged the Colossians to do just this: "Continue in prayer, and watch in the same with thanksgiving; withal praying also for us, that God would open unto us a door of utterance, to speak the mystery of Christ, for which I am also in bonds: that I may make it manifest, as I ought to speak" (Col. 4:2–4).

No man can do this in his own strength. How can a mere creature, apart from the Spirit of Christ, make manifest the mystery of Christ? Pray that the glories of Christ that you have come to rely upon and relish might be proclaimed by your pastors for the full salvation of God's elect.

FELLOW PASTOR

Let us not lose sight of the glorious extent of God's gospel plan. God's intent is that His church be a great multitude from all the nations and peoples of the earth: "After this I beheld, and, lo, a great multitude, which no man could number, of all nations, and kindreds, and people, and tongues, stood before the throne, and before the Lamb, clothed with white robes, and palms in their hands; and cried with a loud voice, saying, Salvation to our God which sitteth upon the throne, and unto the Lamb" (Rev. 7:9–10).

Is the church that you serve representative of such an aim, in principle even if not yet in experience? Are you seeking, under God, to construct a microcosm of this great gathering? Perhaps you live in an area that has only one culture or one race within reach. Do your prayers extend further? Perhaps you live in a richly multicultural environment, where the peoples of the world are milling about on every street. Does your endeavor and expectation extend to them all? Let no national or social narrowness intrude into our congregations. Paul delighted in being the minister of Christ's gospel to the peoples of the world, and that should be our delight also.

Consider also the privilege that has been given to you. Like Paul, yours is the honor of making known what once was hidden but which our God has brought to light in Christ Jesus:

> Unto me, who am less than the least of all saints, is this grace given, that I should preach among the Gentiles the unsearchable riches of Christ; and to make all men see what is the fellowship of the mystery, which from the beginning of the world hath been hid in God, who created all things by Jesus Christ: to the intent that now unto the principalities and powers in heavenly places might be known by the church the manifold

wisdom of God, according to the eternal purpose which he purposed in Christ Jesus our Lord: in whom we have boldness and access with confidence by the faith of him. (Eph. 3:8–12)

Do we capitalize on this privilege? If I am a believer, "I am crucified with Christ: nevertheless I live; yet not I, but Christ liveth in me: and the life which I now live in the flesh I live by the faith of the Son of God, who loved me, and gave himself for me" (Gal. 2:20). If I am a minister of the gospel, that reality is going to have its distinctive outworking in what I preach and how I preach it. We are called to speak the mystery of Christ (Col. 4:3) as the means of presenting every man perfect in Christ Jesus. God has not only been pleased to put Christ in us, the hope of glory, but to make us His ambassadors in the ongoing declaration of that wonderful truth. Go and tell someone about Jesus!

Furthermore, this means that we do not need to guess at the motive, manner, matter, or mode of our ministry. Brothers, we do not need to stick a wet finger in the air to sense the present cultural currents, the flavor *du jour*, the latest fads and fashions of spiritual appetite and expectation. When we are trying in all sincerity to figure out how to "do church," we can rejoice to know that God has already given us the answer, and the beating heart of that answer is the fulfillment of God's Word, making known extensively and intensively the living, dying, rising, reigning, returning Son of Almighty God. The circumstances in which we carry out the task have altered somewhat, but the task itself has not changed. You do not preach in Colosse, but you preach where God has put you to men and women with sinful hearts, some of them already being saved by grace, all of them needing to be warned and taught with a view to the final revelation of Christ in His glory.

We cannot abandon the preaching of the Word of God for something else. We cannot bring someone other than Jesus into the pulpit to exalt. Many churches have an inscription on the pulpit from which the minister preaches: "Sir, we would see Jesus" (John 12:21). Should that not be before our eyes and in our hearts every time we declare the good news? We have a heavenly calling; a divine assignment has been given to us. We are to preach the Word, being ready in season and out of season (2 Tim. 4:2). This is the gospel ministry.

If you are a young man considering the ministry, then bring yourself to this touchstone: Is this what you desire? Is this your aim? Can you conceive of a higher privilege than the declaration of the things concerning Christ which God has made known, speaking them to the world at large and the people of God in particular? Are you going to give yourself to the arduous task of poring over the Scriptures, digging deep in them so that you can feed your people with God's own Word, week in and week out? Will you "study to shew thyself approved unto God, a workman that needeth not to be ashamed, rightly dividing the word of truth" (2 Tim. 2:15)?

This is what it means to be a preacher of the Word of God. Pretty sermonettes will not do. We are called to feed the sheep of Christ (John 21:15–17). The Word of God is the primary means that God has given us so that we may grow spiritually (1 Peter 2:1–3). Let us not forsake our high calling by pursuing that which our God has not sanctioned. The way to "do church" is not to float on the prevailing currents of church practice, let alone secular notions, or even to weave together multiple spiritualities and religious ideas in the hopes of striking home with some. The way to do church is to open the Bible and study it and obey it: to preach who and what you find in it, and to follow the Jesus whom it declares in what you say and what you do, to the praise of God's glorious grace.

6 | THE SUBJECT OF PAUL'S MINISTRY

Whom we preach, warning every man, and teaching every man in all wisdom . . .
— COLOSSIANS 1:28

You have been pursuing an education of mind and heart, preparatory to the office of a minister of the gospel. You are now upon the threshold of that sacred work. How far your ministry will be that of a faithful "steward of the mysteries of God" will depend on how far it shall be the faithful preaching of Jesus Christ. No inquiry, therefore, in the course of your preparation, or at this stage of your career, should seem to you of such importance as that which seeks a full understanding of the work of preaching Christ Jesus our Lord and Saviour, according as it is taught in the Scriptures and set forth before us in the example of the Apostles. It is an inquiry with which the work of a minister of Christ will be more and more identified as he himself shall grow in the mind of his Master, and in a personal experience of the power and preciousness of the grace revealed in him.[1]
— CHARLES P. MCILVAINE

It is Monday afternoon, March 25, 1861. A young man stands to speak in the pulpit of a newly constructed church building, designed to hold the thousands already thronging to hear his ministry. The man will go down in history as the Prince of Preachers. Already much blessed of God, he will continue to be mightily used by the Lord to the saving and sanctifying of multitudes of sinners. His labors for the advance of Christ's kingdom will be prodigious: after twenty-five years in London, he will preside over sixty-six institutions founded on gospel principles

---

1. Charles P. McIlvaine, *Preaching Christ: The Heart of Gospel Ministry—An Address to Those Entering the Christian Ministry* (Edinburgh: Banner of Truth, 2003), 1–2.

and operating from gospel motives. Books and articles will pour from his pen and be readily consumed; his sermons will be heard by thousands, written down and then distributed—many in translation—and eagerly read to the ends of the earth for decades after his death. He will be described by competent judges in glowing terms: "Never since Paul died has so much work and so much success been crowded into so small a space of time."[2]

Who is this man, and what lies at the root of his gospel effectiveness? He is Charles Haddon Spurgeon, and his secret is quickly revealed as he opens his mouth to utter the first formal words of a sermon in the Metropolitan Tabernacle, preaching on Acts 5:42: "And daily in the temple, and in every house, they ceased not to teach and preach Jesus Christ." He says:

> I do not know whether there are any persons here present who can contrive to put themselves into my present position, and to feel my present feelings. If they can effect that, they will give me credit for meaning what I say, when I declare that I feel totally unable to preach. And, indeed, I think I shall scarcely attempt a sermon, but rather give a sort of declaration of the truths from which future sermons shall be made. I will give you bullion rather than coin; the block from the quarry, and not the statue from the chisel. It appears that the one subject upon which men preached in the apostolic age was *Jesus Christ*.... In the days of Paul it was not difficult at once, in one word, to give the sum and substance of the current theology. It was Christ Jesus. Had you asked anyone of those disciples what he believed, he would have replied, "I believe Christ." If you had requested him to show you his Body of Divinity, he would have pointed upward, reminding you that divinity never had but one body, the suffering and crucified human frame of Jesus Christ, who ascended up on high....
>
> I would propose (and O may the Lord grant us grace to carry out that proposition, from which no Christian can dissent), I would propose that the subject of the ministry of this house, as long as this platform shall stand, and as long as this house shall be frequented by worshippers, shall be the person of Jesus Christ. I am never ashamed to avow myself a Calvinist, although I claim to be rather a Calvinist according to Calvin, than after the modern debased fashion. I do not hesitate to take the name of Baptist. You have there [pointing to the baptistery] substantial evidence that I am not ashamed of that ordinance

---

2. Pilgrim Publications, B. H. Carroll, Memorial Address, 1892, quoted in "Introduction to C. H. Spurgeon," http://www.pilgrimpublications.com/about/c-h-spurgeon-biography-page/introduction-to-c-h-spurgeon/, (accessed May 25, 2009).

of our Lord Jesus Christ; but if I am asked to say what is my creed, I think I must reply: "It is Jesus Christ." My venerable predecessor, Dr. Gill, has left a body of divinity admirable and excellent in its way; but the body of divinity to which I would pin and bind myself for ever, God helping me, is not his system of divinity or any other human treatise, but Christ Jesus, who is the sum and substance of the gospel; who is in himself all theology, the incarnation of every precious truth, the all-glorious personal embodiment of the way, the truth, and the life.[3]

What lay at the heart of Charles Spurgeon's wide-ranging and powerfully effective gospel ministry? The answer is quite simple: Jesus Christ. Jesus Christ was the focal point of all his preaching. Spurgeon loved Christ, followed Christ, obeyed Christ, and, as a true minister of the gospel, he proclaimed Christ. Spurgeon was in good company, standing in a long tradition of faithful men who had also embraced the same cause and preached the same glorious person.

As Spurgeon makes plain, he follows the apostle Paul, who preached the Jesus who died but rose again. In Colossians 1:27 Paul had spoken of God's intention that the riches of the glory of the age-old mystery of the redemption of the Gentiles in Jesus the Messiah should be made known. Now, in verse 28, he discloses that this great Savior "whom we preach" is Himself the absolute core and definitive summary of all his proclamation. The will of God for the making known of His Son in the earth finds its human counterpart in the work of Paul and his fellow servants.

We must recognize the polemical point being made by the apostle as he refutes the false teachers who were attacking this church with their flawed notions of salvation. These errorists had much to say about the supposed virtues of circumcision, angel worship, and asceticism as ways to obtain a right standing with God (see Colossians 2:14–23). In this, they denied Christ's preeminence and His exclusive role as the only way to the Father. Paul says, in effect, "Away with these counterfeit saviors! There is but one Savior, the Lord Jesus Christ, and He is, therefore, the sum and substance of my preaching and teaching."

So must it be for all true pastors. In these words, Paul is emphasizing the difference between his preaching and that of the false teachers. The very order of Paul's words is intended to get this message across, although not every translation communicates its force. He might very naturally say, "We preach Christ," and the sense would be fundamentally the same. However, Paul puts

---

3. Charles Spurgeon, "The First Sermon in the Tabernacle" in *The Metropolitan Tabernacle Pulpit* (1861; reprint, Pasadena, TX: Pilgrim Publications, 1995), 7:169.

Jesus up front where He belongs: "*Him* we preach." Jesus Christ the Lord is the great burden of Paul's preaching. He is the one whom Paul and his companions were unashamedly proclaiming to all and doing so by means of "warning" and "teaching" (Col. 1:28).

Paul is here setting out the tools that he employs in making known Jesus Christ: proclamation, admonition, and instruction. The apostle's work is *constant*: his language indicates that it is his habitual and ongoing practice to engage in the work by these means, the overarching demand of proclaiming Jesus, and the subsidiary demands of warning and teaching. Paul's work is *broad*: he uses these tools on "every man." There is none of the false exclusivity that characterized the Colossian errorists, no sense of a spiritual aristocracy. All truth is brought to bear, without exception, on all men—whether Greek or Jew, circumcised or uncircumcised, barbarian, Scythian, slave, or free (Col. 3:11). Furthermore, Paul's work is *focused*: these tools are individually employed. Paul deals with individuals, such as Philemon and Onesimus, the former a member of this church and the latter his runaway but now converted slave. These gospel means are for every man and are brought to bear upon particular men, each being the object of their particular and intelligent application.

Proclamation

What does it mean to preach? The word Paul uses when he declares "whom we preach" indicates an official, authoritative declaration that is to be proclaimed or announced. The word can refer to the message of one who speaks on behalf of another, such as an ambassador or herald. It literally means "to make known," "to tell out," "to communicate," or "to proclaim," bringing a message aloud or publicly. You might almost describe it as the technical term for what some today would call missional preaching—the preaching that brings the gospel clearly to bear upon those who have never before come face to face with Christ in all His saving fullness.

Paul is speaking of the solemn, public declaration of authoritative truth. As an apostle of Jesus Christ, he was authorized by the Lord to communicate on His behalf. As one of heaven's ambassadors, he—commissioned in the same way as the other apostles—would go from town to town publicly declaring the message that Jesus had called him to deliver. Paul's task was to make Christ known to fallen humanity, to those estranged from God. Traveling across the Roman Empire, he proclaimed to all what Jesus had done to procure peace with an offended God through His sacrificial death, making known the personal terms of reconciliation with this holy, just, and gracious Sovereign.

Paul and his fellow ministers did not merely mutter their words quietly to a few. They did not just gather a group of people for a little chat or a gospel talk (although this task does not necessarily demand a great crowd in order to accomplish it). This was not simply conversation; it was not even primarily public dialogue and debate, although both conversation and debate clearly were weapons in the apostolic armory. Rather, Paul is speaking here of how he and his comrades, in reliance upon God the Holy Spirit, boldly and fearlessly announced the message about the only Savior of sinners, Jesus Christ our Lord.

What does it mean to preach Christ?

This declaration of Jesus is the central duty of the true servant of the Lord. So what does this actually mean? To preach Christ is to proclaim the great truths about and the profound implications of His glorious person and finished redemptive work in the place of sinners on the cross of Calvary, making Him known as He is set forth in the entirety of the Scriptures.

The message declared is God's saving purpose in Christ. Paul and those who genuinely follow him never proclaim a mere system or a set of rules, still less the muddled nonsense being spewed out by heretics. Paul and his fellow laborers do not preach philosophy. They do not preach politics. They do not preach positive thinking. They do not preach themselves. Preaching is not the exercise of the preacher's fancy, the fevered labor of an overwrought imagination. It is not empty speculation about spiritual hierarchies and angelic powers. There is no specious spinning out of superficial theories that do nothing but excite and tantalize carnal minds.

Gospel ministers declare a person, a living person who is the source of all true life, in whom is found the hope of glory, the only fulfillment of the deepest needs of sinful men. That person is Jesus Christ, the incarnate Son of God, the only redeemer of God's elect. Remember that Paul has already set Him forth in some of the highest and brightest Christology of the New Testament, declaring Him to be God's

> dear Son: in whom we have redemption through his blood, even the forgiveness of sins: who is the image of the invisible God, the firstborn of every creature: for by him were all things created, that are in heaven, and that are in earth, visible and invisible, whether they be thrones, or dominions, or principalities, or powers: all things were created by him, and for him: and he is before all things, and by him all things consist. And he is the head of the body, the church: who is the beginning, the firstborn from the dead; that in all things he might have the preeminence.

For it pleased the Father that in him should all fulness dwell; and, having
made peace through the blood of his cross, by him to reconcile all things
unto himself; by him, I say, whether they be things in earth, or things in
heaven. (Col. 1:13–20)

It is this Jesus and none other, the head of the first creation and the head of
the new creation (Col. 1:15–16), who indwells His people from every kingdom
and tribe and tongue and nation and is their hope of glory. He is the sum and
substance of the message proclaimed.

This matter reveals the crucial difference between a true servant of Christ
and a false one. This standard remains absolute and is no less important in
our day than it was in Paul's. From many of the world's pulpits chaff is sown
instead of seed, and people are fed the dry husks of manmade religion rather
than Christ-centered truth through Christ-saturated sermons. Neither Paul
nor his fellow workers would ever be party to such a thing. Where Christ is
marginalized, all true, biblical, genuinely Christian religion is quickly lost,
shrouded in bewildering clouds of mystical emptiness. The liquid that is offered
to sinners under such circumstances claims to quench the thirst, but men are
easing their spiritual appetites not with living water but with virulent poison.
Such teaching produces no salvation.

When Christ is proclaimed, it is made plain that all that is necessary for
salvation in the fullest and most complete sense is found in Him alone. Such a
message necessarily excludes everyone and everything else and exalts Him solely:
"Neither is there salvation in any other [but in Jesus Christ of Nazareth]: for
there is none other name under heaven given among men, whereby we must be
saved" (Acts 4:12). John Eadie writes:

> This Christ, so glorious in person and perfect in work—the incarnate
> God—the bleeding peacemaker—the imperial governor of the
> universe—it is He, none else, and none besides Him, whom we
> preach. Not simply His doctrine, but Himself; and He was preached,
> not by Paul alone, but by all his colleagues. This Christ is the one and
> undivided object of proclamation; and if He be the hope of glory, no
> wonder that they rejoice to proclaim Him wide and far, and on every
> possible occasion. The apostolic preaching was precise and definite....
> Christ, as the one deliverer, conferring pardon by His blood, purity by
> His Spirit, and perfection by His pledge and presence, securing defence

by His power, comfort by His sympathy, and the hope of glory by His residence in the believing heart.[4]

This was always the gospel message. We find such a message in the teaching of our Lord Himself, as well as of His apostles.

It may seem odd to state that Jesus preached Himself, but there is nothing strange or inherently arrogant in such activity. As the incarnate Son of God, He alone is warranted—indeed, required—to proclaim Himself. We thus find Him expounding Himself to others.

Consider two key passages. The first is found in the gospel according to John. Chapter 5 records that our Lord has been pleased to heal a man at the pool of Bethesda on the Sabbath. This gives rise to violent antagonism from and a heated debate with the religious leaders of the day. We read that, on account of this healing and its immediate aftermath, "the Jews persecute Jesus, and sought to slay him, because he had done these things on the sabbath day. But Jesus answered them, My Father worketh hitherto, and I work. Therefore the Jews sought the more to kill him, because he not only had broken the sabbath, but said also that God was his Father, making himself equal with God" (John 5:16–18). As our Lord goes on to validate His undeniable equality with the Father, he says to these leaders, "The Father himself, which hath sent me, hath borne witness of me. Ye have neither heard his voice at any time, nor seen his shape. And ye have not his word abiding in you: for whom he hath sent, him ye believe not. Search the scriptures; for in them ye think ye have eternal life: and they are they which testify of me" (John 5:37–39).

The Lord Jesus points out the key reason the Jewish leaders had not responded favorably to Him. It was not that they lacked information. Indeed, they had the right information—the very oracles of God (Rom. 3:2)—but they read it wrongly. He says to them that they were searching the Scriptures, because in them they thought that they had eternal life, and—says our Lord—these Scriptures "are they which testify of *me.*" These religious leaders did a right and necessary thing in reading their Bibles. Nevertheless, these diligent readers and teachers of the Old Testament fell short when it came to understanding those Bibles. This was no slight hermeneutical defect, but a soul-damning flaw. Their study of the Old Testament missed the mark completely because it missed the main Actor. They were like men studying the solar system by means of accurate

---

4. John Eadie, *A Commentary on the Greek Text of Paul's Letter to the Colossians* (Birmingham, AL: Solid Ground Christian Books, 2005), 101–102.

diagrams but without ever recognizing the centrality of the sun and without ever enjoying its light and feeling its heat. All their efforts did not lead them to look to Jesus as Messiah, did not prompt them to lay hold of the salvation that is found in Him alone.

Our Lord tells them in no uncertain terms that if they had correctly understood their Bibles then they would have come to Him to be saved, for it is He of whom the Scriptures speak: "They...testify of me." The Bible in its entirety—the Scriptures of both the Old and New Testaments—is the full revelation of God the Son. Jesus says to these deluded and angry men that a correct reading of the Old Testament would have led them to see plainly that He was the promised Messiah of God.

The Bible remains a closed book to those who do not embrace its main focus. When a person turns to the Lord the veil is taken away, but until then the veil remains (2 Cor. 3:15–16). The Lord Christ reiterates that He is the beating heart of the Old Testament and its primary concern when in this same chapter He tells his opponents that "had ye believed Moses, ye would have believed me: for he wrote of me. But if ye believe not his writings, how shall ye believe my words?" (John 5:46–47). F. F. Bruce effectively summarizes the grievous reality of this encounter: "The tragedy was that these people, for all their painstaking exploration of the sacred writings, had never found the clue which would lead them to their goal. The goal at which they aimed was eternal life, but that life could be received only through him to whom the Scriptures bore witness."[5]

Leon Morris agrees: "Rightly read, the Old Testament leads to Christ. But the scribes of his day, with their wooden reverence for the letter of the Scripture, failed to understand the wonderful thing it was saying and thus were quite unable to recognize him to whom the Scriptures pointed."[6]

Consider next a passage from Luke's gospel. After the death of Jesus, the disciples were thoroughly downcast, and all talk of the resurrection seemed to them like idle chatter (Luke 24:11). On the very day of Jesus' resurrection, two disciples were traveling out to Emmaus, speaking of the recent events, when He drew alongside them. Jesus gently quizzed these disciples about their sad faces and intense conversation, and one disciple, Cleopas, asked the risen Lord of heaven and earth one of the most notably and unintentionally ironic questions in all of Scripture: "Art thou only a stranger in Jerusalem, and hast not known the

---

5. F. F. Bruce, *The Gospel of John* (Grand Rapids: Eerdmans, 1983), 136.

6. Leon Morris, *Reflections on the Gospel of John* (Peabody, MA: Hendrickson Publishers, 1986), 200.

things which are come to pass there in these days?" (v. 18). One can only imagine the look on Christ's face as He graciously asked, "What things?"

The disciples explained to Him that they were hoping that it was the mighty prophet Jesus of Nazareth who was going to redeem Israel. Jesus had died; reports had come through of His resurrection, and the tomb had been searched and found empty, but of Jesus there was no trace.

Our Lord gently rebukes these men and sets out to instruct them concerning what had happened in Jerusalem over the past few days: "O fools, and slow of heart to believe all that the prophets have spoken: ought not Christ to have suffered these things, and to enter into his glory? And beginning at Moses and all the prophets, he expounded unto them in all the scriptures the things concerning himself" (Luke 24:25–27).

What a sermon this must have been! Of all those conversations upon which we might wish to eavesdrop, surely there are few Christians—fewer preachers— who would not wish to have been a fourth traveler on the road to Emmaus. Can you imagine how our Lord must have taken these disciples to those wonderful passages, which—by means of types and shadows, prophecies and predictions— all pointed to Him?

He might have begun with Genesis 3:15 and that wonderful promise set forth in what is often called the protoevangel, that glorious diamond shining in the filth of the curse on the serpent, that there should be a Seed of the woman who would crush the head of the serpent, though in the act He would also feel the strike of the dragon against His heel.

Did He then show them that the Christ was the promised seed of Abraham in whom all the families of the earth should be blessed? Or tell the tale of Abraham offering up Isaac, his son, his only son, tracing all the Godlike and Christlike patterns of the action? Did He explain Jacob's expectation of the scepter not departing from Judah until Shiloh comes? What echoes of the messianic character and calling did He find in Joseph the Preserver and Moses the Deliverer, the great prophet of His people? How did He explain the profound significance of the Passover lamb? What meaning did He find in the great wealth of the levitical sacrifices and rituals? What would He say about the fiery serpent raised up, that those who looked to it should not die but live? What significance did He find in Balaam's prophecy that a star should come out of Jacob and a scepter should rise out of Israel, one who would destroy His enemies and have dominion? What foreshadowings would He see in the judges and deliverers of Israel? What glimmerings of light did He reveal in God's gracious dealings with David? What did He see in the constantly dashed expectations of God's people as they looked to David's line in anticipation of one who would rule forever, time after time confessing, "He is not the one," and the growing sense of the prophets that they were looking for something far more glorious than had been expected? What wonders of divine faithfulness did He demonstrate in the covenant care of the people of God and the bloodline of David? Was persevering Job wonderfully vindicated in his faithful expectation that his eyes would see God? What wealth of instruction would Christ have drawn from the songs of Israel, finding constant testimonies of His person and work? With what piercing insight would He have spoken of Isaiah's Suffering Servant or Daniel's Son of Man? In what rich strains did faithful Jeremiah and exiled Ezekiel figure in His discourse? Did the minor prophets begin to sound their major chords as He unpacked the glories of His name as they had set Him forth? Did Hosea's pains and comforts come alive as He explained them? Did the stern warnings of the bold prophets suddenly make sense in the eternal scheme? What did Jonah's experience yield to His teaching? Did Bethlehem Ephrathah gain a luster that Micah had never given it before? Did Habakkuk's faith gleam brighter than ever before? Did Zechariah's cleansing fountain seem to flow sweeter, and did the Pierced One appear more excellent than He had until then? Did Malachi's ardent anticipations open up and yield abundant fruit at His holy touch? What wonders the Law and the Prophets must have revealed as Jesus spoke!

Whatever passages formed the substance of His discourse, we see that our Lord set forth Himself. Jesus preached Jesus: "beginning at Moses and all the prophets, he expounded unto them in all the scriptures the things concerning himself" (Luke 24:27).

If we are going to preach Christ, then we must do what Christ Himself did. To preach Christ is to open up the whole of Scripture and show how it all points to and connects with our Savior. Our Lord reiterated this when He said, "These are the words which I spake unto you, while I was yet with you, that all things must be fulfilled, which were written in the law of Moses, and in the prophets, and in the psalms, concerning me" (Luke 24:44).

Jesus shows us that the whole Word of God testifies that He is the Son of God, the promised Christ, the glorious Redeemer. Jesus says that He is the great end and ultimate fulfillment of all that the Old Testament writers were expressing. He is the focal point and central theme of Holy Scripture. As our model for ministry, Jesus shows us that the essence of preaching is the preaching of His own person, and the apostles followed in His footsteps.

They were true disciples, approaching their work no differently from their Lord. They were content to be like their Lord, following the same path without deviation. They preached Jesus of Nazareth from the whole Bible as God's Messiah. They preached Him in the fullness of His person and work: Jesus as Christ, promised, living, dying, rising, and reigning was their theme and song (1 Cor. 15:1–4).

We see it in all the records of apostolic ministry. From the moment of Paul's conversion, we find him in the synagogues, preaching the Christ, that He is the Son of God (Acts 9:20), and persuading men that Jesus was that very Christ (v. 22). In Pisidian Antioch, he traces God's dealings with His people, narrowing in on David and coming swiftly to Jesus: "Of this man's seed hath God according to his promise raised unto Israel a Saviour, Jesus" (Acts 13:23). Thereafter the whole sermon is all about Him, closing with the great declaration and challenge:

> Be it known unto you therefore, men and brethren, that through this man is preached unto you the forgiveness of sins: and by him all that believe are justified from all things, from which ye could not be justified by the law of Moses. Beware therefore, lest that come upon you, which is spoken of in the prophets; behold, ye despisers, and wonder, and perish: for I work a work in your days, a work which ye shall in no wise believe, though a man declare it unto you. (Acts 13:38–41)

We find him in the Thessalonian synagogue, where he "reasoned with them out of the scriptures, opening and alleging, that Christ must needs have suffered, and risen again from the dead; and that this Jesus, whom I preach unto you, is Christ" (Acts 17:2–3). There he is before Agrippa: "Having therefore obtained help of God, I continue unto this day, witnessing both to small and great, saying none other things than those which the prophets and Moses did say should come: that Christ should suffer, and that he should be the first that should rise from the dead, and should shew light unto the people, and to the Gentiles" (Acts 26:22–23). We watch him in prison, speaking with the Jews "to whom he expounded and testified the kingdom of God, persuading them concerning Jesus, both out of the law of Moses, and out of the prophets, from morning till evening" (Acts 28:23) and declaring Christ also to the Gentiles: "And Paul dwelt two whole years in his own hired house, and received all that came in unto him, preaching the kingdom of God, and teaching those things which concern the Lord Jesus Christ, with all confidence, no man forbidding him" (Acts 28:30–31).

The opening words of the letter to the Romans set the tone for all his epistles: "Paul, a servant of Jesus Christ, called to be an apostle, separated unto the gospel of God, (which he had promised afore by his prophets in the holy scriptures,) concerning his Son Jesus Christ our Lord, which was made of the seed of David according to the flesh; and declared to be the Son of God with power, according to the spirit of holiness, by the resurrection from the dead" (Rom. 1:1–4).

We find nothing different in any of the other biblical records of apostolic preaching. We hear the same message from the mouth of Peter on the day of Pentecost, as he speaks of "Jesus of Nazareth, a man approved of God among you by miracles and wonders and signs, which God did by him in the midst of you, as ye yourselves also know," sweeping through the testimony of Scripture before rising to the piercing keynote of his address: "Therefore let all the house of Israel know assuredly, that God hath made that same Jesus, whom ye have crucified, both Lord and Christ" (Acts 2:22, 36).

We hear it in Solomon's porch:

> But those things, which God before had shewed by the mouth of all his prophets, that Christ should suffer, he hath so fulfilled. Repent ye therefore, and be converted, that your sins may be blotted out, when the times of refreshing shall come from the presence of the Lord; and he shall send Jesus Christ, which before was preached unto you: whom the heaven must receive until the times of restitution of all things, which God hath spoken by the mouth of all his holy prophets since the world began. For Moses truly said unto the fathers, A prophet shall the Lord your God raise up unto you of your brethren, like unto me; him shall ye hear in all things whatsoever he shall say unto you. And it shall come to pass, that every soul, which will not hear that prophet, shall be destroyed from among the people. Yea, and all the prophets from Samuel and those that follow after, as many as have spoken, have likewise foretold of these days. Ye are the children of the prophets, and of the covenant which God made with our fathers, saying unto Abraham, And in thy seed shall all the kindreds of the earth be blessed. Unto you first God, having raised up his Son Jesus, sent him to bless you, in turning away every one of you from his iniquities. (Acts 3:18–26)

The same note is sounded repeatedly: "To him give all the prophets witness, that through his name whosoever believeth in him shall receive remission of sins" (Acts 10:43). In similar fashion the whole body of the New Testament plays out.

These examples—and they could be multiplied many times—show us that preaching Christ's person and work as set forth in the entire Bible was the heart of all that constituted apostolic preaching. Such preaching is nothing novel. Jesus and His apostles have set the standard from the beginning, and the best of those who follow are those who have adhered most closely to this model. Joel Beeke reminds us of this fact:

The experimental preaching of the Reformers and Puritans focused on preaching Christ. As Scripture clearly shows, evangelism must bear witness to the record God has given of his only begotten Son (Acts 2:3; 5:42; 8:35; Romans 16:25; 1 Corinthians 2:2; Galatians 3:1). The Puritans thus taught that any preaching in which Christ does not have the pre-eminence is not valid experiential preaching. William Perkins said that the heart of all preaching was to 'preach [only] one Christ by Christ to the praise of Christ'. According to Thomas Adams, 'Christ is the sum of the whole Bible, prophesied, typified, prefigured, exhibited, demonstrated, to be found in every leaf, almost in every line, the Scriptures being but as it were the swaddling bands of the child Jesus'. 'Think of Christ as the very substance, marrow, soul, and scope of the whole Scriptures', advised Isaac Ambrose. In this Christ-centred context, Reformed and Puritan evangelism was marked by a discriminating application of truth to experience.[7]

The great evangelical Anglican, Bishop J. C. Ryle, concurs: "Let it be a settled principle in our minds, in reading the Bible, that Christ is the central sun of the whole book. So long as we keep Him in view, we shall never greatly err in our search for spiritual knowledge. Once losing sight of Christ, we shall find the whole Bible dark and full of difficulty. The key of Bible knowledge is Jesus Christ."[8]

For us to preach Christ means that our preaching is always to be anchored on the rock of Jesus' person and work as set forth in the entirety of Scripture. The entire Bible points to Him. He is to be the grand theme of our ministry. We must preach the Bible christologically and christocentrically.

True ministers of God are to preach Christ and His gospel—that good news about our Lord who is fully divine and fully human, a sinless person who perfectly kept God's law for His people and who has borne His Father's righteous judgment in their place. The gospel is all about that person. The *what* of the good news depends upon the *who*: it concerns Jesus Christ the Son of God who came into the world to save sinners (1 Tim. 1:15).

What does it not mean to preach Christ?

Are we to conclude at this point that we are to preach nothing but "Calvary sermons" and that all other preaching is illegitimate? Are all of our sermons to

---

7. Grace Online Library, "What Is Reformed Experimental Preaching?" Joel R. Beeke, http://www.graceonlinelibrary.org/articles/full.asp?id=42|42|394 (May 14, 2009).

8. J. C. Ryle, *Expository Thoughts on the Gospels: Luke 11–24* (Grand Rapids: Baker, 2007), 501.

sound the same? Are we constantly to sound the same note with the same tone and at the same pitch and volume?

Of course not! The same apostle who made it his business to know nothing but Christ and Him crucified (1 Cor. 2:2) could also say that he had, in the course of his time in Ephesus, declared the whole counsel of God (Acts 20:27).

Preaching Christ does not at all preclude us from preaching other great themes found in the Bible such as the doctrines of justification, sanctification, glorification, and providence. All of these topics are to be heralded from the pulpit on a regular basis. However, if we are to be true to the examples of Jesus and the apostles, we must always preach them in the light of Christ and find the road that brings us back to our Savior. Whatever text or topic is the focus of our preaching at a given time, we display it so that Christ is seen, tracing it back to our glorious Lord and Master. Preaching Christ is not merely tacking Him on as an addendum to our messages or as part of a random gospel appeal; He is not just a name to be repeated time after time. Rather, we are to see all the truths that we expound as connected to Jesus. Alexander Maclaren stated this well:

> A ministry of which the Christ who lived and died for us is manifestly the
> centre to which all converges and from which all is viewed, may sweep a
> wide circumference, and include many themes. The requirement bars out
> no province of thought or experience, nor does it condemn the preacher
> to a parrot-like repetition of elementary truths, or a narrow round of
> commonplace. It does demand that all themes shall lead up to Christ,
> and all teaching point to Him.... Preaching Christ does not exclude any
> theme, but prescribes the bearing and purpose of all; and the widest
> compass and richest variety are not only possible, but obligatory for him
> who would in any worthy sense take this for the motto of his ministry,
> "I determine not to know anything among you, save Jesus Christ and
> Him crucified."[9]

It is no agony to find Christ in the Bible and to bring Him into our preaching and pastoring. One of the old masters of pastoral theology, William Taylor, exhorts us accordingly:

> The Gospel, as Paul preached it, was far-reaching enough in its appli-
> cation to touch at every point the conduct and experiences of men. The
> Cross, as he used it, was an instrument of the widest range and of the
> greatest power. When, therefore, I insist that you like him should "preach
> Jesus Christ and Him crucified," I do not mean to make the pulpit for

---

9. Alexander Maclaren, *The Expositor's Bible* (Grand Rapids: Eerdmans, 1956), 6:224.

you a battery, of such a nature that the guns upon it can strike only such vessels as happen to pass immediately in front of its embrasures [openings in battlements]. On the contrary, I turn it for you into a tower, whereon is mounted a swivel-cannon, which can sweep the whole horizon of human life, and strike down all immorality, and ungodliness, and selfishness, and sin. I do not shut you into a small chamber having but one outlook, and even that into a narrow court; but I place you in an observatory with a revolving telescope that can command the landscape round and round, and sweep, besides, the hemisphere of the stars. I do not mean that you should keep continually repeating the words of "the faithful saying" like a parrot-cry, until every particle of meaning has dropped out of them; but rather, that you should make application of the great principles that lie beneath the Cross, to the ever-varying circumstances and occurrences of life, and that in such a way as at once to succor the Christian and arrest and convert the sinner.[10]

Taylor has grasped what is evident in the apostolic writing. Search the Scriptures and see how these men of God, time and time again, brought every issue of doctrine and practice, every question of faith and life, back to Christ and Him crucified and resolved it at the foot of the cross. Did Paul find divisions in the church? Between races? Between factions? Between individuals? Was there creeping legalism? Were libertinism and antinomianism insinuating themselves? Were there false teachers preaching any of a range of heresies? Were there sad and doubting Christians? Believers needing comfort or exhortation? The right response to any of these dangers and difficulties was and always is Jesus. He is not only the entrance into the kingdom, He is its abiding life principle. There is nothing in the Christian life that is divorced from Him. He is the golden hub of the gospel wheel, and the whole is only true and balanced insofar as He is kept at its center.

When we get this right, it keeps us from losing our way in the preaching and teaching of the truth as it is in Jesus. Sometimes preachers, even with the best intentions, fall into a habit of mere moralizing in their sermons. Often Old Testament narratives or New Testament episodes become nothing more than examples of how to live or not to live, examples of goodness or badness. Morality and duty and example are on the pages of our Bibles, but there is more than these things, and such things must always be located where they belong, in

---

10. William Taylor, *The Ministry of the Word* (Harrisonburg, VA: Sprinkle Publications, 2003), 102–103. This entire chapter on "The Theme and Range of the Pulpit" would bear close reading in this regard.

their right relation to Christ. Such sermons should take us to Calvary and not to Sinai. What can be sometimes lacking is the legitimate movement from, for example, great David to great David's greater Son. The rich tapestry of divine grace pointing to and prefiguring Christ in countless ways can too easily become a one-dimensional manual for a morality that cannot be pursued apart from the Lord Christ. We must not forget that these are the pages from which Christ preached *Himself*.

Others boast of finding Jesus in all the Scriptures but fail to enforce the demands of holiness that the Scriptures issue to every child of God. Some are so busy tracing out these things that they lose sight of the fact that God intends that we be conformed to the image of His Son, a perfection of holiness: Jesus of Nazareth is what it looks like when the holiness of God completely characterizes a man, for in Jesus the holy God has become a man.

We must recognize that it is easy to issue legitimate Bible demands to God's people without rooting them in the realities of God's saving work in His incarnate Son, Jesus, and the Spirit of the Lord indwelling the heart of all God's redeemed children. It is also easy to hold Christ before men without ever pressing Him into their consciences, to present Him as Savior and to bypass him as Lord not in theory, but in the practice of the individual lives of His saved people.

The Lord Jesus is the motive and means to all true morality. The morality of the true saint is called holiness, and it has its starting point at the cross of Calvary. We must always begin there, delight to be there, and often return there, at the same time remembering that it is the cross that is taken up in walking the road of the true disciple who should be becoming more like his Savior day by day. Mere moralizing from the pulpit, the commendation of the shell of holiness as an end in itself, apart from the life that is in Jesus Christ, is a fool's errand, both for the man who promotes it and the one who desires it.

Furthermore, the preaching of Christ keeps us from the preaching of our own opinions. It means that not only do we not parade ourselves, but we do not promote our own ideas when we step into the pulpit or, for that matter, into the parlor or any other place. It is too easy to find sermons peppered with "I think" and "I feel." Let us be frank: who cares what a mere man thinks or feels when his business is to make known what God Himself has revealed to be true? There is a place for wise counsels prayerfully grounded in the truth, for suggesting that while we cannot speak with the certainty of a truth plainly revealed, we think we also have the Spirit of God (cf. 1 Corinthians 7:40). But the pulpit is not the place for a man called to be an ambassador of the living Lord of glory to weave his own flawed speculations into God's perfect revelations, to taint the pure streams of God's truth with the oozing of his own fallen mind. The pulpit provides a too ready platform for the man with a psychological need to make his own opinions known to as many people as he can and provides some shred of that authority that such mistaken, sometimes pathetic, spirits crave for themselves. But it is not the place for anything other than holding up the Lord Jesus as the beginning and pattern of all true life, just as God has made Him known.

Charles Spurgeon never lost his focus upon the Lord Jesus. Early on in his labors he told this story:

> A young man had been preaching in the presence of a venerable divine, and after he had done he went to the old minister, and said, "What do you think of my sermon?" "A very poor sermon indeed," said he. "A poor sermon?" said the young man, "it took me a long time to study it." "Ay, no doubt of it." "Why, did you not think my explanation of the text a very good one?" "Oh, yes," said the old preacher, "very good indeed." "Well, then, why do you say it is a poor sermon? Didn't you think the metaphors were appropriate and the arguments conclusive?" "Yes, they were very good as far as that goes, but still it was a very poor sermon." "Will you tell me why you think it a poor sermon?" "Because," said he, "there was no Christ in it." "Well," said the young man, "Christ was not in the text; we are not to be preaching Christ always, we must preach what is in the text." So the old man said, "Don't you know young man that from every town, and every village, and every little hamlet in England, wherever it may be, there is a road to London?" "Yes," said the young man. "Ah!" said the old divine, "and so from every text in Scripture, there is a road to the metropolis of the Scriptures, that is Christ. And my dear brother, your business is when you get to a text, to say, 'Now what is the road to Christ?' and then preach a sermon, running along the road towards the great metropolis—Christ. And," said he, "I have never yet found a text that had not got a road to Christ in it, and if I ever do find one that has not a road to Christ in it, I will make one; I will go over hedge and ditch but I would get at my Master, for the sermon cannot do any good unless there is a savour of Christ in it."[11]

To the end, Spurgeon followed the road to Christ. In the last message he preached at the Metropolitan Tabernacle, delivered on the morning of the Lord's Day, June 7, 1891, the steadfast preacher said,

---

11. Charles Spurgeon, "Christ Precious to Believers" in *The New Park Street Pulpit* (1860; reprint, Grand Rapids: Baker Books, 1994), 5:140. Also told, in slightly different form in *The Soul Winner* (Grand Rapids: Eerdmans, 1964), 106–107.

If you wear the livery of Christ, you will find him so meek and lowly of heart that you will find rest unto your souls. He is the most magnanimous of captains. There never was his like among the choicest of princes. He is always to be found in the thickest part of the battle. When the wind blows cold he always takes the bleak side of the hill. The heaviest end of the cross lies ever on his shoulders. If he bids us carry a burden, he carries it also. If there is anything that is gracious, generous, kind, and tender, yea lavish and superabundant in love, you always find it in him. His service is life, peace, and joy. Oh, that you would enter on it at once! God help you to enlist under the banner of Jesus Christ![12]

From the beginning until the end of his ministry, Spurgeon held to his proposed "subject of the ministry in this house, as long as this platform shall stand, and as long as this house shall be frequented by worshippers"—Jesus Christ. By God's unfailing grace, Spurgeon had a Christ-centered ministry, and God richly blessed him and those who were under his ministry because of it.

Admonition and instruction

We will be further helped in this matter of preaching Christ if we look more closely at the two currents that run in this great stream of truth: Paul speaks of Christ, "whom we preach, warning every man, and teaching every man in all wisdom" (Col. 1:28). As noted before, these are the means that Paul employed, under God, to bring his proclamation of Christ close to the hearts of men.

The sense of "warning" is more definite than we might immediately understand it. A more accurate word might be *admonishing*, but we still need to lay hold of the right idea, which is of having something put into the mind or laid to the heart. One writer has described this action as "putting sense into someone's head." This word has to do with counseling a straying person— whether a believer or not—about correct belief or behavior. It has to do with setting the disposition of someone in proper order with a view to helping that person.

This is activity designed to drive deep into the will and the affections, to hang something prominently before the eye of the mind. It will include warning, rebuke, exhortation, and comfort in order to correct, rouse, or cheer the soul.

The intensity of this word is apparent in Acts 20:31, where Paul—on the back of a series of plainly expressed concerns of the highest order—calls upon the Ephesian elders to watch, remembering that for three years he did not cease to

---

12. Charles Spurgeon, "The Statute of David for the Sharing of the Spoil," in *The Metropolitan Tabernacle Pulpit* (1892; reprint, Edinburgh: Banner of Truth, 1970), 37:324.

warn [admonish] everyone night and day with tears. A slightly different nuance is apparent in 1 Corinthians 4:14, where Paul describes Apollos and himself as servants of Jesus, saying with earnest paternal tones, "I write not these things to shame you, but as my beloved sons I warn you."

The intention is to awaken a man, to arouse the soul, to stimulate reflection and promote repentance. Sin will be identified and addressed, error exposed and warned against, holiness portrayed and encouraged, behavior that reflects underlying attitudes promoted where right and corrected where wrong. It is pastoral care that looks into a man's eyes and brings the issues of sin and holiness to bear, ensuring that they penetrate, are recognized, and then acted upon. It will bring eternity near, be always conscious of the great and terrible day of the Lord, and the judgment that all must face. It brings Christ Jesus before the eye in all His splendor, emphasizes the necessity of faith in Him, and holds Him in the mind.

In the same way the minister gives himself to "teaching." This is instruction or training, whether in a formal or informal setting. It means to explain or expound something to another person and is typically connected to the work of teaching the objective truths of God's Word. Here the preacher works upon the understanding. Christ is proclaimed by means of careful and systematic instruction, definite truth and clear direction issued and imparted to the inquiring mind, demonstrating a pastor's ability to teach (1 Tim. 3:2). If the minister as admonisher is salt, pungent and penetrating, as instructor he is light, searching and illuminating. The truth of Christ is clearly, plainly, warmly laid out. All the fullness of His person and work, everything the prophets declared Him to be, all that God the Father reveals Him to be, is made known with all the distinctness that a preacher can muster.

These means are to be used "in all wisdom." Paul identifies the manner of warning and teaching Christ. In writing to the Colossians, the apostle is much concerned with wisdom, referring to it several times (1:9; 2:3; 2:23; 3:16; 4:5). The commandments and doctrines of the false teachers "have indeed a shew of wisdom in will worship, and humility, and neglecting of the body: not in any honour to the satisfying of the flesh" (2:23). But when Paul speaks about preaching "in all wisdom" the Christ who is himself the totality of wisdom (2:3), he is subtly assaulting and opposing the counterfeit wisdom of men. Paul did not warn and teach every man according to his native human wisdom or rationality. Rather, he did these things in the wisdom that God the Holy Spirit gave him (1 Cor. 2:13). This is spiritual wisdom that is from God and is found in His Word.

Thus equipped, the minister is to work at appropriate seasons and use effective means. He must discern particular needs and the corresponding gospel counsels that are required. He is to be engaging, interesting, accessible, earnest, and colorful, as a means of performing his work to God's glory in Christ. He must root men out of every refuge of falsehood and lies in order to bring them to the knowledge of the truth. By these means he guides sinners to Jesus and directs the child of God in matters of faith and life, keeping Christ always at the center of the wheel.

|| FELLOW CHRISTIAN   Are you sitting under a Christ-centered, Christ-saturated, Christ-magnifying ministry? Are you hearing about Him in the fullness of His person: the God-man, who is Prophet to teach us, Priest to atone and intercede for us, and King to rule over us as His people? Are you hearing about His work? Is His life of sinless obedience held up to you? Do you learn of His atoning death, bearing God's wrath in our place? Do you hear of His resurrection from the dead? What of His glorious rule as He reigns over heaven and earth? A faithful minister will bring these things often before you, directly and indirectly. You are, because of God's grace, entitled to such a ministry, and entitled to require it of the man who ministers to you. The Lord intends that His people should be shepherded by men concerned for the salvation and subsequent spiritual maturity of those who hear them. He will hold to account those who neglect this calling and thereby end up with blood on their hands. God has appointed His gospel ministers to employ proclamation, with admonition and instruction, for His glory and your good, pressing Christ home upon your minds and hearts honestly, earnestly, and closely. We should pray for regiments of such men to be raised up and thrust out into the harvest.

The ministry of a faithful man will have the savor of Christ about it. The Lord Jesus will be set forth, explicitly and implicitly, as the one who came to save His people from their sins (Matt. 1:21), as the one from whom we receive all of our life as the children of God (John 15:4–5), as the one who promises to keep us—and will keep us—in His ways all of our days until the very end (John 10:27–28). This is the Christ that you need to hear about in the church that you attend. This is the one whose voice you are to hear and in whose steps you are to follow as you hear Him proclaimed in the Scriptures from the man or men preaching before you week in and week out.

Settle for nothing less! The eternal well-being of your soul is at stake. Christ must be all in all. Are you, perhaps, looking for a pastor and preacher for the church where you worship? When interviewing a man for the position, ask him directly, "What do you think about Christ?" Take heed to his answer and the spirit in which he gives it. If Jesus is this man's all in all, then at least the foundation is laid for him to be a good undershepherd for the congregation; if not, then peek beneath the fleece to make sure that you are not inviting a wolf to take care of the flock.

Listen to a man's preaching. Does he belt out only the commands and demands of Scripture and leave you battered and broken by them? Or does he also, in Christ, bind up that which is broken, connecting legitimate duties and requirements to our Lord Jesus, showing how, with, and in Him we can carry these things out (Col. 2:6–7)? Does a candidate, when he proclaims publicly and preaches privately, constantly point you back to Jesus as the one who can meet all your spiritual needs, the one from whom you are to derive comfort? Does he bring the light of instruction to bear on your soul and rub the salt of admonition into your heart?

This is something of what it means to preach Christ in the fullness of His being. It is the model for all gospel witness. You yourself have opportunities to declare Christ to others. This responsibility in its broadest sense is not the task only of ordained men. When the Lord gives you a door for the Word, whether at the workplace, the library, the store, at your child's bedside, or in the pew after the sermon, have you told others about Him? This was the pattern in the early church, even in the midst of fierce persecution and principled opposition: "Therefore they that were scattered abroad went every where preaching the word" (Acts 8:4). Remember in this regard that there is also a duty to one another within the congregation in terms of instruction and warning. Writing to the maturing saints in Rome, Paul said, "And I myself also am persuaded of you, my brethren, that ye also are full of goodness, filled with all knowledge, able also to admonish one another" (Rom. 15:14). The church in Colosse is encouraged to carry out this duty in their sung worship: "Let the word of Christ dwell in you richly in all wisdom; teaching and admonishing one another in psalms and hymns and spiritual songs, singing with grace in your hearts to the Lord" (Col. 3:16). The church in Thessalonica, fighting a different battle, is encouraged to admonish the one who does not obey apostolic directives: "Note that man, and have no company with him, that he may be ashamed. Yet count him not as an enemy, but admonish him as a brother" (2 Thess. 3:14–15).

But remember also that such a ministry to you—whether from a faithful pastor or fellow member—will never lead to an easy time or a casual life. If a man is faithful to your soul, you will not hear stories and jokes all the time. You will not always feel good about yourself. At times, you may see yourself as the least worthy sinner who ever crawled the earth. You may often weep over sin. You will not only hear about your privileges and blessings but will have responsibilities and obligations pressed upon your soul. You will be humbled as well as lifted up; you will often mourn before you rejoice. You will be called to walk in the footsteps of the crucified Jesus as a faithful disciple and brought back into the way when you stray from it.

The "downside" of praying for and finding such a ministry is that you ought to receive it. Every Christian likes the idea of holiness and applauds the notion of a faithful ministry, but we are not always so keen when we feel its scriptural force. We are ready, perhaps even eager, to see others admonished and instructed, but there will almost certainly come a day when a loving, faithful servant of Jesus will look us in the eye and put something in our mind, will impart truth to us and will not let us shake it off, but will press it home until it penetrates, hold it up until it illuminates. Then what a multitude of excuses we make, what a list of reasons we offer to ignore the truth, how many evasions and self-delusions we will conjure to avoid the truth and its demands.

When you pray that you might enjoy the privileges of a faithful gospel ministry, pray also that you will be disposed to receive it. Pray for its fruitful effect upon you and for the pulling down of all barriers to faithful warning and teaching, seeking that the Word of the Lord may run freely and be glorified (2 Thess. 3:1). It is a disaster to lack such a ministry; it is a terror to reject it; it is an unparalleled blessing to receive it and embrace it.

FELLOW PASTOR We must be fundamentally and profoundly Christ-centered. We are to see and put Christ in all His glory at the very heart of our ministry, bringing Him to bear, as Paul and the other apostles do, upon situations great and small. We are, by these God-appointed means, to labor for the salvation and spiritual maturity of all those before us. Our duty is to make Christ known, publicly to proclaim Him, impressing Him upon the lives of men and women, boys and girls, closely, effectually, earnestly, and prayerfully, by the pointed tools of admonition and instruction. This is how we in our turn fulfill the Word of God (Col. 1:25). Nothing is to dissuade us; nothing is to deter us; nothing should bring us to despair. As we will see in coming chapters, there is a glorious end in view though a great deal of hardship is involved, and we must therefore pursue this calling ardently and faithfully.

What hinders us, then, from preaching Christ more fully and more freely in our ministries? Surely we love Him, do we not? Do we not esteem Him as precious above all things? If this is so, how is it that we do not preach Him as we should? Is there some reason He has not been the subject of our ministries in recent days, or even months, or perhaps years? Could it be our pride that hinders us, our desire to share the glory that Christ will not share with another? Could it be our self-centeredness that holds us back, that we want to spare ourselves the effort of preparing to preach like this and of pastoring in the aftermath of such sermons? Could it be fear, fear of outcomes, fear of the response of the people, or fear of our own insufficiency to address such a high theme—an implicit uncertainty in the Spirit's ability to make us sufficient?

Here we must take stock. Can you say with the apostle, "Him we preach"? Is your ministry centered on Jesus, His glorious person and His finished work, as you declare Him from all the Scriptures as the only Savior of sinners? Does He have the preeminence in all things in your ministry (Col. 1:18), both in principle and in practice? The outstanding Baptist theologian of the eighteenth century, Andrew Fuller, assures the fearful preacher that he may rest here:

> If you preach Christ, you need not fear for want of matter. His person and work are rich in fulness. Every Divine attribute is seen in him. All the types prefigure him. The prophecies point to him. Every truth bears relation to him. The law itself must be so explained and enforced as to lead to him.... The preaching of Christ will answer every end of preaching. This is the doctrine which God owns to conversion, to the leading of awakened sinners to peace, and to the comfort of true Christians. If the doctrine of the cross be no comfort to us, it is a sign we have no right to comfort. This doctrine is calculated to quicken the indolent, to draw forth every Christian grace, and to recover the backslider. This is the universal remedy for all the moral diseases of all mankind.[13]

To proclaim Christ Jesus our Lord is to preach Him by whom the kingdom advances, in whom is the power of God to salvation, through whom comes life and peace and blessing to the church. He alone answers every need of the church in every time and place. He is the Savior whom we are to present to our people, crying with the apostle John, "Behold! The Lamb of God who takes away the sin of the world!" Preaching duty alone is not preaching Christ; preaching the

---

13. Andrew Fuller, "Preaching Christ" in *Complete Works* (Harrisonburg, VA: Sprinkle Publications, 1988), 1:503–504. See also Fuller's letter on "The Uniform Bearing of the Scriptures on the Person and Work of Christ" (1:702–704) for some reasonable and balanced advice.

law alone is not preaching Christ; preaching a principle alone is not preaching Christ; we must preach Christ Himself.

Furthermore, we must preach Christ in a Christlike manner. We must pray God to grant us a Christlike spirit of meekness and boldness, of loving firmness and principled tenderness. A duty to proclaim and a responsibility to admonish and instruct must never become an excuse to lash out unrestrainedly or to brutalize the people of God. We need the wisdom that is from above (James 1:5; 3:17–18) for the discharge of our duty and the employment of our ministerial tools. We need the grace that God supplies to keep us from growing weary in this well-doing, to maintain honesty and integrity, to keep our eye fixed on the purpose of this sometimes painful labor.

If you preach in this way, you may see sinners bored, frustrated, irritated, and angered, but you must esteem Christ too highly and their souls too precious to hold back that which, under God, will also prove the means of their being humbled, convicted, and converted. You may see even the saints appear to be shaken, troubled, rebuked, ashamed, rebellious, resistant, and proud as Jesus is declared: sins will be uncovered, duty instilled, holiness displayed, and grace upheld as the cross is pressed into the saints' lives so as to leave an indelible imprint. Remaining sin in God's people will kick hard against "Christ crucified" applied to their whole lives, but He is to have the preeminence in all things, and we love the people of God too much to allow them to go on in ignorance and sin. Preach Christ to Christ's people: they need Him desperately, and He will do them good.

Consider again that plaque that sits on many pulpits. Remember its inscription: "Sir, we would see Jesus" (John 12:21). Make it so. Make it your goal to hold Him up in all His splendor and worthiness in all you do as a preacher and pastor.

How shall we accomplish this? To begin with, we need simply to spend more time with Him. The Christian's love for the unseen Christ grows by communion with Him. He is a person, a real person, a living Lord and Savior, who has promised to be with us all of our days. We must spend time with Him daily, and as we do, we will be overwhelmed with His greatness and glory to the end that we will want to tell others about Him.

This is not only a matter of the time that we put into our sermon preparation for the Lord's Day or other ministerial duties. We must not read the Bible for our "professional" needs, as a lawyer might turn to his statute books. Hear Andrew Fuller once more in his counsel to a young minister at his ordination:

Live the life of a Christian, as well as of a minister.—Read as one, preach as one, converse as one—to *be profited*, as well as to profit others. One of the greatest temptations of a ministerial life is to handle Divine truth as ministers, rather than as Christians—for others, rather than for ourselves. But the word will not profit them that *preach* it, any more than it will them that hear it, unless it be "mixed with faith." If we study the Scriptures as Christians, the more familiar we are with them, the more we shall feel their importance; but if our object be only to find out something to say to others, our familiarity with them will prove a snare. It will resemble that of soldiers, and doctors, and undertakers with death; the more familiar we are with them, the less we shall feel their importance.[14]

Let us not handle the Scriptures in our studies as mere scholars, but receive them as humble saints. Let our efforts not be only for others, but let us preach Christ first to ourselves. We need to have constant and fresh dealings with our Lord if we are going to preach Him to others with fervor.

How will we do this? We must read the Word of God with a Christian appetite, as a fiancée reads the love letters of her groom-to-be, poring over the pages, reading and re-reading the love-laden phrases. We must meditate on the truth as it is in Jesus; we must memorize and chew over the Scriptures. We must be much in prayer, conversing with the Author of the book, and seeking the Spirit's illumination that more and more we might be given eyes to see "the light of the knowledge of the glory of God in the face of Jesus Christ" (2 Cor. 4:6). Only then will we be able to preach not ourselves, but Christ Jesus the Lord, and ourselves the servants of God's people for Jesus' sake (2 Cor. 4:5).

If we are to preach our Lord to others, we must have an ever increasing heart attachment to Him. God has called us into the fellowship of His Son (1 Cor. 1:9; 1 John 1:3). We are called to grow in the grace and knowledge of Him (2 Peter 3:18). We are to be "changed into the same image from glory to glory, even as by the Spirit of the Lord" (2 Cor. 3:18). As this glorious process takes place, our preaching of Christ will not be like the flow of water resulting from the mechanical pressures of an artificial fountain, perhaps correct and even, but emotionless and routine. Rather, it will be the bubbling natural spring of a soul taken up with Jesus, the spontaneous outflow and overflow of a heart enraptured by Christ.

---

14. Andrew Fuller, "Spiritual Knowledge and Love Necessary for the Ministry," *Complete Works*, 1:482, original emphasis. He gives similar counsel repeatedly to preachers in a series of sermons and addresses directed to men entering or already in the gospel ministry.

It is Christ alone whom we are to preach and Christ only who can enable us, by His Spirit, to preach in this way. Do you feel the weight of this duty? Good! Then we are ready to fall on our faces and plead with God to equip us in mind and heart and soul and strength to serve His glory by exalting His Son, Jesus Christ. The hymn writer John Berridge expressed such desires in potent words. Let us pray them home:

> The means of grace are in my hand,
> The blessing is at God's command,
> Who must the work fulfil;
> And though I read, and watch and pray,
> Yet here the Lord directs my way,
> And worketh all things still.
>
> I cannot speak a proper word,
> Nor think aright, but from the Lord
> Preparing heart and tongue;
> In nature I can see no good,
> But all my good proceeds from God,
> And does to grace belong.
>
> I see it now, and do confess
> My utter need of Jesus' grace,
> And of His Spirit's light;
> I beg His kind and daily care;
> O Lord, my heart and tongue prepare
> To think and speak aright.
>
> Prepare my heart to love Thee well,
> And love Thy truth which doth excel,
> And love Thy children dear;
> Instruct me how to live by faith,
> And feel the virtue of Thy death,
> And find Thy presence near.
>
> Prepare my tongue to pray and praise,
> To speak of providential ways,
> And heavenly truth unfold;
> To strengthen well a feeble soul,
> Correct the wanton, rouse the dull,
> And silence sinners bold.

7 THE GOAL OF PAUL'S MINISTRY

Whom we preach, warning every man, and
teaching every man in all wisdom; that we may
present every man perfect in Christ Jesus . . .
— Colossians 1:28

We do not limit the infinite extent and power of Divine grace, when we
speak of the necessity of the Christian Ministry. These uses of the sacred
institution are not and cannot be necessary to God, as if he were unable
to work without them. But they are such as he has appointed and made
necessary in the constituted order of means, for the accomplishment of
his own purposes of mercy to the world.... This, therefore is the ordained
means of conversion, and of subsequent establishment in every stage of
the Christian life; and its necessity must continue, while there is a single
sinner to be brought into the family of God, or a single grace in the heart
of the saint to advance to perfection.[1]   — Charles Bridges

As a servant of the living God, Paul has been pressing home on the Colossians his burden for them. He feels a deep sense of responsibility toward them. He is profoundly conscious of his duty. His earnestness and tenderness toward them has given him an open door into their hearts to deal closely with them, as the situation demands.

As previously mentioned, since Paul is a fellow worker with God, we should expect to find—and do indeed find—a full and precise correspondence between God's plan and Paul's intention. Nowhere is that plainer than when we consider the ultimate aim of the gospel minister's task: to "present every man perfect in Christ Jesus." Paul has identified the three tools of the gospel minister: the

---

1. Charles Bridges, *The Christian Ministry: With an Inquiry into the Causes of Its Inefficiency* (Edinburgh: Banner of Truth, 1967), 10.

proclamation of Jesus Christ with the complementary means of admonition and instruction. He himself employed this ministerial equipment vigorously and lovingly, seeking to drive truth into the will, understanding, and affections of his hearers. He sought, by all truly wise means, to shake them from lethargy, to stir them to endeavor, and to guide them in holiness.

Paul used these tools constantly, comprehensively, and specifically, both to reach the lost and to teach the reached. His scope is as vast as the revealed will of God, and so Paul labors to bring every man into the kingdom and to nurture all those within the kingdom.

Why do Paul and those who imitate him as ministers of the gospel give themselves to this task so assiduously? Is it because they are no good at anything else? Are they opinionated and argumentative know-it-alls who will not rest until everyone thinks like them? Do they, like Diotrephes, love to have the preeminence (3 John 1:9)? Are they interfering and intrusive busybodies? Are they inherently aggressive, liking nothing more than a good argument—apart, of course, from winning a good argument?

These and many other charges might be flung at the faithful minister as he goes about his gospel business. Granted, he is not without sin. At times he may be inclined to overstate a particular element of his case, while at other times he is just as readily inclined to avoid necessary conflict. He may become frustrated. He will often be weary. He may be misguided at times. He may speak less wisely, less graciously, less carefully, less tenderly, than he intended or hoped. But if he is a true man of God, such harsh charges as those above will be fundamentally false. He will have a far higher and nobler purpose than those who impute evil to him might ever imagine.

Why, then, does he give himself tirelessly to this task? Why does he strive not to be deterred, dissuaded, or dejected? Why does he resist despair? What carries him always forward?

The concern for true godliness

Paul's language in writing to the Colossians denotes a clear purpose. The English word *that* connects the gospel minister's tools (preaching, warning, and teaching) with his task. Paul is directing our attention to the end that he has in view in the gracious exercise of all these tools. He points to the governing principle that dictates the employment of all the pastor's gospel equipment. The end, the goal, of all his proclamation, admonition, and instruction is simply this: "to present every man perfect in Christ Jesus."

In every preaching and pastoring effort, this purpose must be consciously entertained; it should lie behind every word that proceeds from the mouth of the man of God. It is to be ingrained in his thinking, becoming a sort of mental "muscle memory" that guides all his proclaiming, warning, and teaching. By keeping this end in view, the servant of the Lord is enabled—under God—to bring to bear all the tools of his holy profession on this one great end. It is the burden of the minister's heart, shining through in his public and private ministry and prayer. So we find faithful Epaphras pleading for this very thing in Colossians 4:12: "Epaphras, who is one of you, a servant of Christ, saluteth you, always labouring fervently for you in prayers, that ye may stand perfect and complete in all the will of God." It is a noble cause that is sufficient to engage the whole redeemed humanity of the man of God. It is this cause that will stimulate his enthusiasm and sustain his endeavor.

Notice the thread of Paul's thinking, the consistent compass of his work. As he aims to preach Christ, warning every man and teaching every man in all wisdom, so here he wishes to present "every man" perfect in Christ.

The errorists perhaps claimed that salvation was for only an elite group of people. By contrast, Paul preached a gospel for all people. The emphatic threefold use of "every man" in this verse stresses the universality of the gospel. Poor and rich, slave and free, male and female, Jew and Gentile—all were on the radar of Paul's gospel labors. As our Lord had commanded, the gospel was for "every creature" (Mark 16:15), so the scope of Paul's work was never limited. There is a principled hopefulness and broad extent in his work. On the one hand, Paul is not foolish or naïve. He recognizes that not every man will bow the knee to Jesus Christ in faith and love. He also reckons with the powerful adversarial activity of his opponents in the human as well as in the spiritual realm. At the same time, he is a servant of the God who "is longsuffering to us-ward, not willing that any should perish, but that all should come to repentance" (2 Peter 3:9). Paul's holy desire is that by preaching and teaching he might see every man come to repentance toward God and faith in Jesus Christ. He mentally excludes none from this prospect—not the most hardened, the most vindictive, the most aggressive, the most antagonistic. When he prays, he prays for all. Why should he dismiss or despair of any? Is he himself not a potent example of the efficacy of God's saving grace in Christ?

> And I thank Christ Jesus our Lord, who hath enabled me, for that he counted me faithful, putting me into the ministry; who was before a blasphemer, and a persecutor, and injurious: but I obtained mercy, because I did it ignorantly in unbelief. And the grace of our Lord was

exceeding abundant with faith and love which is in Christ Jesus. This is a faithful saying, and worthy of all acceptation, that Christ Jesus came into the world to save sinners; of whom I am chief. Howbeit for this cause I obtained mercy, that in me first Jesus Christ might shew forth all longsuffering, for a pattern to them which should hereafter believe on him to life everlasting. (1 Tim. 1:12–16)

So there is a divinely inspired desire driving this divinely mandated labor, all carried out with a divinely patterned end in mind.

The cultivation of mature holiness

Paul wishes to "present every man perfect in Christ Jesus." This immediately demands an answer to the question, "What is this perfection?"

Is Paul saying that he anticipates people living entirely without sin? In a very careful and specific sense, yes, that is Paul's ultimate desire. Let us remember that Paul is living constantly with that legitimate tension between the ideal and real, between the Lord God's appropriately high aims for His creation and the sober facts of life in a fallen world. There is a sense in which Paul is aiming progressively toward the sinless perfection that will only be accomplished fully in glory. He has in view that day when God brings all His chosen ones to complete and glorious likeness to His Son, Jesus Christ (1 John 3:2).

For now, however, we must consider that there is another way to use this word, and it is this sense that Paul has primarily in mind as he writes. This perfection can be properly described as maturity, a completeness in faith and character. The word has to do with intactness or wholeness. The sense is of a man who is fully grown in Christ so that he can appear before God without confusion in the day of judgment.

If we look back to our Old Testament, we will find some help in understanding what Paul means when he talks about perfection. Consider first two passages from the first book of the Kings. In one, King Solomon is blessing the gathered people of God at the inauguration of the temple of the Lord. His concluding request is this: "Let your heart therefore be perfect with the LORD our God, to walk in his statutes, and to keep his commandments, as at this day" (1 Kings 8:61). Again, in 1 Kings 11:4, we find the same notion employed in a much sadder testimony, for Solomon himself had departed from this standard: "For it came to pass, when Solomon was old, that his wives turned away his heart after other gods: and his heart was not perfect with the LORD his God, as was the heart of David his father." The word *perfect* here might be translated "loyal"—loyalty to the Lord God, having a heart wholly tuned to God's will and in step with His Word, demonstrated by walking in His statutes and keeping His commandments. This is the language of perfection.

Next, consider two examples from Genesis and Deuteronomy. In Genesis 6, we read of the terrible spiritual gloom of the days when men spread across the face of the earth, and Noah alone found grace in the eyes of the Lord. This faithful man of God is described in this way: "Noah was a just man and perfect in his generations, and Noah walked with God" (Gen. 6:9). Compare this with the command of Deuteronomy 18:13: "Thou shalt be perfect with the LORD thy God." The sense here is "blameless." The lives of God's chosen people were to contrast starkly with the abominable practices of the heathen nations of Canaan. They were to be marked by a spiritual wholeness, entirely free from the foulness of idolatry that characterized the surrounding paganism. These passages deal respectively with the perfection of Noah—clearly a man with remaining sin, as his subsequent history demonstrated—and the perfection of the people of God before Him when in the land. They speak of being sound, in the sense of possessing full-orbed health, of being intact and unblemished. This is a character that is sincere and honest, with nothing grossly objectionable about it. The word describes a man who is bound fully to God, walking with Him without offense.

Moving back to Paul's language, in Colossians 1:22 we find the apostle speaking of the ultimate purpose of Christ's redeeming work. Christ died in order that sinners like us, once alienated from God and enemies in our minds by wicked works, being reconciled to God through Christ's death, might be presented holy and blameless and irreproachable in His sight. Here again is the very concept that we have just been considering. We have mentioned already the prayer of Epaphras that Paul records with such approval. This prayer is entirely in keeping with the declared purpose of Almighty God, even down to the very terms employed: "Epaphras, who is one of you, a servant of Christ, saluteth you, always labouring fervently for you in prayers, that ye may stand perfect and complete in all the will of God" (Col. 4:12). Paul and Epaphras, together with Timothy—and, following them, every true gospel minister—are praying toward the divinely appointed goal in full accord with the declared will of God, and they are working accordingly.

We can therefore see that the perfection that Paul primarily has in mind is not a sinless perfection, the utter lack of anything obnoxious to God. Rather, he is speaking of a sincere, principled, balanced holiness of life, an honest and comprehensive loyalty to the Lord our God. He is pointing to a life of careful and cheerful obedience to God's commandments, demonstrating a heart wholly attuned to the Lord and in step with His Word. Fundamentally, this is that mature and full-orbed godliness that declares before God, men, and angels that here is "an Israelite indeed" (John 1:47), a true child of the living God, the Holy One.

Paul speaks of the same task and the same end more expansively in writing to the Ephesians:

> And he gave some, apostles; and some, prophets; and some, evangelists; and some, pastors and teachers; for the perfecting of the saints, for the work of the ministry, for the edifying of the body of Christ: till we all come in the unity of the faith, and of the knowledge of the Son of God, unto a perfect man, unto the measure of the stature of the fulness of Christ: that we henceforth be no more children, tossed to and fro, and carried about with every wind of doctrine, by the sleight of men, and cunning craftiness, whereby they lie in wait to deceive; but speaking the truth in love, may grow up into him in all things, which is the head, even Christ: from whom the whole body fitly joined together and compacted by that which every joint supplieth, according to the effectual working in the measure of every part, maketh increase of the body unto the edifying of itself in love. (Eph. 4:11–16)

We must recognize that remaining sin in our hearts and the sin-sodden environment in which we live combine to militate against such a purpose. Sin and errors abound within and without, forming obstacles to genuine Christian progress. When the minister strives toward this goal, he must overcome all the obstacles that will arise against him (in himself and others).

Given such a context, we must be persuaded that this is a legitimate goal. We must be confident that, as servants of God, our Lord has called us to accomplish His stated purposes by His appointed means of proclamation, admonition, and instruction. Are you so persuaded? Do you accept that God expects His servants to call His people ever onwards and upwards toward full-orbed spiritual maturity? Do you accept that preachers are entitled—indeed, obliged—to warn, instruct, reprove, correct, and urge all men with this end in view?

There was a lie in Colosse, being perpetrated by the false teachers, that there was a mystical perfection, a spiritual completeness, an advanced and assured attainment, that belonged only to a spiritually elite class of people. Such ideas gave grounds for some to fall into puffed-up delusion, as if they had already arrived on the highest plane of spiritual accomplishment. Others might have ceased to pursue godliness in a spirit of Christian endeavor, perhaps convinced that they were outside the sacred circle and so doomed to low attainments in godliness.

This same lie of the devil exists still. We hear it whispered when we put certain people on a pedestal, praising their attainments in holiness as if beyond the reach of regular people like us: "Well, I am just an ordinary Christian. Surely no one would expect such a life of me." Do you hear those words? "Just an ordinary Christian." But there is no one who is just an ordinary Christian. There are only those who, contrary to all deserving, are the blood-bought sons of the living God, reconciled to Him through the atoning death of the Son of His love, our Lord and Savior Jesus Christ. There are degrees of progress and maturity; there are particular callings and offices; there are specific duties and opportunities given to some. However, there are no ranks or classes in salvation. This lie tempts some to think that they have already arrived, and so they coast through a life that demands constant combat. Others assume that they can never attain to such heady heights and cease to strive toward them. Perhaps for some it is just an easy way out—a cloak to mask their laziness, an excuse not to bother with the hard graft of sanctification.

That is why Paul makes plain that he wants to present every man "perfect *in Christ Jesus.*" Here is the great and necessary qualifier, the sphere in which all this operates. Here should be an end to all pride and despair and laziness. This goal is bound up with and dependent on the indwelling Christ. The progress that any Christian makes is by virtue of union with Him. All the power of the universe is here! Who can deny the presence of all needful grace and strength when in union with Jesus? Who can dismiss the hope of glory when it is "Christ in you"? It is in fellowship with the Lord Jesus that the Christian advances in godliness. It is through power derived from Him that the believer overcomes sin and grows in grace. It is a character that consists in likeness to Him that the child of God pursues and receives by the inward working of the Holy Spirit. This ties together the natural end and the spiritual power of the man who has been grafted into Christ: "For whom [God] did foreknow, he also did predestinate to be conformed to the image of his Son, that he might be the firstborn among many brethren" (Rom. 8:29). This is that life eternal which consists in knowing God in Christ, and Christ in God (John 17:3).

It is the task of pastors and preachers to bring the God-appointed tools of the gospel ministry to bear on men and women to the end that every man might come to Christ and then come in Christ to that spiritual maturity that derives from and depends on Jesus the Lord. Such mature holiness is manifest in a consistent and increasing likeness to Jesus, which glorifies the God of our salvation.

The consciousness of Christ's return

Paul's God-directed, God-patterned mission is grounded in a definite eschatological expectation and carried out with a decided eschatological edge. When he looks forward to presenting every man perfect in Jesus Christ, he is acting as a man profoundly conscious of the second coming of our Lord and the judgment that will occur in that day. This is the day that will put all other judgments in perspective: "For we shall all stand before the judgment seat of Christ" (Rom. 14:10). The apostle is conscious of it in all his work as a preacher and teacher. It always presses upon his soul: "Wherefore we labour, that, whether present or absent, we may be accepted of him. For we must all appear before the judgment seat of Christ; that every one may receive the things done in his body, according to that he hath done, whether it be good or bad. Knowing therefore the terror of the Lord, we persuade men; but we are made manifest unto God; and I trust also are made manifest in your consciences" (2 Cor. 5:9–11).

Paul lived his life with the end of the world and the judgment of souls in view. Every gospel minister should live accordingly. God's reconciliation of His people to Himself in Christ was carried out with this day in mind (Col. 1:22–23), and Paul has it always hanging before him.

Paul is not content merely with beginnings; he is greatly concerned with endings. In this, he must be imitated. When John Bunyan, the great Baptist preacher and allegorist of the seventeenth century, put pen to paper with the aim of depicting the style and trajectory of Christian life and combat, he did not call his book *The Sluggard's Stagnation* but *The Pilgrim's Progress*. None of us have finished the race until we have arrived at the Celestial City. God's servants, knowing that there is "a way to hell, even from the gates of heaven, as well as from the City of Destruction,"[2] cannot rest until those committed to their care are safe at home. No true shepherd of souls can rest content with self-satisfied Christian dwarfishness; he cannot be at ease with indolence, idleness, and ignorance in matters of sin and holiness. Paul—together with those who labor alongside him in this task that lasts until time comes to an end and eternity dawns—is called upon to "present every man perfect in Christ Jesus." Men hear Christ proclaimed and bow the knee to Him as the only Mediator between God and man, the great and effective Redeemer of God's elect, and so enter into His kingdom. Once there, they are to be cared for with a view to being delivered over to God in a state

---

2. John Bunyan, *The Pilgrim's Progress* in *Works* (Edinburgh: Banner of Truth, 1991), 3:166. These are almost the last and very sobering words of the first part of the tale. They exemplify the warning ministry that the true man of God faithfully undertakes.

of spiritual health and maturity "in the day when God shall judge the secrets of men by Jesus Christ according to my gospel" (Rom. 2:16).

It is the faithful minister's greatest concern that this work should be done, and done well. It is the abiding pressure on his soul that as an undershepherd of Christ he should not fail to bring his Master's sheep safely and soundly home. He has no greater desire than that those entrusted to his care should come at last to that Mount Zion above, arriving there in a state that plainly declares them to be God's healthy and happy children.

Therefore Paul unashamedly exhorts the Philippians: "Do all things without murmurings and disputings: that ye may be blameless and harmless, the sons of God, without rebuke, in the midst of a crooked and perverse nation, among whom ye shine as lights in the world; holding forth the word of life; that I may rejoice in the day of Christ, that I have not run in vain, neither laboured in vain" (Phil. 2:14–16).

Again, he writes with passionate pastoral heart to the Thessalonian church, explaining his cares and conflicts and concerns: "But we, brethren, being taken from you for a short time in presence, not in heart, endeavoured the more abundantly to see your face with great desire. Wherefore we would have come unto you, even I Paul, once and again; but Satan hindered us. For what is our hope, or joy, or crown of rejoicing? Are not even ye in the presence of our Lord Jesus Christ at his coming? For ye are our glory and joy" (1 Thess. 2:17–20).

The coming of Christ is when the perfection of complete sinlessness swallows up the perfection of holy maturity. In that day, at that very moment, all God's purposes will be finally revealed, fully accomplished, and entirely realized. That is the final and ultimate aim of the gospel minister: to see God bring all His chosen ones to complete and glorious likeness to His Son, Jesus Christ (1 John 3:2). He looks forward to rejoicing in the day of Christ that he has not run or labored in vain. It is the day he lives for, and it is the day he is ready and even willing to die for. William Still asserts, "Every temptation to be sidetracked from the task of eternity which is the task of the hour—your hour—must be seen in relation to the finished product. What is the end of what you are doing? The God-appointed end?"[3]

Let us consider carefully that the gospel ministry is God's appointed means for the salvation and sanctification of His people. It is the Holy Scriptures "which are able to make thee wise unto salvation through faith which is in Christ Jesus."

---

3. William Still, *The Work of the Pastor* (Edinburgh/Fearn, Ross–shire: Rutherford House/Christian Focus, 2001), 136.

Furthermore, "All scripture is given by inspiration of God, and is profitable for doctrine, for reproof, for correction, for instruction in righteousness: that the man of God may be perfect, thoroughly furnished unto all good works" (2 Tim. 3:15–17). The preacher-pastor brings the Scriptures to bear, in prayerful dependence on the Spirit of Christ and His powerful working, to accomplish God's saving purposes. The proclamation of Jesus Christ, with admonition and instruction, is necessary for entry into the kingdom of God and spiritual advance within the kingdom. When it comes to salvation, the beginning is Romans 10:14–15: "How then shall they call on him in whom they have not believed? and how shall they believe in him of whom they have not heard? and how shall they hear without a preacher? And how shall they preach, except they be sent? as it is written, How beautiful are the feet of them that preach the gospel of peace, and bring glad tidings of good things!" The continuing is John 17:17: "Sanctify them through thy truth: thy word is truth." The assured ending—itself a new and glorious beginning—is 1 Corinthians 15:50–58:

> Now this I say, brethren, that flesh and blood cannot inherit the kingdom of God; neither doth corruption inherit incorruption. Behold, I shew you a mystery; we shall not all sleep, but we shall all be changed, in a moment, in the twinkling of an eye, at the last trump: for the trumpet shall sound, and the dead shall be raised incorruptible, and we shall be changed. For this corruptible must put on incorruption, and this mortal must put on immortality. So when this corruptible shall have put on incorruption, and this mortal shall have put on immortality, then shall be brought to pass the saying that is written, Death is swallowed up in victory. O death, where is thy sting? O grave, where is thy victory? The sting of death is sin; and the strength of sin is the law. But thanks be to God, which giveth us the victory through our Lord Jesus Christ. Therefore, my beloved brethren, be ye stedfast, unmoveable, always abounding in the work of the Lord, forasmuch as ye know that your labour is not in vain in the Lord.

FELLOW CHRISTIAN God expects His servants to call His people ever onwards and upwards toward full-orbed spiritual maturity. Do you believe and accept this fact? Are you persuaded that your pastor's concern for your spiritual maturity is a biblically legitimate one?

It is vital that the whole church of Jesus Christ be united in this aim. The healthy congregation is one in which every saint is laboring together toward God's purpose for His people. Do you live with the determined aim of perfection in Christ Jesus? Peter calls every child of God to such a life, lived in the light of the coming day of judgment:

> Seeing then that all these things shall be dissolved, what manner of persons ought ye to be in all holy conversation and godliness, looking for and hasting unto the coming of the day of God, wherein the heavens being on fire shall be dissolved, and the elements shall melt with fervent heat? Nevertheless we, according to his promise, look for new heavens and a new earth, wherein dwelleth righteousness. Wherefore, beloved, seeing that ye look for such things, be diligent that ye may be found of him in peace, without spot, and blameless. (2 Peter 3:11–14)

Do you sit under the sound of the Word of God and receive pastoral counsel with this awareness and disposition in your soul? You cannot coast to heaven, and you will not reach glory by standing still. You must change, you must advance, and you will be greatly aided in doing so if you accept that your pastors are God's servants to assist you toward Christian maturity, and not officious bystanders poking their noses into your business.

Do you accept that pastors and preachers are not only entitled but obligated before God to warn, instruct, reprove, correct, and urge all men with this end in view? How, then, do you hear them? It will not always be pleasant and will certainly be, at times, painful to have the cancer of sin addressed and the cross of a crucified Christ pressed afresh into your tender soul. There will, by God's grace, be times when your soul is lifted up, when your heart burns within you, when glory seems near, Christ appears precious, the church most excellent, and all things worth bearing for the sake of the glory of God. But, if you have a faithful minister, there may also be times when your face blanches, when your teeth clench, when your cheeks redden, when your stomach churns, when your heart falls, when your excuses rise, and when your defenses go up. There may be times when you are tempted to go home and rail against your pastor for his barefaced cheek and blinding audacity. You may be tempted to hurl fire at the elders after the latest pastoral visit. Pause, then, and consider: What is the truth of the matter? Are these men really throwing their weight around and abusing their authority? Or could it be that they are seeking to discharge the weighty responsibility of seeing you safely to glory?

Is your pastor speaking to you as a man called, equipped, and deeply concerned to see you grow in the grace and knowledge of Jesus Christ? If he is a man of God, there will be no joy in your struggling and tears, except insofar as they prove stepping stones toward greater godliness. There will be no delight in your distresses as he holds the line of truth and righteousness. He should righteously refuse to give in to your implicit or explicit entreaties that you be spared the effort of pursuing godliness. After all, your soul's health is at stake. This is a man whose "hope, or joy, or crown of rejoicing" is your being "in the presence of our Lord Jesus Christ at his coming"—you are his "glory and joy" (1 Thess. 2:19–20). With paternal care he is pouring out the energies of his soul with a view to seeing sinners won to Jesus and then advancing in godliness, for their great blessing and the glory of our God and Savior.

Yes, pastors are sinful men. They will at times err in the manner or matter of their speaking, but listen to them opening their hearts in the words that they speak. Pray God to help His servants—who are your servants for Jesus' sake—to keep this great purpose, this state of Christian maturity, always fixed in their minds. Ask God that they might labor with the awesome occasion of Christ's return in their hearts. Pray that they will be given wisdom and humility never to employ their gospel tools for anything but their high and holy task. Plead with God that they will never abuse their position or authority but will only labor to make you fit for glory. Pray for the identification and mortification of every sinful or shallow motive that would distort their purpose or distract from their goal.

You may come to search for a faithful man who will preach to you and pastor your soul. You may need to seek out a church where your soul, and perhaps the souls of your family, will be cared for. When you do, pray for and hunt out a true man of God who will be gracious but tenacious, who will act in a Christlike fashion with the heartfelt desire that you be saved from your sins, together with as many others as God has appointed. Seek out a man who wants you to be sanctified, changed from glory to glory as he proclaims Jesus to you, admonishing and instructing you. Determine that he is a man who lives with eternity in view and acts accordingly.

Finally, reckon with eternity yourself. We must all appear before the judgment seat of Christ, that each one may receive the things done in the body, according to what he has done, whether good or bad (2 Cor. 5:10). You must come to Christ and cling to Christ and walk with Christ if you are to be happy in that day. The mere existence of a pastor who cares for your soul will not in itself accomplish that. You cannot rely on the fact that you hear good preaching or commend yourself simply for being in the orbit of a faithful ministry. You must yourself receive the Jesus who is proclaimed and heed the warning and teaching that is issued out of love for your soul. There are many who have had faithful, earnest, and loving servants of God seeking to shepherd their souls who have finally found hell gaping to swallow them because they never received the faithful teaching. It is Christ alone who will save you, not His servants, however gracious or gifted. You must be sure that the Savior to whom they point is your Savior. You must, if you value your soul, trust in Him and follow in His footsteps.

FELLOW PASTOR God expects us to call His people ever onwards and upwards toward full-orbed spiritual maturity. We must accept this fact. We must appreciate that our authority is God-constituted and that we are both entitled and obliged faithfully to discharge our calling. We will be answerable for its use and abuse. Disregard of our duty and brutality in our shepherding are equally fearful crimes. Neglecting or attacking the sheep is just as bad as ignoring or encouraging the wolves. William Still points out, "A shepherd is no mere warder-off of wild beasts. To save the sheep from wild beasts and all other dangers is not to feed them; and if they are not fed, what matters whether they are safe or not? What is the good of being saved to starve?"[4] Conscious of the eye of God upon us, we must give ourselves to Christ-centered, Christ-honoring proclamation, admonition, and instruction with eternity in sight.

Are you, then, persuaded that you have a definite purpose in hand that calls forth all the strength that God gives you? When we consider this, we feel pressing upon us a task that demands the consecration of our whole redeemed humanity to a cause of eternal significance.

Are you persuaded that God has called you into fellowship with Him in pursuing—for yourself and for those committed to your care—a sincere, principled, balanced holiness of life? You are to cultivate in your own and every heart that honest and entire loyalty to the Lord our God which consists in being wholly attuned to Him and in step with His Word. You are to promote an attachment of profound love to God in Christ that is worked out by and demonstrated in a careful and cheerful obedience to His commandments. God has put His people under our rule and care so that they come to a mature godliness that declares before God, men, and angels that they are true children of the living God. We are to work so that God's people may view the coming day of judgment without the fear of the unbeliever and might stand before Christ without confusion.

Are you persuaded that your life's work is to be carried out with this definite occasion in view? Consider this: "When the Son of man shall come in his glory, and all the holy angels with him, then shall he sit upon the throne of his glory: and before him shall be gathered all nations: and he shall separate them one from

---

4. Ibid., 135.

another, as a shepherd divideth his sheep from the goats: and he shall set the sheep on his right hand, but the goats on the left" (Matt. 25:31–33).

Brother, that is the day in which you will see those whom you have pastored giving an account of their life and work to Jesus. It is the day on which you must do the same. Their account will reflect on your work as well. You and I must stand before the judgment seat of Christ, and there we will answer for what we have been not only as men but also as ministers. We must know it and reckon with it and so preach as if the Lord were pleading through us, "Be reconciled to God." Knowing, therefore, the terror of the Lord, let us persuade men.

Let these things constrain us to a tender and Christlike discharge of our duty with all faithfulness and righteousness. We must love to be tender, and loathe being terrible, but we are constrained above all to be tenaciously true for the well-being of immortal souls. Let us remember that genuinely fatherly spirit that characterized the apostle Paul:

> But we were gentle among you, even as a nurse cherisheth her children: so being affectionately desirous of you, we were willing to have imparted unto you, not the gospel of God only, but also our own souls, because ye were dear unto us. For ye remember, brethren, our labour and travail: for labouring night and day, because we would not be chargeable unto any of you, we preached unto you the gospel of God. Ye are witnesses, and God also, how holily and justly and unblameably we behaved ourselves among you that believe: as ye know how we exhorted and comforted and charged every one of you, as a father doth his children, that ye would walk worthy of God, who hath called you unto his kingdom and glory. (1 Thess. 2:7–12)

Do not lose sight of the preciousness of souls and your commission to proclaim Jesus to them. You may face temptations to be deterred by the frowns of men, by their anger and disgust. You will be coaxed by the smiles and charms of flattery to water down your faithful dealings. The pressure to be dissuaded from a righteous course will grow, whether by a fear of the consequences or the sheer labor and effort involved. As you preach and warn and teach, you may become dejected at the little progress that is made. You might be grieved at the unwillingness of sinners to hear, let alone repent and believe, and distressed by the dullness of the people of God. You may even struggle with despair, asking yourself, "What is the point? Why do I bother?"

You will bother because you have a great and glorious calling. You will bother because you are called to "present every man perfect in Christ Jesus" (Col. 1:28). The Jesus who gave His blood for His people will not allow you or them to fall away. All for whom He died will be gathered into His kingdom, and none shall be lost. Jesus Christ will never leave or forsake you but will strengthen you, help you, and cause you to stand. You will find and prove His grace sufficient for your every need: for courage, for energy, for hope, for joy, for strength, and for perseverance in righteousness. He is your Lord and your God, and you are His servant for the sake of His people. Do not let Him down; do not let them down. He has appointed you to care for His sheep and to see them safely home, and He will equip you for and uphold you in the discharge of your duty.

You know this. Even at the worst of times, you know that you cannot turn away. You feel the weight of being a preacher. You may be ready to throw up your hands. You may be considering what other calling you might pursue. Then there will come that message on the phone, that knock on the door, that e-mail into the inbox, and you will go out into the night like the Good Shepherd before you, to give your life (albeit by degrees) for the sheep.

And you will know this at the best times. You will know times when you see the light of understanding dawn in the eyes of one who has been walking in darkness. You may receive notes or hear reports or even look into the face of someone who says without any intention but the glory of God that your feeble, sin-wracked efforts were employed by God to bring a sinner into the kingdom. You will see spiritual gloom brighten as a child of God begins to enjoy his gospel privileges. You will see saints who have struggled for years with particular sins make discernible progress. You will see sinners saved and simply leaving behind sins that you might have imagined would dog their steps all the way to glory. You will see believers struggle with particular doctrines, for the first time or the hundredth time, and you will be privileged to see the Spirit of God grant clearer sight of the truth as it is in Jesus. You will see scriptural realities work into their souls and work out in their lives. You will see angry men and women become more tender, and proud men and women by degrees demonstrating the mind that was in Christ Jesus. You will see broken marriages restored, rotten families made gradually whole, wrecked relationships built up, and failing friendships made strong. You will see the hearts of hard people break over sin as the hammer of God's Word strikes them. You will see Christians suddenly or slowly appreciate some gospel privilege and watch the tears spring into their eyes or the smiles light up their faces. You will be shyly informed that your preaching struck the precise note needed by some frail sheep at some particular time. You will hear, from time to time, expressions of deep gratitude and appreciation that make you ask, "Who am I to be made such a means of blessing?" and cry out in humble thanksgiving to God.

You will, in short, see the gospel taking root in men's souls and watch as those roots press ever deeper into the bedrock of the soul, and that once dry and withered tree begins to bud and bloom and bring forth the fruit of the Spirit to the glory of God. You will see the truth of genuine spiritual happiness: "Blessed is the man that walketh not in the counsel of the ungodly, nor standeth in the way of sinners, nor sitteth in the seat of the scornful. But his delight is in the law of the LORD; and in his law doth he meditate day and night. And he shall be like a tree planted by the rivers of water, that bringeth forth his fruit in his season; his leaf also shall not wither; and whatsoever he doeth shall prosper" (Ps. 1:1–3). You will have those reminders that you are not beating the air or running in vain, and you will remember that you do this with an eye upon the end of all things and the beginning of all things.

Let eternity press upon your soul. Meditate on the coming day. Consider the significance of that hour for every soul that has lived, is living, or will live. Remember that there is a way to hell even from the very gates of heaven, as well as from the City of Destruction. You cannot rest until those committed to your care are safe at home, and you will be kept by Christ in the faithful discharge of that duty. Like your Lord, love and serve His redeemed people to the end.

8 | THE STRENGTH OF
PAUL'S MINISTRY

Whereunto I also labour, striving according to his working, which worketh in me mightily.
— COLOSSIANS 1:29

God does not work instead of our working, but through our working. God does not energize instead of our having energy; he energizes our energy. Therefore it is unbiblical and irrational to say that because the grace of God produces an active trust in God, we don't need to exert an active trust in God. At the end of your life, after decades of loving ministry, however God uses you to stir up the obedience of faith in others, what are you going to say about the grace of God and your lifelong labors? Are you going to boast? No. You are going to use the words of Paul in Romans 15:18, "For I will not presume to speak of anything except what Christ has accomplished through me, resulting in the obedience of the Gentiles." You will say something like a paraphrase of 1 Corinthians 4:7, "What did I have that I did not receive? If then I received it, why should I boast as if it were not a gift?"[1]
— JOHN PIPER

Shortly after I left secular employment to enter vocational pastoral ministry I received an e-mail from a friend:

What is your weekly schedule like as a pastor, Rob? Is it still an 8-hour day? I've always wondered what they do during the week. I figured mostly night hours are necessary and that daytime is spent for studying a bit, writing sermons and tanning. I'm basically wondering what most evangelical pastors would actually do during the week. I would really,

---

1. John Piper, *A Godward Life (Book Two): Savoring the Sustenance of God in All of Life* (Sisters, OR: Multnomah Publishers, 1999), 331–32.

really like to know the schedule of my current pastor, but of course, I
could never ask or know such a thing, because it is too rude to ask them.
What's your experience on that?

Many ministers of the gospel will eventually be asked the question, "So what
exactly does a pastor do?" From the perspective of the world looking in, and even
sometimes for the people of God looking on, understanding the work of a pastor
can be difficult. Some people who assess the work of the ministry seriously
underestimate the demands of a true preacher's calling, seeing it as something
that takes place on Sunday mornings, in public meetings, in front of people. It is
judged to last a few minutes, at most a few hours.

The Christian ministry, faithfully undertaken, is neither for lightweights nor
for the fainthearted. It is and ought to be hard work. If a man is going to minister
diligently and effectively for the good of souls and for the glory and praise of
God, then being enlisted in Christ's service will cost him his all—but it will
prove a worthy endeavor.

The apostle Paul gave his all for those to whom he ministered. We never
see the apostle kicking back and adopting a take-it-easy, nonaggressive mentality.
Paul was not sipping smoothies on the promenade deck of a cruise ship. Paul was
always manning his station, doing all that he could for his great Captain and for
all those who belonged to Him. The apostle was inflamed with the great passion
of spending and being spent for the people whom God had committed to his
watchful care. Just as an arrow is shot towards a single target, so Paul's one aim was
bringing Jesus' people to Him in good spiritual health. He exerted and expended
all of his faculties towards this great and worthy goal. Clearly, the apostle had
the best interests of the people in view. As we have seen, his great desire was to
present them all perfect—spiritually mature in that great and final day.

However, the God-appointed means are not easily employed or His ends
effortlessly achieved. Often when we think about Paul and all that he accomplished
for the good of the church, we are left spellbound and even ashamed. We scratch
our heads, asking, "How in the world did he do all of that work?" Was Paul one
man or five? Where did he get the ability or find the time to accomplish what
he did? Was he, after all, a "super-apostle"? Was he simply superhuman? Paul
himself answers the question. Having told us about the goal of his preaching,
he humbly but pointedly testifies to his labors and reveals the source of his vigor
and vitality for the carrying out of the various tasks that were assigned to him
by the living Christ.

Paul's effort

Paul says, "Whereunto [that is, with this great objective in view of presenting every man perfect in Christ] I also labour, striving" (Col. 1:29). It is interesting to note Paul's change from the plural in verse 28—"that *we* may present every man perfect in Christ Jesus"—to the singular: "*I* also labour, striving (emphasis added)." Paul is highlighting his own pastor's heart for people. He is setting himself apart from the errorists in Colosse who were seeking to deceive these believers (Col. 2:4) and draw them away from the true Jesus whom they first believed (Col. 2:6). It is possible that these false teachers were maligning the apostle. Paul says here in essence, "Before you take into account what others have to say about me and my message, please remember that in all that I do, I myself exert my all with your highest good in view." Even more likely is the probability that these errorists had little if any true regard for the Colossian believers, being more interested in their own reputation and advancement. They might have professed concern for others, but their labors were on their own behalf. Against such an attitude, it is as if Paul says, "However else you may think of me, know this: I personally strive and labor to present every one of you perfect in Christ."

The apostle Paul was not ashamed to set the record straight when it came to declaring the truth of a matter. He was not embarrassed by his labors. He wanted these Colossians believers (and all the people for whom he bore any responsibility) to hold fast to the Jesus he proclaimed. To this end, at various points in his letters, he needed to describe his own life and labors so that they would not be duped by counterfeit messages from bogus messengers. To be sure, Paul took no pleasure when forced to boast (2 Cor. 11:16–21). Nevertheless, as a means of helping others stay on track and as a matter of principle and example, he would make the truth plain. He had a clear conscience about the fact that, by God's grace, he was a sincere man: "But as we were allowed of God to be put in trust with the gospel, even so we speak; not as pleasing men, but God, which trieth our hearts. For neither at any time used we flattering words, as ye know, nor a cloke of covetousness; God is witness" (1 Thess. 2:4–5).

Paul was not a spiritual charlatan or con artist. He was not in the ministry in order to make merchandise of people. Quite the opposite! Paul worked hard for the cause of Jesus and His people, and if any called this fact into question he was quick to speak in righteous defense. Paul was quite willing to appeal to the highest witness to attest to the sincerity and straightforwardness of his ministry. He was conscious that he lived before God.

First, I thank my God through Jesus Christ for you all, that your faith is spoken of throughout the whole world. For God is my witness, whom I serve with my spirit in the gospel of his Son, that without ceasing I make mention of you always in my prayers. (Rom. 1:8–9)

Now he which stablisheth us with you in Christ, and hath anointed us, is God; who hath also sealed us, and given the earnest of the Spirit in our hearts. Moreover I call God for a record upon my soul, that to spare you I came not as yet unto Corinth. Not for that we have dominion over your faith, but are helpers of your joy: for by faith ye stand. (2 Cor. 1:21–24)

For God is my record, how greatly I long after you all in the bowels of Jesus Christ. (Phil. 1:8)

Ye are witnesses, and God also, how holily and justly and unblameably we behaved ourselves among you that believe. (1 Thess. 2:10)

Paul was a man who lived the entirety of his life *coram Deo*. This Latin phrase simply means "before the face of God," or "in the presence of God." It speaks of a profound and abiding awareness of the eye of God piercing to the depths of our being. In entertaining such an awareness, Paul was helped to speak and do the truth and nothing but the truth. Thus he can say without bluff, bluster, or embarrassment that he labored, striving on behalf of others.

With his eye fixed on the prospect of presenting every man spiritually mature in Christ Jesus at the great day of the Lord, Paul bends his back to the task. The word *labor* that Paul uses is the language of consistent exertion, of wearisome and steady toil. It implies a felt physical weariness as the result of persistent and severe work. It may be that you have enjoyed the privilege of giving yourself to some real physical work, perhaps a major project in or outside the home or some job in construction or landscaping, as an individual or as part of a team. Under various pressures and constraints, you must press on to get that task finished, so all your strength is engaged, exerted, and expended to that end. Finally, at the close of day or even late at night, you reach the end of your task and slowly and painfully put away your tools. You are left at the point of exhaustion; you feel as if you have been beaten. You drop into bed to enjoy the sweet rest of the laboring man (Eccl. 5:12). This description is representative of the gospel minister's exertion in a task that is never finished until he is discharged from his responsibilities, he goes to his eternal rest, or the day of the Lord comes.

Furthermore, Paul says that in this labor he is "striving," expending unsparing effort. Paul speaks as a man involved in an athletic contest or military combat. His language indicates concentrated and intense struggle at maximum engagement.

It is this Greek word from which we get the idea of agonizing, of fighting with all our effort toward something. This is the runner in the last few paces of the race pushing for the finish line. It is the athlete inches away from scoring the points that will win the game, with the clock counting down the final seconds, straining every nerve and sinew to secure the victory. It is the soldier who keeps moving forward with sweat in his eyes and pain in his muscles, perhaps even with metal in his body and blood flowing from his wounds, caught up in a desperate firefight, and still ready to engage with the enemy.

Such intense effort is the minister's way of life: it is his consistent, rather than his occasional, contribution. He competes in the face of fierce opposition. That opposition is definitely spiritual and extends into the physical realm:

> For we wrestle not against flesh and blood, but against principalities, against powers, against the rulers of the darkness of this world, against spiritual wickedness in high places. Wherefore take unto you the whole armour of God, that ye may be able to withstand in the evil day, and having done all, to stand. (Eph. 6:12–13)

> Are they Hebrews? so am I. Are they Israelites? so am I. Are they the seed of Abraham? so am I. Are they ministers of Christ? (I speak as a fool) I am more; in labours more abundant, in stripes above measure, in prisons more frequent, in deaths oft. Of the Jews five times received I forty stripes save one. Thrice was I beaten with rods, once was I stoned, thrice I suffered shipwreck, a night and a day I have been in the deep; in journeyings often, in perils of waters, in perils of robbers, in perils by mine own countrymen, in perils by the heathen, in perils in the city, in perils in the wilderness, in perils in the sea, in perils among false brethren; in weariness and painfulness, in watchings often, in hunger and thirst, in fastings often, in cold and nakedness. Beside those things that are without, that which cometh upon me daily, the care of all the churches. (2 Cor. 11:22–28)

Such an attitude is required because the world opposes the Christian, his own fleshly inclinations hinder him, and the devil stands against him. The minister of the gospel does not have an easier time of it than others; if anything, the opposition against him is intensified on every front because he is caring for the flock, and if he can be brought down, the sheep can in some degree be exposed if not scattered.

In short, then, the gospel minister is called to a life of total strain on the total man, every faculty engaged at every moment, as required. Without a doubt, this is the exertion and effort demanded of him as a servant of Jesus Christ and His church. That is why so many pastors break, or come close to breaking, under the burden of their work. Whether or not other people are aware of such exertions, these demands expose the folly of imagining that the pastoral life is one of ease and relaxation.

Every true gospel minister, and every man who would be such, must recognize this and commit himself to it. He must know this before he begins in order that he might not be quickly overcome when he joins the battle or be deterred by the dangers, distresses, and disappointments that will come. The gospel ministry is not for the careless, casual, or lazy man. This is not about the difference between an intense personality and a more laidback character. It is about the engagement of the whole man in truth, whatever character God has given him. He who desires this position in the church desires a good work (1 Tim. 3:1), not a gentle rest.

It is unmistakable that, when it came to getting things done for the Lord, Paul did not see himself as a mere channel through whom God worked apart from or in spite of himself. Rather, the apostle was actively involved in fulfilling his ministerial calling, which was assigned to him by God. His words could not be clearer: "I also labour, striving."

Both of these terms demonstrate that, as a true minister of the gospel, Paul worked aggressively and assertively for others, whether in his preaching to them or by praying for them. It is no accident that the bulk of Paul's metaphors for Christian living and ministerial effort are military and athletic. The strain and demand of those two spheres is the closest analogy to the life of faith. Remember, too, that Paul had a competitive spirit: as an unbeliever, it is certainly possible that the covetousness with which he so often struggled (Rom. 7:7) was a desire to hold the highest rank. He would strain every sinew to attain and maintain such a position: this is the man who "profited [or advanced] in the Jews' religion above many my equals in mine own nation, being more exceedingly zealous of the traditions of my fathers" (Gal. 1:14), who used to boast that he was "circumcised the eighth day, of the stock of Israel, of the tribe of Benjamin, an Hebrew of the Hebrews; as touching the law, a Pharisee; concerning zeal, persecuting the church; touching the righteousness which is in the law, blameless" (Phil. 3:5–6). But he has learned something of the mind of Christ. Now, as a saved man, esteeming others better than himself (Phil. 2:3), that same earnest and fiery spirit finds its outlet in being poured out as a drink offering (Phil. 2:17) on behalf of Christ and His people.

This striving for others was by no means a matter of occasional zealous exertion. Rather, it was the constant tenor of his ministry. The New Testament record is plain, demonstrating Paul's diligence as a servant of Christ. For example:

> I beseech you, brethren, (ye know the house of Stephanas, that it is the firstfruits of Achaia, and that they have addicted themselves to the ministry of the saints,) that ye submit yourselves unto such, and to every one that helpeth with us, and laboureth. (1 Cor. 16:15–16)

> Giving no offence in any thing, that the ministry be not blamed: but in all things approving ourselves as the ministers of God, in much patience, in afflictions, in necessities, in distresses, in stripes, in imprisonments, in tumults, in labours, in watchings, in fastings. (2 Cor. 6:3–5)

> Are they ministers of Christ? (I speak as a fool) I am more; in labours more abundant, in stripes above measure, in prisons more frequent, in deaths oft. (2 Cor. 11:23)[2]

It is plain from Paul's language that the apostle was tireless and diligent in his efforts for the good of the church and the glory of Christ. To Paul the work of the ministry was not a gentle stroll. On the contrary, it was a hard race of often painful effort.

It is a desperately sad thing that many believers—ministers included—have embraced a view of the Christian life that advocates "letting go and letting God." The idea that lies behind this popular expression has its roots in the Keswick Movement that reached its zenith during the last decades of the nineteenth century. Still current, this so-called Higher Life teaching says, in essence, that in our lives as believers we need to reach the point of absolute or total surrender to God. We are told that victorious Christian living—triumph over our remaining sins and usefulness in the hands of God—comes only when we are entirely yielded to God, consecrated to Him in every aspect of our lives. This surrender is complete passivity, a call to exert no conscious effort of our own in the Christian life but rather to abandon ourselves to the power of Christ, accomplishing real triumph in a "surrendered" walk with the Lord.[3]

This teaching is an unbiblical and unsafe view of the Christian life. Paul never embraced such a notion or taught such a thing, though we acknowledge that some who hold to this teaching are sincere, if mistaken, saints. When it

---

2. See also Galatians 4:11; 1 Timothy 4:10; 2 Timothy 4:7.

3. For a fuller treatment of this subject, see Benjamin B. Warfield's *Perfectionism* (Philadelphia: Presbyterian & Reformed, 1958). It is worth noting that J. C. Ryle's *Holiness* was written primarily to counter these vapid teachings of the Keswick Movement.

came to living a holy life and accomplishing things for the Lord, His cause and His people, Paul took the bull by the horns. He actively engaged and eagerly sought to marshal his entire redeemed humanity to accomplish the work that God had given him to do.

Paul viewed the work of regeneration as *monergistic*. That is, God is the one who alone accomplishes the work (Col. 1:12–14; 2:13). However, when Paul spoke of sanctification—our progressive growth in grace and increasing likeness to Christ—he viewed it as *synergistic*. In other words, not only is God at work in us but at the same time we also—as renewed creatures—are working out our own salvation with fear and trembling (Phil. 2:12–13). When God redeems us, He does not neuter us and live His life *through us* so as to bypass our bodies and souls purchased with the blood of Christ. Rather, He lives *in us* and we—in prayerful dependence on the Spirit of Christ—work together with Him, to live, labor, and serve for His glory and honor: "Sanctification is a progressive work of *God and man* that makes us more and more free from sin and more like Christ in our actual lives."[4] This being so, Robert Reymond says:

> Throughout his life, from the moment of his regeneration and conversion to the moment of his final elevation to heavenly glory, the Christian, by virtue of his union with Christ's death and resurrection and through the power of God's word and Spirit dwelling within him, will necessarily experience progressive sanctification, this process to be understood *negatively* in terms of putting to death the deeds of the flesh which still remain in him and *positively* in terms of growth in all saving graces.[5]

This teaching is plain throughout the Scriptures. At times, the Holy Spirit emphasizes God's part in our sanctification:

> Sanctify them through thy truth: thy word is truth. (John 17:17)

> And the very God of peace sanctify you wholly; and I pray God your whole spirit and soul and body be preserved blameless unto the coming of our Lord Jesus Christ. (1 Thess 5:23)

> Looking for that blessed hope, and the glorious appearing of the great God and our Saviour Jesus Christ; who gave himself for us, that he

---

4. Wayne Grudem, *Systematic Theology: An Introduction to Biblical Doctrine* (Grand Rapids: Zondervan, 1994), 746, emphasis added.

5. Robert L. Reymond, *A New Systematic Theology of the Christian Faith* (Nashville: Thomas Nelson, 1998), 768–69.

might redeem us from all iniquity, and purify unto himself a peculiar people, zealous of good works. (Titus 2:13–14)[6]

At times, the Holy Spirit emphasizes our part in our sanctification:

For if ye live after the flesh, ye shall die: but if ye through the Spirit do mortify the deeds of the body, ye shall live. (Rom. 8:13)

And they that are Christ's have crucified the flesh with the affections and lusts. (Gal. 5:24)

Mortify therefore your members which are upon the earth; fornication, uncleanness, inordinate affection, evil concupiscence, and covetousness, which is idolatry. (Col. 3:5)[7]

Again, the Holy Spirit sometimes emphasizes the work of God together with the renewed man himself in our sanctification:

A new heart also will I give you, and a new spirit will I put within you: and I will take away the stony heart out of your flesh, and I will give you an heart of flesh. And I will put my spirit within you, and cause you to walk in my statutes, and ye shall keep my judgments, and do them. (Ezek. 36:26–27)

But ye have not so learned Christ; if so be that ye have heard him, and have been taught by him, as the truth is in Jesus: that ye put off concerning the former conversation the old man, which is corrupt according to the deceitful lusts; and be renewed in the spirit of your mind; and that ye put on the new man, which after God is created in righteousness and true holiness. (Eph. 4:20–24)

Wherefore, my beloved, as ye have always obeyed, not as in my presence only, but now much more in my absence, work out your own salvation with fear and trembling. For it is God which worketh in you both to will and to do of his good pleasure. (Phil. 2:12–13)

Paul embraces all this scriptural truth in his view of Christian living and Christian service, not least for pastors and preachers. He therefore assures the Colossian believers that he labors, striving. If the Christian life and especially the Christian ministry were all about coasting, if it were simply an opportunity to "let go and let God," then Paul would not bother with such vigorous and active

---

6. See also, for example, Ephesians 5:25–26; 2 Thessalonians 2:13.
7. See also Romans 6:11; 1 John 3:3.

terms as these. However, Paul's language completely dismantles notions of ease: as a minister, a servant of Christ, he labors, he strives.

"But," you might say, "this is a recipe for disaster. This is a call to burnout! It is a simply unsustainable model for ministry." Certainly such a model does not cut across other biblical commands and principles and the wisdom of legitimate respite. Like the athlete, the preacher must rest and recreate if he is to perform at his peak; like the soldier, he must at times come off the front line in order that he might return to it restored to fighting condition. The sixth commandment applies as much to preachers of the gospel as it does to anyone else and is perhaps the most plain and prominent demand for us to preserve our own health and life. Let no man of God neglect the cultivation of his physical well-being, enabling him (under God) to work hard, serve effectively, and recover quickly. Even the apostle John prayed that his friend Gaius might "prosper and be in health, even as thy soul prospereth" (3 John 1:2). There is no need to set up an unbiblical (essentially platonic) antagonism between the degrees of health in any or every part of a man's redeemed humanity. Nevertheless, there is a further and even sweeter answer to the despairing cries we might utter when we face these weighty demands, for Paul does embrace both sides of the coin of sanctification: he holds in biblical tension the two strands of truth laid out above. Paul is working, but so is God.

Paul's energy

Having described his active effort as a minister of the gospel—laboring and striving with all of his being—Paul has more to say. His testimony to his own laboring and striving has given us half the truth, and Paul will not leave out the other half. From the Scriptures that we have just considered we get the entire picture.

Those passages show that the working out of our lives as believers in Christ has two elements: God Himself is working, and so is the Christian. There is a legitimate and holy concurrence of the divine and the human at this point; once the Lord in His mercy has saved the sinner and made him alive, the spiritually alive believer now works in accordance with God's working in him.

Imagine what Paul must have thought after receiving his commission from Jesus at his conversion:

> And I said, Who art thou, Lord? And he said, I am Jesus whom thou persecutest. But rise, and stand upon thy feet: for I have appeared unto thee for this purpose, to make thee a minister and a witness both of these things which thou hast seen, and of those things in the which I will appear unto thee; delivering thee from the people, and from the

Gentiles, unto whom now I send thee, to open their eyes, and to turn them from darkness to light, and from the power of Satan unto God, that they may receive forgiveness of sins, and inheritance among them which are sanctified by faith that is in me. (Acts 26:15–18)

How could he possibly pursue such a monumental responsibility in his own strength? He might have had a holy desire, but his frail best would simply not sustain the demands that would be put upon him. What man living could do this in his own strength alone? Indeed, the more one contemplates such a task, the weightier and more awesome it appears.

No mere man could have begun to accomplish this work, but the man who knows the almighty power of God at work in and through him can and will set out to accomplish just such a task, and—in Christ—he will know fruit from his labors.

When we seek to answer the question of how ministers are energetically and aggressively to carry out the work of the ministry, we must hear the whole truth: Paul says, "I also labour, striving *according to his working, which worketh in me mightily*" (Col. 1:29, emphasis added).

If Paul pointed only to his own labor and striving, there would be countless dangers for the Christian minister. On the one hand, he might get the idea that working hard out of his own resources would be sufficient. What pride he might fall into if he imagined that he were accomplishing anything in his own strength! On the other, he might quickly realize the limitations of those resources. What hopeless disillusionment would follow when he reached the end of himself!

But, thanks be to God, Paul gives us the full account of how he did all he did. Paul is laboring to the limit not so much of his own strength as of the strength that God Himself has supplied. Where man is toiling, God is mightily working.

Christ in Paul is the source of the power to work effectively, and that power is at work dynamically. This word for *working* is the source of the English word *energy*, whereas "mightily" has to do with strength and force. Paul did not run on his own batteries. His energy was not self-produced but Christ-bestowed: it was the reality of the Holy Spirit at work in him. This is true not just of Paul but of all the saints, and Paul prays that they will be "strengthened with all might, according to his glorious power" (Col. 1:11). He can do all things through Christ who strengthens him (Phil. 4:13). God's grace in Christ is working in the apostle, equipping and supplying him for the gospel minister's toil. The man is by no means superhuman, but the energy that supplies him is undeniably supernatural. It is this that makes a minister fit for his duties, ready to endure, and able to bring forth fruit.

There is no "either-or" to this working. It is "both-and." Paul wholeheartedly labors, and God is at work in and through him to enable him, sustain him, and produce fruit by him. His self-determination and achievements derive from his complete dependence upon and faith in the living Christ. Without Christ's strength working powerfully in him, nothing will be accomplished for the glory of the Lord.

Paul provides here a potent example to follow as Christians, not least as ministers of the gospel. In all that we do and in all that we accomplish for the Lord, we are to freely and joyfully acknowledge that whatever we have done that was good was because God gave us the will and ability to do it. Such a God-exalting testimony resounds repeatedly from God's servants:

> I have therefore whereof I may glory through Jesus Christ in those things which pertain to God. For I will not dare to speak of any of those things which Christ hath not wrought by me, to make the Gentiles obedient, by word and deed. (Rom. 15:17–18)

> That the Gentiles should be fellowheirs, and of the same body, and partakers of his promise in Christ by the gospel: whereof I was made a minister, according to the gift of the grace of God given unto me by the effectual working of his power. (Eph. 3:6–7)

> If any man speak, let him speak as the oracles of God; if any man minister, let him do it as of the ability which God giveth: that God in all things may be glorified through Jesus Christ, to whom be praise and dominion for ever and ever. Amen. (1 Peter 4:11)

> According to the glorious gospel of the blessed God, which was committed to my trust. And I thank Christ Jesus our Lord, who hath enabled me, for that he counted me faithful, putting me into the ministry. (1 Tim. 1:11–12)

As redeemed people we do all that we do because God, through Christ, by the Holy Spirit, works in us powerfully by His free and sovereign grace.

Christ again is at the forefront. It is by Christ's strength that Paul proclaims Christ. The Spirit of God is in Paul and at work in him (Col. 1:29). It is by Him that the labor is carried out. Apart from Christ's power we have nothing to offer: "Not that we are sufficient of ourselves to think any thing as of ourselves; but our sufficiency is of God; who also hath made us able ministers of the new testament; not of the letter, but of the spirit: for the letter killeth, but the spirit giveth life" (2 Cor. 3:5–6). Christ alone is our strength and hope: "I am crucified with Christ: nevertheless I live; yet not I, but Christ liveth in me: and the life which I now live in the flesh I live by the faith of the Son of God, who loved me, and gave himself for me" (Gal. 2:20). Our frailty becomes the platform on which He displays His glorious strength (2 Cor. 12:9). Only in this way does the man of God maintain his ministry:

> But we have this treasure in earthen vessels, that the excellency of the power may be of God, and not of us. We are troubled on every side, yet not distressed; we are perplexed, but not in despair; persecuted, but not forsaken; cast down, but not destroyed; always bearing about in the body the dying of the Lord Jesus, that the life also of Jesus might be made manifest in our body. For we which live are alway delivered unto death for Jesus' sake, that the life also of Jesus might be made manifest in our mortal flesh. (2 Cor. 4:7–11)

Colossians 1:29 is at once unambiguous and complete. As with the work of sanctification as a whole, so in carrying out the work of the ministry there is a concurrence between the labors of the Spirit-enlivened man and the ongoing work of the God who made him alive. We must labor with all of our might, all the while depending on and acknowledging that it is God who works in us. Behind and foundational to the sweat of the minister's brow is the might of an all-powerful God, providing strength to stand, energizing us powerfully for the accomplishment of the task to which He Himself has called us. John Eadie observes,

> It was, indeed, no sluggish heart that beat in the apostle's bosom. His was no torpid temperament. There was such a keenness in all its emotions and anxieties, that its resolve and action were simultaneous movements. But though he laboured so industriously, and suffered so bravely in the aim of winning souls to Christ and glory, still he owned that all was owing to Divine power lodged within him—
>
> > The work to be perform'd is ours,
> > The strength is all His own;
> >
> > 'Tis He that works to will,
> > 'Tis He that works to do;
> > His is the power by which we act,
> > His be the glory too.[8]

---

8. John Eadie, *A Commentary on the Greek Text of Paul's Letter to the Colossians* (Birmingham, AL: Solid Ground Christian Books, 2005), 105.

"But by the grace of God I am what I am: and his grace which was bestowed upon me was not in vain; but I laboured more abundantly than they all: yet not I, but the grace of God which was with me" (1 Cor. 15:10).

|| FELLOW
|| CHRISTIAN

When it comes to practical daily living in the world, what has been your approach to salvation?

What does our Lord say to those who would get into heaven? He says, "Strive to enter in at the strait gate: for many, I say unto you, will seek to enter in, and shall not be able" (Luke 13:24). The word *strive* here is from the same word that Paul uses in Colossians 1:29 concerning diligent effort. We must not separate what God has joined together. There is no contradiction here: "The kingdom of heaven suffereth violence, and the violent take it by force" (Matt. 11:12). If you would have Christ, then go after Him wholeheartedly, knowing that it is God who gives, stirs up, sustains, and finally meets such desires. Some declare that they wish to see Jesus and quickly complain, "Well, I asked and nothing happened!" Did you labor? Did you strive? God will do His part, but your whole being must be engaged in accordance with divine power.

What about the path to glory? Have you been passive when it comes to serving God and being holy before Him? Have you forgotten the great biblical imperatives to be actively engaged in continually becoming a more holy person? The great abolitionist William Wilberforce wrote of the attitude all too common in professing Christians under the heading "Inadequate Conceptions of Practical Christianity":

> Yet thus life rolls away with too many of us in a course of "shapeless idleness." Its recreations constitute its chief business. Watering places—the sports of the field—cards! never-failing cards!—the assembly—the theater[9]—all contribute their aid—amusements are multiplied, and combined, and varied, "to fill up the void of a listless and languid life;" and by the judicious use of these different resources, there is often a kind of sober settled plan of domestic dissipation, in which with all imaginable decency year after year wears away in unprofitable vacancy. Even old age often finds us pacing in the same round of amusements which our early youth had tracked out. Meanwhile, being conscious that we are not giving into any flagrant vice, perhaps that we are guilty of

---

9. For a modern paraphrase, try "pubs and bars and clubs, loitering, computer/online gaming, the idolatry of sports, television, running with a gang, hanging out, cinemas, and DVDs."

no irregularity, and it may be, that we are not neglecting the offices of Religion, we persuade ourselves that we need not be uneasy. In the main we do not fall below the general standard of morals, of the class and station to which we belong, we may therefore allow ourselves to glide down the stream without apprehension of the consequences.[10]

Do you have inadequate conceptions of practical Christianity? The Bible teaches us that the Christian life is a fight (2 Tim. 4:7), a race (1 Cor. 9:24–27), and a wrestling match (Eph. 6:12). If you are going to see real victory in such a life, then you must aggressively seek to do battle and "let not sin therefore reign in your mortal body" (Rom. 6:12). The true Christian knows how fierce that battle can be. Sometimes it is profoundly surprising and deeply perplexing.

> How strange is the course that a Christian must steer!
> How perplext is the path he must tread!
> The hope of his happiness rises from fear,
> And his life he receives from the dead.

> His fairest pretensions must wholly be waiv'd,
> And his best resolutions be crost;
> Nor can he expect to be perfectly sav'd,
> Till he finds himself utterly lost.

> When all this is done, and his heart is assur'd
> Of the total remission of sins;
> When his pardon is sign'd, and his peace is procur'd,
> From that moment his conflict begins.[11]

There is nothing in our conscious engagement in the Christian life about which we are to be passive: we neither enter into the kingdom nor advance in it without effort and exertion.[12] Our entire life as believers is to be lived out in the full employment of heart and soul and mind and strength. Have you been diligent in your walk with the Lord to wage "the good warfare" (1 Tim. 1:18), to "make not provision for the flesh" (Rom. 13:14), "perfecting holiness in the fear of God" (2 Cor. 7:1)?

Can you say these words with the psalmist: "Thou art my portion, O LORD: I have said that I would keep thy words. I intreated thy favour with my whole heart: be merciful unto me according to thy word. I thought on my ways, and

---

10. William Wilberforce, *A Practical View of Christianity* (Peabody, MA: Hendrickson, 1996), 98–99.

11. Joseph Hart, *Hart's Hymns* (Choteau, MT: Old Paths Gospel Press, 1965), no. 29.

12. Readers interested to study this further might consider Mark Chanski's books *Manly Dominion* and *Womanly Dominion* (Calvary Press).

turned my feet unto thy testimonies. I made haste, and delayed not to keep thy commandments" (Ps. 119: 57–60)?

These are the things that the Word of God calls us to daily. But how do we pursue this? The answer is "according to His working which works in us mightily." God has not left us alone in this life as His people but has fully equipped us with all that we need in this life to walk well pleasing to Him (2 Peter 1:3).

God has given us His Word, His Spirit, the various means of grace—prayer, preaching, baptism, the Lord's Supper, and fellowship, for example—to be channels whereby we are kept in the way of truth and built up in our most holy faith. As we daily put off the old man and "put on the new man, which is renewed in knowledge after the image of him that created him" (Col. 3:10) we are, by His working in us, more and more conformed to Jesus' blessed image.

Christ—by His Spirit—dwells within every Christian, and He strengthens us in the inner man (Eph. 3:16). God's power is exceedingly great toward us who believe, according to the working of His mighty power (Eph. 1:19). Brother or sister, when you are feeling weak and unable to walk strongly, cast yourself afresh upon the free mercies of God in Jesus and learn by experience that they are "new every morning" (Lam. 3:23).

He promises that He will "never leave thee, nor forsake thee" (Heb. 13:5), and, having begun a good work in you, He will go on working until the day of Jesus Christ so as to bring that work to completion (Phil. 1:6). Christ is our great help; He is the fountain of all of our strength. Always remember that we are to "run with patience the race that is set before us, looking unto Jesus the author and finisher of our faith" (Heb. 12:1–2).

Furthermore, having considered the hard work to which pastors are called, are you not called to labor as well? Is the work of the kingdom only for those who have been duly recognized and called, or are all of the people of God called to labor hard for the cause of Christ Jesus our Lord? When Paul calls Timothy to this way of life—"Let no man despise thy youth; but be thou an example of the believers, in word, in conversation, in charity, in spirit, in faith, in purity. Till I come, give attendance to reading, to exhortation, to doctrine" (1 Tim. 4:12–13)— he does so not as an isolated individual but as a visible example to all. Timothy is to be a paradigm for the church he serves.

Repeatedly we see in the Bible that God's people work hard for the glory of Jesus. This is not the work that secures salvation. That is Christ's work, and it is entirely accomplished. Christ has secured our approval from God, and we do not need to and cannot increase it. Rather, this is the life now lived in the flesh that is lived out for the Christ who loved us and gave Himself for us; it is the outworking of love, done not to gain favor but as the response of the favored heart. It is seen all through the New Testament. In Romans 16:3–4, Paul writes, "Greet Priscilla and Aquila my helpers in Christ Jesus: who have for my life laid down their own necks: unto whom not only I give thanks, but also all the churches of the Gentiles." In verse 6 he writes, "Greet Mary, who bestowed much labour on us." The apostle commands in Philippians 1:27, "Only let your conversation be as it becometh the gospel of Christ: that whether I come and see you, or else be absent, I may hear of your affairs, that ye stand fast in one spirit, with one mind striving together for the faith of the gospel." Again, in 1 Thessalonians 1:2–3, Paul says, "We give thanks to God always for you all, making mention of you in our prayers; remembering without ceasing your work of faith, and labour of love, and patience of hope in our Lord Jesus Christ, in the sight of God and our Father." In Colossians 4:12, he says, "Epaphras, who is one of you, a servant of Christ, saluteth you, always labouring fervently for you in prayers, that ye may stand perfect and complete in all the will of God."

All true Christians are called to labor, striving for the glory of our God and the advance of the kingdom of Christ. None of us are to be lazy servants saying in our hearts, "My lord delayeth his coming" (Matt. 24:45–51). None of us is free to do nothing. A pastor seeking—like Timothy—to be an example to the believers (1 Tim. 4:12–13) must answer for the example that he gives you, but you must answer for the manner in which you follow good examples.

You may not be a vocational minister, but you are a servant of the living God, and you are called to bring Him your all and consecrate yourself as a living sacrifice to Christ. Now is the time to work diligently for Jesus, doing all we can do to evangelize the lost, spread the gospel, plant churches, and minister to God's people. This is not extreme Christianity or mere fanaticism. It is normative biblical Christianity (Matt. 28:16–20; Mark 5:19–20; John 4:39; Acts 8:1–13; Gal. 6:9–10; Heb. 10:23–25).

However, some may be involved in the process of identifying vocational elders for a particular church. Most believers will at some point have a responsibility to identify overseers of the flock, whether or not they are financially fully supported by the church. Perhaps you now are or may one day be on a pulpit committee. As you discharge these vital responsibilities, what counsel might we offer?

First, get a man who is not afraid to work hard. A lazy man is a curse to the cause of Christ and to His people. Ministers are called to "labour in the word and doctrine" (1 Tim. 5:17). Seek a working man for yourself, and when you find one, thank God for him and esteem him very highly in love for his work's sake (1 Thess. 5:12–13).

Second, if you find such a man, encourage him in his labors. Do not seek to flatter him or to pander to his pride, but do seek to assist him any way that you can, and acknowledge what God is doing in and through him. He, like you, is a man whose sufficiency is of God. A humble man will not become prideful when he receives words of gratitude and encouragement but will praise God for His mercy, that God has made such a wretch as he a profitable servant. If you do not want such a man to burn out, be sure that he gets a fair amount of time off every year with his family so that he can be refreshed in his own body and soul. Remember that those on the front line need opportunity for rest and recuperation if they are to continue to be effective soldiers of Christ.

Third, do not expect more from a pastor than does God in His own Word. Familiarize yourself with the biblical qualifications for an elder, as found in such places as 1 Timothy 3, Titus 1, and 1 Peter 5. By all means hold him to this standard, and nothing less, but do not demand more than God requires of him, especially if God has not equipped him beyond the minimum. No pastor is or ever will be Superman.

Do not cripple your pastor by imagining him superhuman and attributing to him what Christ alone supplies. Do not trip him up by the flattery of looking to man for what belongs to God. How foolish the people who look to the arm of men for help, and how foolish the pastor who boasts in his own strength or wisdom, who undertakes the work in the imagined power of his nonexistent might, who relies upon carnal resources.

Finally, as we have asked repeatedly, pray for your pastor. If he is a faithful laborer in God's vineyard, he will toil in the heat of the day and will know his need of God's grace upholding and enabling him. Often he will ask, "Brethren, pray for us" (2 Thess. 3:1). Do not deny him.

FELLOW PASTOR We cannot speak for you, but we can speak for ourselves: such a spirit as Paul's condemns us. These words and this example expose our sins. Like Peter, we are ready to plead and confess before Christ, "Depart from me; for I am a sinful man, O Lord" (Luke 5:8). What in other spheres would be enthusiasm is, in the service of Christ, restraint: "when ye shall have done all those things which are commanded you, say, We are unprofitable servants: we have done that which was our duty to do" (Luke 17:10). Let us not imagine that there is no admonition and instruction for us in the Scriptures, for we are as much exposed and exhorted as any others.

Who is sufficient for these things? It is the Spirit of Christ who makes us adequate for the accomplishment of the task to which we have been called. We must look to God and walk closely with Christ and rely entirely upon the Spirit if we are to be faithful and fruitful ministers of the new covenant.

And what a blessed and joyful service that is. It is hard and often painful, but still blessed and truly joyful, to spend and be spent in the service of the King of kings. We have been called to a good work (1 Tim. 3:1). We are fighting a good fight (2 Tim. 4:7). Let us take heed to Paul's example and examine our principles and practices.

First, have you been giving your all and your best for the people whom God has committed to your care? Our calling in life is that of "a workman that needeth not to be ashamed" (2 Tim. 2:15). Have you been ashamed, as you have read this chapter, seeing slothfulness in your own life? Let us pause to note again that there is a balance to be achieved. Robert Murray M'Cheyne declared that "the oil of the lamp in the temple burnt away in giving light; so should we."[13] He served accordingly. However, toward the end of his life, his health destroyed, he is reported to have said, "God gave me a message to deliver and a horse to ride. Alas, I have killed the horse and now I cannot deliver the message." Here, there is some recognition that a more careful stewardship of his physical health might, under God, have been the means of longer and even more effective service for his Lord and Savior.

The call to Christ's service is not, as we have said, a call to neglect the sixth commandment. Costly service is not the same as suicidal service. You do not have to pander to your limits, but you ought to recognize them. You need also to recognize the effect of your call, not just on your own life but, if you are married, on the life of the woman who has become "one flesh" with you (Eph. 5:28), as well as on your family and friendships. A pastor has a particular responsibility to his wife and any children God has given him. The discharge of this calling is part of his qualification for the work of the ministry (1 Tim. 3:2–5). If a man is called to the ministry and pursuing marriage, it is well for his wife also to recognize the demands that will be placed upon him and—by extension and necessity—her. The husband too must recognize and respond to the additional demands that will be placed upon him in encouraging and nurturing his wife through their life. Children are not to be neglected, for bringing them up in the training and admonition of the Lord is the ultimate responsibility of fathers (Eph. 6:4).

---

13. Andrew Bonar, *Memoir and Remains of Robert Murray M'Cheyne* (Edinburgh: Banner of Truth, 1966), 160.

The apostles had varying circumstances. Their freedom extended to their family arrangements: "Have we not power to lead about a sister, a wife, as well as other apostles, and as the brethren of the Lord, and Cephas?" (1 Cor. 9:5). Paul recognized that his own situation gave him a certain scope for gospel commitment that others might not have: "But I would have you without carefulness. He that is unmarried careth for the things that belong to the Lord, how he may please the Lord: but he that is married careth for the things that are of the world, how he may please his wife" (1 Cor. 7:32–33). But let us not make what is one of the greatest blessings of many ministerial lives an excuse not to give ourselves to the work of ministry. Read the testimony of Calvin regarding the comfort and help he received from his wife, or consider the family life of a man like Jonathan Edwards, of whom Samuel Miller wrote, "Perhaps no event of Mr Edwards' life had a more close connexion with his subsequent comfort and usefulness than this marriage [to Sarah Pierrepont],"[14] and you will see that these men were made happier and more effective laborers by their families. Indeed, our lives with and before our families ought to be a sermon to all who see us, demonstrating the gospel in the very relationship itself as well as preaching true consecration to Jesus Christ both with regard to our responsibilities to them and to the wider sphere of labor that the Lord has given us.

Taking all these things into account, Spurgeon was right when he said, "It is our duty and our privilege to exhaust our lives for Jesus. We are not to be living specimens of men in fine preservation, but living *sacrifices*, whose lot is to be consumed; we are to spend and to be spent, not to lay ourselves up in lavender, and nurse our flesh."[15]

Someone may assume that as a pastor and preacher you have it easy, that you work one day a week, on Sunday, maybe an hour or two at most. However, your life ought to reveal this as a misunderstanding, whether or not the truth is ever known by anyone but God. On the other hand, perhaps someone says, "Oh, you work too hard!" Really? Yes, it is possible, and yes, you should take care to preserve your health and life so that they can be fully spent for the Lord. At the same time, remember that man is a lazy creature, and ours is a lazy age. Look at the life of Christ, of Paul, of Peter, and say that the cause of God is worthy of any less exertion now than it has ever been! Brother, do you really think you are

---

14. Quoted in Iain H. Murray, *Jonathan Edwards: A New Biography* (Edinburgh: Banner of Truth, 1987), 91.

15. Charles Spurgeon, "The Minister's Fainting Fits" in *Lectures to My Students* (Edinburgh: Banner of Truth, 2008), 182.

risking the possibility of ending your life bemoaning the fact that you worked too hard for Jesus your Savior? We do not see that danger for ourselves. Far more likely is a cry of earnest forgiveness for so many wasted hours and opportunities out of a spirit of godless laziness or carnal self-preservation.

One thing we can hope for: if our people know that we are eager to see Christ formed in them and have them truly blessed, then they will put up with our many other shortcomings in living and serving. We are far from being perfect men. However, if we are diligent men, if we are serious men, if we are men who are bent on nothing but the good of our people, men who set a good example of diligent service for Christ, then they might love us and be all the more ready to heed what we tell them and follow what God calls them to do in His Word.

Could it be that you have slipped into cruise control? Have you become used to frittering away minutes and even hours on the apparently harmless frivolities of life? Under the umbrella of "knowing the times" have you begun to indulge in a mental freefall through countless Websites, movies, magazines, newspapers, TV shows, and other largely pointless pastimes? If so, ask the Lord to forgive you even now. There will be times in our ministries when things might be a bit slower and less active in the providence of God, but surely even in these times there are things that we can do on behalf of our Lord and His people. Walk the streets and witness to the people; write an article; dig in to that enormous theological tome; visit the sick, widows, and orphans; assist at some organized ministry of mercy; lead a neighborhood Bible study; give time to dedicated prayer. Daniel tells us that "the people that do know their God shall be strong, and do exploits" (Dan. 11:32). May that be our testimony!

Second, do you sometimes or often feel like you are at the end of your tether? Do you feel utterly sapped, as if all your strength has been drained away? If so, look again to Christ. How quickly we feel our creatureliness! We must learn to come back to Jesus time and again, to our gracious Jehovah who gives power to the weak. Remember that "to them that have no might he increaseth strength. Even the youths shall faint and be weary, and the young men shall utterly fall: but they that wait upon the LORD shall renew their strength; they shall mount up with wings as eagles; they shall run, and not be weary; and they shall walk, and not faint" (Isa. 40:29–31).

From Him we will and do receive all the help and strength and power that we need to fulfill our tasks as undershepherds of His flock. Our Lord says to us, "Abide in me, and I in you. As the branch cannot bear fruit of itself, except it abide in the vine; no more can ye, except ye abide in me. I am the vine, ye are the branches: He that abideth in me, and I in him, the same bringeth forth much fruit: for without me ye can do nothing" (John 15:4–5). These absolute declarations are crucial for us to grasp. The word *abide* means to remain, to dwell or to depend. The sense is that if we are to know God's help in our lives and be genuinely fruitful in a God-honoring way, then we must rely entirely on the Lord for His strength as we go about the faithful discharge of our God-given calling. If we are to know vigor and vitality as pastors of the flock, then we need constantly to go to Him for it. John Owen, the great Puritan, captures the thrust:

> If a branch be so separated from the root and body of the vine as that it receives not continual supplies of nourishment from them, if their influence into it be by any means intercepted, it proceeds not in its growth, it brings forth no fruit, but is immediately under decay. It is so, saith our Saviour, with believers in respect unto him. Unless they have continual, uninterrupted influences of grace and spiritually vital nourishment from him, they can do nothing. "Without me," expresseth a denial of all the spiritual aid that we have from Christ. On supposition hereof "we can do nothing,"—that is, by our own power, or by virtue of any habit or principle of grace we have received; for when we have received it, what we can do thereby without farther actual assistance, we can do of ourselves. "Ye can do nothing," that is, which appertains to fruit-bearing unto God. In things natural and civil we can do somewhat, and in things sinful too much; we need no aid or assistance for any such purpose;—but in fruit-bearing unto God we can do nothing. Now, every act of faith and love, every motion of our minds or affections towards God, is a part of our fruit-bearing; and so, unquestionably, are all external works and duties of holiness and obedience. Wherefore, our Saviour himself being judge, believers, who are really sanctified and made partakers of habitual grace, yet cannot of themselves, without new actual aid and assistance of grace from him, do any thing that is spiritually good or acceptable with God.[16]

Let us then daily humble ourselves and always look to God in Christ for all the help that moment by moment we need. In our own strength, apart from His, we will utterly fail; in and with His strength we can do all of God's holy will for us. In Jesus is "all the fulness of the Godhead bodily" (Col. 2:9). Why should we not always go to Him for help? Paul did this, and Jesus helped him. Will not our Lord do the same for us? Our God is no more a respecter of persons in this than in anything else (Acts 10:34).

---

16. John Owen, *Works* (Edinburgh: Banner of Truth, 1965), 3:531.

Paul models characteristics for us to follow. We have seen his holy aggression for God as well as his righteous reliance upon God. These are equally valid perspectives that we must always keep before us as we labor as ministers of the gospel. Let us press on in the things of God, and let us not grow weary while doing good, for in due season we shall reap if we do not lose heart (Gal. 6:9). God is on our side, and greater is He who is in us than he who is in the world (1 John 4:4). Read the histories of great days, great achievements, and great wars, or the biographies of those who participated in them. Will the men of this world give themselves so entirely, so inventively, so diligently, and so sacrificially for things that will fade away with a passing world, and shall we not labor, striving with an eye upon the crown that Christ will dispense, our gaze fixed upon that "inheritance incorruptible, and undefiled, and that fadeth not away, reserved in heaven for you, who are kept by the power of God through faith unto salvation ready to be revealed in the last time" (1 Peter 1:4–5)? Let us not grow dull or cold in the service of our King.

These things will motivate us to continue in our hard efforts on behalf of Jesus and His bride. One day in glory, our Lord will reward you for your faithful service to Him. Paul knew this. With his body full of cold and weariness and his heart full of happy expectation, he writes to Timothy: "For I am now ready to be offered, and the time of my departure is at hand. I have fought a good fight, I have finished my course, I have kept the faith: henceforth there is laid up for me a crown of righteousness, which the Lord, the righteous judge, shall give me at that day: and not to me only, but unto all them also that love his appearing" (2 Tim. 4:6–8). What a day that will be! "For which cause we faint not; but though our outward man perish, yet the inward man is renewed day by day. For our light affliction, which is but for a moment, worketh for us a far more exceeding and eternal weight of glory; while we look not at the things which are seen, but at the things which are not seen: for the things which are seen are temporal; but the things which are not seen are eternal" (2 Cor. 4:16–18).

If we are exhausted here in this life, eternal glory will make up for it in an instant. "Therefore, my beloved brethren, be ye stedfast, unmoveable, always abounding in the work of the Lord, forasmuch as ye know that your labour is not in vain in the Lord" (1 Cor. 15:58).

Do not let your life give credence to the assumption that pastors have a cakewalk. More positively, and more importantly, let your life and its toil—and, when it comes, your death—tell the tale of the excellence of the Master you serve, the worthiness of Jesus to receive all you are and all you have.

9 | THE CONFLICT OF PAUL'S MINISTRY

For I would that ye knew what great conflict I have for you, and for them at Laodicea, and for as many as have not seen my face in the flesh; that their hearts might be comforted, being knit together in love, and unto all riches of the full assurance of understanding, to the acknowledgement of the mystery of God, and of the Father, and of Christ; in whom are hid all the treasures of wisdom and knowledge.
— COLOSSIANS 2:1–3

I long exceedingly to know if the oft-spoken-of match betwixt you and Christ holdeth, and if ye follow on to know the Lord. My day-thoughts and my night-thoughts are of you: while ye sleep I am afraid of your souls, that they be off the rock. Next to my Lord Jesus and this fallen kirk, ye have the greatest share of my sorrow, and also of my joy; ye are the matter of the tears, care, fear, and daily prayers of an oppressed prisoner of Christ. As I am in bonds for my high and lofty One, my royal and princely Master, my Lord Jesus; so I am in bonds for you.... Oh, if any pain, any sorrow, any loss that I can suffer for Christ, and for you, were laid in pledge to buy Christ's love to you! and that I could lay my dearest joys, next to Christ my Lord, in the gap betwixt you and eternal destruction!... My witness is above; your Heaven would be two heavens to me, and the salvation of you all as two salvations to me.[1]
— SAMUEL RUTHERFORD

Why does a pastor need the strength that only God can give for the work of the ministry? The simple answer is, because of the nature of the ministry in which he is engaged. In the second chapter of the Colossian letter, Paul tells the church of his great conflict on their behalf. He takes a magnifying glass to focus

---

1. Samuel Rutherford, "Letter CCXXV.—To his Parishioners" in *Letters of Samuel Rutherford* (Edinburgh and London: Oliphant, Anderson and Ferrier, 1894), 438–39.

the rays of his pastoral affection upon this particular congregation, bringing the realities of his service to bear on them especially. It might be that some would only slowly be persuaded of his true regard for their well-being. Perhaps the false teachers had attempted to drive a wedge between the apostle and the Colossian Christians. Paul puts holy hooks in their hearts: his words get attention, breed expectation, and solicit affection. Having declared in Colossians 1:29 that he, by God's grace, exerts all his energies for God's people, Paul now proves and explains that assertion, saying, "For I would that ye knew..." (Col. 2:1). This is a formal phrase of disclosure, as Paul unveils his heart of love for God's people.

Paul's fervent heart for the Colossians

Most commentators suggest that Paul had never visited the Colossian church in person, although it is plain that he had at least traveled through the region, and he clearly knew some of its members well (for example, Philemon, to whom he also wrote a personal letter). It may be that he had at some point preached in or near Colosse and Laodicea, two cities situated in what was called the Lycus Valley. Whatever the extent of Paul's personal contact, certainly Epaphras and Archippus had ministered apostolic truth with an apostolic spirit. They might even have been Paul's formal co-laborers in the area. As a result of this preaching, sinners had been saved and the churches were established and growing (Col. 1:6–7; 4:17).

Now Paul wants the Colossians to know that they are *the concern of his heart*. This church in Colosse (and, incidentally, the church in Laodicea) is exposed to grave spiritual danger, and Paul wants these brothers and sisters to know the greatness of his regard for them. He writes to say, in effect, "I agonize over you, Colosse, and over Laodicea, including those whom I have never met." With such words he burrows into their souls, he embraces them all. Laodicea was about twelve miles from Colosse, and this letter will be exchanged with one that he is writing to the church there (see Col. 4:15–16). Though many of these believers living in the Lycus Valley had never seen Paul, and he had never laid eyes on them, his striving encompasses them all.

Here is the largeness of his heart and the breadth of his embrace. There is a total absence of favoritism. He has a comprehensive concern on the basis of spiritual affinity and gospel unity, not merely on the grounds of personal knowledge and geographical proximity. Distance is not the issue; cultural distinctives do not prove an obstacle; one-on-one relationships are not required. All that is needful is a pastor's heart in the face of a report that God's people are in trouble. The real battles and felt needs of God's true saints call forth all the energies of the true pastor's heart, and here they demand the fervent engagement of the apostle Paul.

And it is indeed a fervent engagement. Paul shows us *the warmth of his heart* by speaking of his "great conflict." There is an echo here of Colossians 1:29, for this concept of "conflict" has the same linguistic root as Paul's language of "striving," an echo that will be heard again in Colossians 4:12, which speaks of the fervent labor of Epaphras. Again, this has to do with agonizing. He is saying, in effect, "You need to understand that my labors are not without point or focus. I do not fight as one beating the air. My efforts are directed toward you with a particular goal in mind."

This is profound travail of soul expressed in the language of deep solicitude and earnest contention. It speaks of spiritual combat. Paul is profoundly aware of their struggles. He is conscious of the assaults being made upon them and he is engaged against the enemy on their behalf. Even while chained in a Roman prison, Paul demonstrates a willingness to meet conflict head on for the sake of God's redeemed people, and he testifies to the Colossians that he is doing so. Such ardent striving should—and, in healthy saints and in a healthy church, does—establish a strong bond between the shepherd and the sheep, between the one who is contending and those for whom he contends. Paul unashamedly declares that he is going into battle on behalf of this church, those whom he knows and those whom he has never seen.

Let us note here that strivings *for* God's people demand enough of a minister apart from strivings *against* God's people. A true shepherd would much rather engage in conflict on behalf of and alongside God's people than against them. When Paul wrote to the Colossians he was able to contend for them because, though they were needy, they were faithful. They were hearing the whisper, "Christ is not enough," but it seems that they had not yet succumbed to it. At other times—writing to the puffed-up Corinthians, for example, or to the deceived and increasingly legalistic Galatians—he had not only to contend for them but also against them. Even reading through those letters, you feel as well as read in Paul's words the grief, tension, and weariness that this produced in his soul.

Nothing more saps the strength of a man of God, nothing more grieves his heart and hinders his work, than contending with God's people as they slide into dullness, error, and sin. He will fight for them with all readiness, but he has no desire that he will ever need to enter battle against them should they become enemies of their own souls or the souls of others.

And what, then, is the outworking of Paul's ardent affection for these saints, known and unknown? Paul does not leave them in the dark, but outlines *the activities of his heart.* This striving shows itself by all legitimate means. Remember, Paul was an apostle: he was entitled to visit the churches and write epistles. We must take care that we do not arrogate to ourselves an apostolic attitude to churches when God has not made us apostles. We must take pains not to throw our weight around in dealing with any church, let alone those not under our care as undershepherds.

Even so, see how Paul demonstrates the manner in which (in accordance with one's calling and circumstances) true heart affection for God's people is worked out. Paul is physically limited in what he can accomplish and is probably also financially constrained (see his letter to Philemon for the evidence). Imprisoned, he cannot visit the church. He cannot preach to them in person. He can send Epaphras back to them with particular encouragements and instructions both for him and the people for whom he cares. He can at least write to them, and he does, using the pen to minister to their souls. But, in this context, it is plain that his agonizing for them has one particular manifestation—prayer.

While true heart affection for God's people will find every legitimate avenue of expression, prayer is always legitimate. This is the man who wrote to the Thessalonian church, "Wherefore also we pray always for you, that our God would count you worthy of this calling, and fulfil all the good pleasure of his goodness, and the work of faith with power: that the name of our Lord Jesus Christ may be glorified in you, and ye in him, according to the grace of our God and the Lord Jesus Christ" (2 Thess. 1:11–12).

Prayer was the unceasing expression of Paul's heart's burden for the Lord's people, and he constantly assures the various churches to whom he writes that he has them on his heart. Here, like Epaphras and with Epaphras, he gives himself to fervent prayer as the primary expression of his battle on behalf of the Christians in Colosse, explaining in the following verses the substance and purpose of those prayers.

But before we move on to consider those things, notice that Paul's prayers are an agony. These are not a few burbled and thoughtless words or a formulaic expression of distant interest. Paul does not offer a vague benediction, and his prayer is no light expression of a lukewarm concern. Paul's pleading at the throne of grace is heated and animated. It partakes of the character of conflict, it is wrestling: "For we wrestle not against flesh and blood, but against principalities, against powers, against the rulers of the darkness of this world, against spiritual wickedness in high places.... Praying always with all prayer and supplication in the Spirit, and watching thereunto with all perseverance and supplication for all saints" (Eph. 6:12, 18).

Here is a vivid insight into a pastor's heart. Love is a key ingredient in the work (2 Tim. 2:10; 1 John 4:21), and Paul's love and zeal are unashamedly and sincerely communicated and readily evident. Love is expressed before the warning is given; Paul wants the saints to know his motive for straight speaking. He therefore emphasizes his affection before he delivers his exhortation. Such active affection is typical of the true undershepherd. We read, for example, of the Scottish preacher, John Welch, who "often in the coldest winter nights rose for prayer, and was found weeping on the ground and wrestling with the Lord on account of his people, and saying to his wife, when she pressed him for an explanation of his distress, 'I have the souls of three thousand people to answer for, while I know not how it is with many of them.'"[2]

By the end of his life, Welch's knees apparently calcified, due in part to the number of nights he spent kneeling in prayer for the glory of God in His kingdom. Such is a faithful pastor's heart for Christ and His people.

But we also have at least a faint picture of Christ's heart. Paul is a mere man, but he is showing us something of what it means to imitate Christ. How much more fervently and effectually Christ prays for His church! His conflict on behalf of His people could not have been more agonizing: "As he saith also in another place, Thou art a priest for ever after the order of Melchisedec. Who in the days of his flesh, when he had offered up prayers and supplications with strong crying and tears unto him that was able to save him from death, and was heard in that he feared; though he were a Son, yet learned he obedience by the things which he suffered" (Heb. 5:6–8).

We have a window into our Lord's heart in the seventeenth chapter of John's gospel:

> Neither pray I for these alone, but for them also which shall believe on me through their word; that they all may be one; as thou, Father, art in me, and I in thee, that they also may be one in us: that the world may believe that thou hast sent me. And the glory which thou gavest me I have given them; that they may be one, even as we are one: I in them, and thou in me, that they may be made perfect in one; and that the world may know that thou hast sent me, and hast loved them, as thou hast loved me. Father, I will that they also, whom thou hast given me, be with me where I am; that they may behold my glory, which thou hast given me: for thou lovedst me before the foundation of the world. (vv. 20–24)

---

2. William S. Plumer, *Pastoral Theology* (Harrisonburg, VA: Sprinkle, 2003), 53.

Christ still offers up such prayers on our behalf. He ever lives to make interces-
sion for those for whom He has died (Heb. 7:25). "Christ is not entered into the
holy places made with hands, which are the figures of the true; but into heaven
itself, now to appear in the presence of God for us" (Heb. 9:24). We, not having
seen Him, love Him and fervently pray for His glory to be made known. He
knows us absolutely and loves us absolutely, and He earnestly desires that we
may be with Him where He is. Does He not long to lay His human eyes upon
His own redeemed host? Here is one who is far better than Paul. Here is *the*
Pastor of the flock. Here is the great Example who is merely reflected in His
faithful servant, the apostle.

Paul's heart—like that of his Savior—opens to reveal fervent feeling for
and earnest contention on behalf of the people of God, even those personally
unknown to him. This passionate, Christlike concern is demonstrated primarily
by agonizing prayer on their behalf.

Paul's protective prayers for the Colossians

But what is the content of that prayer? Paul's petitions for the Colossians are
comprehensive and magnificent. They are not petty, narrow, or shallow, but
rich, deep, scriptural, penetrating, both Christ-centered and Christ-exalting.
We need to learn to pray like this for the church and against the devil and his
minions. With true largeness of heart, Paul enters into the particular needs and
concerns of the Colossian believers and does so with a definite design (literally,
in Colossians 2:2, he tells us that he prays "in order that…"). He is offering up
specific and significant petitions for things that are vital to the well-being of the
Colossians and other saints.

Here are three petitions for things that are inseparably bound together. All
of them have to do with the heart of the believer. This is not the physical organ,
or even the heart considered—after the current mode of thinking—as simply
the seat of emotion or affection. Rather, this is the center of the personality.
It is the place of thought, reason, and deliberation. It is the source not only of
affection or emotion, but of will and thought. The heart, in Paul's view, is the very
core of our inner being. Paul knows his Old Testament: "Keep thy heart with all
diligence; for out of it are the issues of life" (Prov. 4:23). He knows the centrality
of the heart in such portions of Scripture as Psalm 119. As Paul records three
potent protective petitions for the Colossians living for Jesus in a deceptively
persuasive world (Col. 2:4), so he teaches us how to pray both for ourselves and

for saints known and unknown, seen and unseen. Paul prays that the Colossians might have strong hearts, united hearts, and assured hearts.

First, he prays for *strong hearts*: "that their hearts might be comforted" (Col. 2:2). The word *comforted* can be translated in a variety of different ways depending on the context, including such notions as "encourage" or "strengthen." Literally, it has to do with calling someone else to your side. In secular Greek literature, it is used, for example, of a general sent to restore the moral fiber of a demoralized regiment, with strong exhortation and by sterling example. The Colossians, under their present circumstances, probably required less in the way of consolation and more in the way of confirmation. In the face of trials and temptations, in an environment in which Christ was being devalued and degraded by pernicious whisperings, Paul prays that they will be invigorated. He wants them to know and feel the benefits of seeing him contending for the truth that they themselves have also embraced. His earnest desire is that they will be spiritually reinforced in the face of initial contact and growing conflict with error.

To live in a perpetually hostile environment is exhausting, sometimes overwhelming. A great need under such circumstances is for our hearts to be invigorated and encouraged. This, then, is nothing less than a prayer for the continuing and progressing operations of the Holy Spirit in the lives of the believers, in accordance with what Paul writes elsewhere, asking "that [God the Father] would grant you, according to the riches of his glory, to be strengthened with might by his Spirit in the inner man" (Eph. 3:16). The Spirit's title of *Comforter* and this verb that Paul uses have the same root sense: help, comforting, strengthening, calling to one's side for the purpose of exhortation and encouragement:

> And I will pray the Father, and he shall give you another Comforter, that he may abide with you for ever; even the Spirit of truth; whom the world cannot receive, because it seeth him not, neither knoweth him: but ye know him; for he dwelleth with you, and shall be in you. I will not leave you comfortless: I will come to you.... But the Comforter, which is the Holy Ghost, whom the Father will send in my name, he shall teach you all things, and bring all things to your remembrance, whatsoever I have said unto you. (John 14:16–18, 26)

> But when the Comforter is come, whom I will send unto you from the Father, even the Spirit of truth, which proceedeth from the Father, he shall testify of me. (John 15:26)

Nevertheless I tell you the truth; It is expedient for you that I go away: for if I go not away, the Comforter will not come unto you; but if I depart, I will send him unto you. (John 16:7)

Notice that the Spirit is from Christ, and observe how the Spirit brings Christ to bear. It is by His Spirit that the risen Lord takes up residence in our hearts (Eph. 3:17). It is the Spirit of Christ, the Holy Spirit, who calls us to His side and bears us up.

But this is also a function of life in the body of Christ. In Luke 22:32 we read our Lord's instructions to Peter: "But I have prayed for thee, that thy faith fail not: and when thou art converted, strengthen thy brethren." In Acts 15:32 and 41, we see the habit of the teachers of the apostolic church: "And Judas and Silas, being prophets also themselves, exhorted the brethren with many words, and confirmed them"; "And [Paul] went through Syria and Cilicia, confirming the churches." Again, the apostle, concerned for the health of God's people, takes steps to secure the good of the Thessalonian church: "Wherefore when we could no longer forbear, we thought it good to be left at Athens alone; and sent Timotheus, our brother, and minister of God, and our fellowlabourer in the gospel of Christ, to establish you, and to comfort you concerning your faith" (1 Thess. 3:1–2). This strengthening is not only something that the Spirit of God works directly in the hearts of men, but it is accomplished with and through the Word of God ministered to and among us.

This being so, it is no surprise that we next find Paul praying for *united hearts*: "being knit together in love" (Col. 2:2). Error is both destructive and divisive. It brings personal declension and breeds corporate dissolution, encouraging suspicion, alienation, and coolness of heart toward one's fellow saints. This is true even in a situation where the healthier members of a church are wondering who might have been infected with some error, and to what degree. Who can be trusted? In such an environment, and facing just such dangers, Paul pleads with God that the hearts of these brothers might be knit together in love, welded tight in unity.

We might ask if this unity is a preparation for strong hearts, or the product of them. The answer is both. Lifeless orthodoxy and loose association are no sure guards against error, but the vibrant realities of life as healthy members of Christ's flourishing body provide just such a defense. This love is not a matter of mere warm feelings or even of sentimental words, but a love of sacrificial deeds, of investment in one another's souls: "But whoso hath this world's good, and seeth his brother have need, and shutteth up his bowels of compassion from him, how dwelleth the love of God in him? My little children, let us not love in word, neither in tongue; but in deed and in truth" (1 John 3:17–18).

We cannot truly know God in an environment where brotherly love is not cultivated. Hearts will never be strengthened where there is an absence of Christian unity because we will be cut off from each other and drive the Holy Spirit far from us. Consider how Paul writes in Ephesians 4:25–5:2, 6:

> Wherefore putting away lying, speak every man truth with his neighbour: for we are members one of another. Be ye angry, and sin not: let not the sun go down upon your wrath: neither give place to the devil. Let him that stole steal no more: but rather let him labour, working with his hands the thing which is good, that he may have to give to him that needeth. Let no corrupt communication proceed out of your mouth, but that which is good to the use of edifying, that it may minister grace unto the hearers. And grieve not the holy Spirit of God, whereby ye are sealed unto the day of redemption. Let all bitterness, and wrath, and anger, and clamour, and evil speaking, be put away from you, with all malice: and be ye kind one to another, tenderhearted, forgiving one another, even as God for Christ's sake hath forgiven you. Be ye therefore followers of God, as dear children; and walk in love, as Christ also hath loved us, and hath given himself for us an offering and a sacrifice to God for a sweetsmelling savour.... Let no man deceive you with vain words: for because of these things cometh the wrath of God upon the children of disobedience.

We cannot underestimate the seriousness of these words or miss the connections that Paul makes in this passage. Because we are members of one another, we are to act accordingly. Paul tells us that we are to avoid certain sins. When we consider their positive, gracious counterparts, a pattern emerges: we are, by implication, called upon to pursue truth, unity, peace, honesty, edification, sweetness, calmness, quietness, and right speech, in a spirit of true, Godlike forgiveness. Love is to characterize us. All these graces are associated, more or less, with the Spirit of Christ. It is His pleasure to nurture these things in us. To neglect these Christlike graces, and to live in the exercise of these corresponding sins is to offend and grieve the One who delights in those graces and abominates the contrary wickedness, and therefore to have Him draw back from us. It is also worth noticing that the majority of the sins identified are closely associated with our speech.

When true brotherly love is cultivated among us, the Spirit of truth draws near. This is a love which acts as a powerful defense against deceitful words of persuasion.

How much need there is for humility in the cultivation of such a love: "Put on therefore, as the elect of God, holy and beloved, bowels of mercies, kindness, humbleness of mind, meekness, longsuffering; forbearing one another, and forgiving one another, if any man have a quarrel against any: even as Christ forgave you, so also do ye" (Col. 3:12–13). Pride and division go together just as surely as do lowliness of mind and unity:

> If there be therefore any consolation in Christ, if any comfort of love, if any fellowship of the Spirit, if any bowels and mercies, fulfil ye my joy, that ye be likeminded, having the same love, being of one accord, of one mind. Let nothing be done through strife or vainglory; but in lowliness of mind let each esteem other better than themselves. Look not every man on his own things, but every man also on the things of others. Let this mind be in you, which was also in Christ Jesus: who, being in the form of God, thought it not robbery to be equal with God: but made himself of no reputation, and took upon him the form of a servant, and was made in the likeness of men: and being found in fashion as a man, he humbled himself, and became obedient unto death, even the death of the cross. (Phil. 2:1–8)

Unloving hearts are no small matter, for only loving hearts are both a root and fruit of strengthened hearts.

Paul's third petition builds on the first two. He prays for *assured hearts*: "And [attaining] unto all riches of the full assurance of understanding, to the acknowledgement of the mystery of God, and of the Father, and of Christ; in whom are hid all the treasures of wisdom and knowledge" (Col. 2:2–3). Paul expands this petition more than the first two, but it is essentially a third door that he is seeking to slam shut against error. Error enters our lives through weak hearts, unloving hearts, and doubting hearts. These three problems are bound together. So, for example, we read that knowledge puffs up, but love builds up (1 Cor. 8:1). Strong faith is related to clear comprehension and genuine love: "[I pray] that Christ may dwell in your hearts by faith; that ye, being rooted and grounded in love, may be able to comprehend with all saints what is the breadth, and length, and depth, and height" (Eph. 3:17–18).

Paul is layering his prayers, asking now for the riches—the spiritual opulence—of the full assurance of understanding: a sure and settled conviction.

Many doubters are seeking for "something," searching for an experience or offer of "fullness"—the very experience being offered by the errorists of Colosse. That fullness is to be found in Christ alone. However, if a person travels in a state of doubt, casting about in constant uncertainty, he will be very susceptible to those who come with the appearance of guides and helpers, but who direct us into wrong paths.

Notice also how Paul fixes assurance in the understanding. Some people boast a great deal of assurance without any true knowledge. It is the equivalent of someone assuring you, "I have great faith!" but not being able to answer the question, "In what or in whom?" True assurance is built upon a degree of accurate understanding. Nevertheless, the problem goes beyond the understanding: assurance lies not merely in the possession of knowledge but in the application of truth. The assurance of which Paul speaks is, as John Eadie explains, "the fixed persuasion that you comprehend the truth, and that it is the truth which you comprehend."[3] It is not merely a happy high, a spiritual boost, a "word from the Lord," or a temporary buzz. It is the confidence that you have truly "got it." It is the reality of genuine *apprehension*, both in the sense that you have understood something and in the sense that you have laid hold of it. This is to grasp the truth accurately with regard to its nature and concretely with regard to its relations. It is the conviction that this truth is of God, and that you have accurately (albeit in accordance with your limitations as a mere man) grasped the mind of God in this thing.

This assurance does not come about as a result of gazing upon or within ourselves, apart from Christ, but it derives from a proper hold of and a joyful dwelling upon Christ. It is a matter of truth grasped by a strengthened heart in a context of Christian community in unity and love, resulting in profound and settled conviction of that truth. Christian health and happiness rest upon and are directly tied to our grasp of the person and work of the Lord Jesus Christ.

What great value there is in possessing strong, united, and assured hearts! Such powerful protective petitions would surely, under God, establish three great barriers to the entrance of error into the church. Hearts such as these contribute mightily to the joy, stability, and usefulness of the saints of God. They establish the health of Christ's church. Many of us can, perhaps, think of brothers and sisters in Jesus, individually or as local churches, for whom such hearts are the means, under God, of keeping them afloat while pounded by waves and storms.

Remember also that it is relatively easy to give the appearance of strength, unity, and assurance without possessing the reality. It is too easy to become satisfied with what we have attained, without going further and deeper. Unless we, like the apostle, seek after and pray for such hearts, we will be fearfully

---

3. John Eadie, *A Commentary on the Greek Text of Paul's Letter to the Colossians* (Birmingham, AL: Solid Ground Christian Books, 2005), 111.

exposed. Do we not feel the chill in our own souls of neglect or poverty with regard to such things? Can we not feel the imbalance and instability that so quickly characterizes us and that is so quickly revealed in us? Have you not watched some who once named the name of Christ drifting from the truth and embracing folly because they did not cultivate or soon abandoned the pursuit of strong, united, and assured hearts?

No wonder, then, that Paul pleads as he does. In an error-soaked world, it is the truth-soaked heart that holds fast. It is the man of stirred-up soul, standing with, striving for, investing in, and united to healthy fellow saints, with a fixed and anchored grasp and sense of the truth, who will love and serve Jesus Christ, the Head of the body, which is His church. How much we need to deal with the heart, for out of it are the issues of life.

Paul's high hope for the Colossians

We have already said that Paul develops the third of these three intertwined petitions more than the first two. He pleads for and promotes strong, united, and assured hearts by all legitimate means. But with what things are such hearts taken up? What is it that such hearts rightly understand and firmly grasp?

Paul makes plain that this assurance of understanding is rooted in and rests upon Christ Jesus. He makes his point in language that he has already used, rehearsing what has gone before so as to gather up the weight of his argument for his first definite and explicit response to the false teaching.

What does it mean to attain to "all riches of the full assurance of understanding" (Col. 2:2)? Paul is at least implying *the necessity of God's revelation*. As we have seen in an earlier chapter, a mystery in the biblical sense is truth revealed by God that would otherwise have remained hidden. Paul spoke of the riches of the glory of the gospel mystery among the Gentiles: "Christ in you, the hope of glory" (Col. 1:27). A full assurance of understanding depends on the revelation of God; you cannot be confident that you comprehend God's truth until He makes it known. We could never attain to any profitable degree of accurate spiritual understanding apart from God's self-revelation. Without the Spirit of God illuminating the Word of God, giving eyes to see what God has made known, we would know nothing of eternal spiritual value. All our own contemplations, all the teachings of cults, all the suggestions of philosophers and psychologists— none of them could help us pierce the mind of God and bring us near to Him. We cannot be saved from sin, made more like Christ, and know that we possess such blessings without the teaching of God Himself. Without the Spirit, we are like blind men in an empty room. God must both fill the room with riches and open our eyes to see them.

We must face honestly the profoundly humbling truth declared by Christ Jesus when He prayed to His Father, "I thank thee, O Father, Lord of heaven and earth, because thou hast hid these things from the wise and prudent, and hast revealed them unto babes. Even so, Father: for so it seemed good in thy sight. All things are delivered unto me of my Father: and no man knoweth the Son, but the Father; neither knoweth any man the Father, save the Son, and he to whomsoever the Son will reveal him" (Matt. 11:25–27).

The truth of God is hidden from the wise and prudent and revealed to babes. No worldly wisdom can discern God so as to be delivered from sin and then to delight in deliverance from sin. You would feel sorry for a brilliant scientist who could perceive the structures of a flower, depict the details of its composition and construction, label all its parts, and generally describe it exhaustively, but who could not delight in its beauty, enjoy its colors, or breathe in its fragrance. So we need God both for perception of and delight in His truth. We are utterly dependent on God's revelation.

What, then, is *the content of God's revelation?* Several commentators identify some difficulty here in working out precisely which words Paul used in the text and in what order. However, it makes little material difference to the sense, not least because Paul has already stated so much and so clearly in Colossians 1:26–27 about this mystery.

This revealed truth is the good news of God made known and brought near in Christ and of us brought near to God by Him. How few would have looked to Jesus of Nazareth for the revelation of God, and yet Paul points to Him as the revealer of God. The treasures of divine truth are hidden in Him. The sense is that these treasures are stored up in Him, deposited securely there, hidden not *from* us but *for* us, and therefore accessible to all His people. In Jesus, the crucified Christ, the glory of God in salvation shines forth to be known by sinners like us. Remember 1 Timothy 3:16: "great is the mystery of godliness"—a mystery that has to do with Christ, which can have only to do with Christ. Again, this lies behind our Lord's prayer in Matthew 11:

> All things are delivered unto me of my Father: and no man knoweth
> the Son, but the Father; neither knoweth any man the Father, save the
> Son, and he to whomsoever the Son will reveal him. Come unto me,
> all ye that labour and are heavy laden, and I will give you rest. Take my
> yoke upon you, and learn of me; for I am meek and lowly in heart: and

ye shall find rest unto your souls. For my yoke is easy, and my burden is light. (vv. 27–30)

Christ reveals God; only through Jesus is the Father known and peace for the burdened soul obtained. Once we saw Him as the world sees Him still, according to the flesh (2 Cor. 5:16): Jesus the Nazarene, the outcast, the accursed. Now, by God's grace, we behold the same Jesus as God's Lord and Christ, as the One in whom God is declaring Himself for salvation and glory.

That brings us to *the riches of God's revelation*. Paul never skimps on language when he speaks of God's gospel revelation (see Col. 1:27). He does not intend to undersell the good news. These are the riches of full assurance, the knowledge—the sense is full and accurate comprehension—of the mystery of God, in whom are hidden all the treasures of wisdom and knowledge (Col. 2:2–3). The apostle may be drawing on the language of Isaiah 33:6, speaking of the gracious activity of the highly exalted Lord: "And wisdom and knowledge shall be the stability of thy times, and strength of salvation: the fear of the LORD is his treasure."

Paul is saying that all that is deepest in God is summed up in Christ Jesus. He is the highest expression of divine self-revelation. This is well borne out by Hebrews 1:1–4:

> God, who at sundry times and in divers manners spake in time past unto the fathers by the prophets, hath in these last days spoken unto us by his Son, whom he hath appointed heir of all things, by whom also he made the worlds; who being the brightness of his glory, and the express image of his person, and upholding all things by the word of his power, when he had by himself purged our sins, sat down on the right hand of the Majesty on high; being made so much better than the angels, as he hath by inheritance obtained a more excellent name than they.

Furthermore, perhaps with a sidelong glance and a subtle dig at his opponents in Colosse and their empty rival claims, Paul makes clear that *all* these treasures, without exception, are stored up in Jesus alone.

"Wisdom and knowledge" in Colossians 2:3 are not so much distinct categories as a summary declaration of divine truth. All that must be known for salvation in its beginning, continuing, and ending is in Christ exclusively. He is, if you will, a complete, accurate, and final salvific encyclopedia: to work through the entries on the pages of this book is to attain to a full, correct, and saving revelation of the mind and heart of God Himself.

God as He truly is—His character and government; His law and grace; His justice and mercy; His righteousness and lovingkindness; His majesty and beauty; His wrath and love; His wisdom and power—these things are shown to us in Christ Jesus in the highest degree and in perfect proportion and in right relationship. John Eadie writes, "And after those combinations of wisdom, power, and love, which characterize the counsels and government of God, have attracted and engaged the inquiring soul through innumerable ages, there will still remain heights to be scanned, and depths to be explored, facts to be weighed, and wonders to be admired."[4] Such are the treasures of God in Christ! In the incarnate Son and nowhere else we are able to comprehend God as our God and Redeemer.

Do you see the futility of man's misguided search for spiritual substance? What time, energy, money, and, sometimes, life itself are poured into the pursuit of the divine, into yearnings after spiritual reality! How men agonize over what can be known, battling, raging, laboring after truth and reality, and yet remaining fools. The thirst for truth is legitimate, the appetite to know is reasonable, but men apart from and against God are drinking at the wrong fountain:

> Ho, every one that thirsteth, come ye to the waters, and he that hath no money; come ye, buy, and eat; yea, come, buy wine and milk without money and without price. Wherefore do ye spend money for that which is not bread? and your labour for that which satisfieth not? hearken diligently unto me, and eat ye that which is good, and let your soul delight itself in fatness. Incline your ear, and come unto me: hear, and your soul shall live; and I will make an everlasting covenant with you, even the sure mercies of David. (Isa. 55:1–3)

If men would only look to Christ, they would live. Philosophy, psychology, religion, morality—all are in and of themselves empty. A man finds nothing of God until he finds it stored up in Christ. There is no genuine holiness or lasting happiness elsewhere. If you are not yet saved, you will only ever know truth if you cast all else aside and look to Jesus of Nazareth as God's Christ and be saved from your sin, knowing in Him a God who saves sinners.

Christians, too, ought to be awed and overwhelmed by what we have in having Christ. In Him we know God; we have God as our God; we obtain true wisdom and knowledge; we lay hold of divine truth; we come into saving contact with Almighty God. Here in Christ Jesus we find the incarnate Son in whom God is made known for salvation. Having Christ, we have God Himself. We say it is true, but do we live as if it were true? Do we live as if Christ is God and we have come to know Him?

---

4. Ibid., 118.

Here is the root of assurance: it is a firm grasp on the Lord Christ in whom is hidden all these treasures of wisdom and knowledge. It is a true apprehending of Jesus Messiah, who reveals the truth of God and the God of truth, who is the all-sufficient Savior of sinners, the sole source of life and peace. There have been countless errors and heresies that have assaulted Christ's church over the centuries, and the key point—time and again—has been a strike upon Christ Himself. Often that assault is deceptive and persuasive, and so Paul seeks that the saints should have hearts so full of Christ, so taken up with Him, so permeated with the Lord Jesus, that there is no room for anyone or anything else. How we should long for such hearts—hearts strong, knit together in love, and granted all the riches of the full assurance of understanding, having grasped the mystery of God in Christ, in whom are hidden all the treasures of wisdom and knowledge.

That is the battle that Paul is fighting for the Colossians. His heart is fully engaged on behalf of his dearly beloved friends, some of whom he has never seen. Kept from them in body, he marches on to the field of combat on his knees. There, he gets to the heart of the matter—the heart. On his face before God, with sweat on his brow and tears in his eyes, he pleads for their health and happiness. To that end, he develops protective petitions of scope and penetration, weighty and purposeful pleas, and brings them before the throne of grace, seeking that the hearts of the Colossians might be strong, united, and assured, that having received Christ Jesus the Lord, they might walk in Him, "rooted and built up in him, and stablished in the faith" (Col. 2:7). Their hope is bound up in Christ. The better they know Him, the closer they are to Him, the more full they are of Him, the more God will be honored and the more secure they will be in the face of many enemies.

This is the apostle's conflict. This is the conflict of every true shepherd of souls.

FELLOW CHRISTIAN Consider that you have a Great Shepherd who prays for you—Jesus Himself. Whatever else may or may not be true, this you can rely on, that your Great High Priest is interceding for you with the aim of seeing your soul made safe and secure in time and for eternity. That Shepherd and Overseer of your souls might presently have sent to you an undershepherd who—with his heart in tune with the Master's—will likewise enter into combat on your behalf. Let none of us underestimate the unspeakable privilege of having a heavenly Intercessor or neglect the importance of having men on earth who enter the throne room of God, through Jesus Christ, for our sakes.

We urge you to give your pastors no grounds to contend against you, but only for you. If you would benefit from the elders' labors on your behalf, then heed the Word of God: "And we beseech you, brethren, to know them which labour among you, and are over you in the Lord, and admonish you; and to esteem them very highly in love for their work's sake. And be at peace among yourselves" (1 Thess. 5:12–13). "Obey them that have the rule over you, and submit yourselves: for they watch for your souls, as they that must give account, that they may do it with joy, and not with grief: for that is unprofitable for you" (Heb. 13:17).

This is not a plea for unthinking following of or slavish obedience to mere men, but for an intelligent, humble recognition of the men whom Christ Himself has appointed and equipped and whom a church of Christ has recognized as overseers of His flock. Let your pastors give their energies for you, not against you.

Furthermore, are you fighting alongside them with the same aims in view? Do you pray like Paul and your elders for the church of which God has made you a part? Every Christian needs to get to the heart in prayer. Are you persuaded of the vital importance of a strong, united, and assured heart, both for yourself and for the members of your church? If you are, you will be pleading for it, for yourself and others, and cultivating it, individually and corporately, lest the devil find a means by which to divide you. You will do all that lies in your power to put to death those sins that particularly offend and grieve the Holy Spirit and to promote an environment in which deep heart-dealings between brothers and sisters in Christ are the norm and not the exception. For example, we must ask ourselves: "Do I struggle in the giving or receiving of Christian love? Am I serving the strengthening of my brothers? Am I failing to do so because of a spirit of pride in me that cuts me off from others—that isolating attitude that rages against wise judgment because it seeks its own desire and will therefore listen only to its own voice (Prov. 18:1)?"

Do you have anything of Paul's concern for the body of Christ at large? Not being apostles, we cannot write or visit as he did. However, we can pray, and we can communicate that we are praying. In this matter, Paul remains a model for us. He shows us that we can and should enter into the trials and travails of churches and Christians even if we have never seen them in the flesh. We must stir up our souls to pray, ensuring that our prayers are not mere lists of names and details, parading degrees of personal knowledge.

We might have heard people pray who can list every country on a particular continent and do so at great and wearying length. We may have heard the prayers of a gentleman who has recently visited a congregation, or who has memorized the names of her elders and deacons, and insists on incidentally regaling those who are forced to sit through his prayers with the tale of all that has been happening, with details that are irrelevant or with names that no one knows and will not remember. Under such circumstances, one is put in mind of the anecdote concerning the man who was praying interminably in a prayer meeting over which Charles Spurgeon was presiding. Wearied by the man's meanderings, he apparently informed those gathered that while Mr. So-and-So finished his prayer, the rest of the congregation would sing a hymn! Such empty verbiage is hard for others to enter into.

What we need to pursue, and what Paul demonstrates, are significant petitions of a wide and well-instructed kind for the well-being of souls. As Matthew Henry said, "We may keep up a communion by faith, hope, and holy love, even with those churches and fellow-christians of whom we have no personal knowledge, and with whom we have no conversation. We can think, and pray, and be concerned for one another, at the greatest distance; and those we never saw in the flesh we may hope to meet in heaven."[5] Are you, then, using scriptural models, concepts, and words to frame your prayers, getting beyond the shallows and plunging into the deeps of biblical prayer?[6]

If you are looking for a church in which you will know the care of a Christlike man or seeking such men for the office of elder in your present congregation, his prayers will tell you much about him. Of course you cannot hear his private prayers, but his public prayers will give you some sense of the overflow of his private wrestling with God.

Does his heart spill over with biblically informed richness when he intercedes with God? Ask him, and expect a faithful man to confess quickly that he does not pray as he wishes, as he should, or as he might. Ask him what he considers to be his priorities in prayer. Ask him what the deepest desires of his heart are for the people of God. Ask him to explain the nature of pastoral prayer. Listen to

---

5. Matthew Henry, *Commentary on the Whole Bible: Acts to Revelation* (Peabody, MA: Hendrickson, 1991), 6:609.

6. Resources that might help include Matthew Henry's *A Method for Prayer*; D. A. Carson's *A Call to Spiritual Reformation: Priorities from Paul and His Prayers*; Gardiner Spring's *The Mercy Seat*; some of the Puritans on the Lord's Prayer, such as Thomas Watson and Thomas Manton, and Puritan works on prayer generally; A. W. Pink, *Gleanings from Paul: The Prayers of the Apostle*; and C. H. Spurgeon's recorded prayers, *The Pastor in Prayer*. Many others might be suggested. Some of these are available online.

his answers to discern whether this man understands his responsibilities to labor in prayer for the saints of God.

Get a sense of his general attitude to pastoral labor. We are not suggesting that you need a man who gets into the pulpit each week mentally clad in combat fatigues and carrying a bazooka and whose idea of pastoral casuistry bears close relation to the tactics of a tank battle. A merely militant mindset is not a requirement for pastoral ministry. At the same time, you want a shepherd who, like David, like Christ, is willing to stand up against the bear and the lion in order to deliver the lambs of the flock. You need a man who knows his weapons of spiritual warfare and is neither slow nor ashamed in the employment of them. You need a man who appreciates what is at stake and recognizes that he is Christ's enlisted man to fight for the glory of his King and the good of the kingdom. The effeminate soul will refuse this; the lazy man will reject it; the carnal man will rebel against it. You need a good soldier of Christ who will strive on your behalf because of a profound attachment to Jesus and His people because he is fighting to love you, and then fighting for you because he loves you. Seek such men.

Furthermore, pray for such men. Pray that God will raise them up, and then pray for those whom God has raised up. Your pastors are soldiers, and soldiers train hard, work vigorously, take risks, receive injuries, and become weary. This man is going into battle for you, employing all legitimate means to secure your eternal well-being. Remember his conflict; pray for him, as he prays for you. Provide for him, and encourage him to take necessary recuperation (breaks and holidays); necessary medicines (food for his own soul); necessary training (conferences and fraternals); necessary weapons (the best books); and necessary companionship (friendships with other men of God of similar spirit, both mentors and peers, and your own friendship as a "brother, and companion in labour, and fellowsoldier" [Phil. 2:25]). These things will help to keep those who watch out for your souls in a healthy, alert, fit condition, ready to serve you and—in serving you—to serve Christ the King.

FELLOW PASTOR Reckon with the fact that your service for Christ and His church deserves the name "agony." Paul, looking back on his ministerial life, made plain his sense of this: "For I am now ready to be offered, and the time of my departure is at hand. I have fought a good fight, I have finished my course, I have kept the faith: henceforth there is laid up for me a crown of righteousness, which the Lord, the righteous judge, shall give me at that day: and not to me only, but unto all them also that love his appearing" (2 Tim. 4:6–8).

Remember your calling. Consider yourself an enlisted man: "Thou therefore endure hardness, as a good soldier of Jesus Christ. No man that warreth entangleth himself with the affairs of this life; that he may please him who hath chosen him to be a soldier. And if a man also strive for masteries, yet is he not crowned, except he strive lawfully" (2 Tim. 2:3–5).

If you are not willing or able to engage accordingly then, in all frankness, perhaps you should resign your commission. Cultivate this spirit as you legitimately can. Cultivate it in the whole man. Learn what it means to strive in the pursuit of victory from reasonable sources, and emulate that spirit. If need be, take time to read a little credible and competent military history. As we have suggested before, read the records of feats of heroic effort and endurance. If you are able, get out on the road or into the gym or, better, the competitive sports arena, even if that means only an occasional contest with a friend. Get a sense, a taste, from life in the world if nowhere else, of the nature of conflict and the pursuit of victory, and let that sense bleed through your whole redeemed humanity. Remember whose you are and whom you serve and to what end. Cultivate a godly, martial spirit, a genuinely masculine attitude to the fight of faith.

Remember your goals: a strong, united, assured church, a people whose hearts are rooted and grounded in Christ. Do not drop your gaze. Do not exchange your target for something shallow or misguided, but maintain the highest hope. Aim where your Bible points you. Do not become content with the norm. Do not sit back and accept the status quo. Strive for the good of the church and the glory of her crowned Head.

Remember your weapons. Employ all scripturally legitimate means to accomplish your ends, and remember the place of prayer above all, "praying always with all prayer and supplication in the Spirit, and watching thereunto with all perseverance and supplication for all saints" (Eph. 6:18). Without God's blessing obtained through prayer, all your other striving will come to nothing. Thomas Murphy points out:

> Above all other Christians, the pastor must be a man of prayer. All others need to be daily at the throne of grace, but he more. He has to do with such purely spiritual things that nothing but the Spirit can qualify him for his exalted work. In the cause committed to him such tremendous interests are involved that he needs constant guidance from on high. Of himself how can he reach such hard and impenitent hearts as he has to do with? His vocation requires him to stand so near to God that he must have the purifying of the Holy Spirit for that awful presence. It is his to intercede for others as well as to pray for himself, and how can he do

that unless he has the aid of that Intercessor who inspires groanings that cannot be uttered? Eminently is he to be a temple of the Holy Ghost; oh how holy, how holy doth it become him to be! Even Christ, the divine Shepherd, spent whole nights in prayer; how much more do those who are mere men, though in the most sacred office, need to tarry long, long in that exercise! Among other ends he had in view in praying so often, and in causing that fact to be recorded, did he not intend to set an example to his undershepherds in all time? Ah, prayer should be their daily breath. Emphatically should it be true of them that they "pray always."[7]

Do you expect to lie on your deathbed, and—if opportunity is given to you for reflection on your life—to voice the regret, "I spent too much time in prayer"? Will you complain, as the curtain comes down on the brief scene of your life, that you gave too much thought and energy to pleading with God for a blessing upon His people, and your labors among them? You may not kneel in prayer as John Welch did, but, if you did, what tale would your knees and the spot where you kneel tell of the time and effort poured out on behalf of the saints of Christ Jesus? We, especially, must furnish our minds and hearts with scriptural models, concepts and words to frame your prayers.[8] We must plead God's promises back to Him, framing our ardent desires with those words and phrases that the Lord Himself has given us as the best and clearest expressions of His will and intent.

Remember your people, those for whom you strive. Show no favoritism among them in your prayers. If anything, make prayer one of those rare occasions on which you practice positive discrimination, and pray most for those whom you find hardest or know to be most troublesome. Plead for God's richest blessings upon the heads of those who make your life the most difficult, whose sins are most aggravating and annoying. This will stir up love, for you will find it almost impossible to have a hard heart towards those for whom you pray in such a fashion. At the same time, do not overlook any member of the flock. Again, it is too easy for the overseers to concentrate on the hard cases and leave the healthy to take care of themselves. Generally, that will result in unhealthiness across the board. Pastors ought to be as much affected by the condition of the flock as they are by their own well-being: "And I will very gladly spend and be spent for you; though the more abundantly I love you, the less I be loved" (2 Cor. 12:15).

---

7. Thomas Murphy, *Pastoral Theology: The Pastor in the Various Duties of His Office* (Audubon, NJ: Old Paths Publications, 1996), 69–70.

8. See footnote 6 for a list of helpful resources.

Do not be afraid to show your heart to God's people. It is good for them to know something of the general and particular labors of God's undershepherds on their behalf. They will derive benefit, not least in coming to appreciate what they receive from you. Do not be afraid to tell them that you care for them and how that compassion and affection work themselves out. Speak it and show it, not only in your prayers, but in your questions, your interactions, your service, with the look in your eyes and the tone of your voice, in the things that you say and do, as well as in the things that you refrain from saying and doing. Let none of the sheep doubt that what you do is done out of love for their souls and a concern for Christ's glory.

Remember your destiny. First the cross, then the crown: "For I reckon that the sufferings of this present time are not worthy to be compared with the glory which shall be revealed in us" (Rom. 8:18). When the fight is hard, when the race is long, when the faith that you hold to and preach is a matter of contention and an occasion for combat, remember the reward: "Henceforth there is laid up for me a crown of righteousness, which the Lord, the righteous judge, shall give me at that day: and not to me only, but unto all them also that love his appearing" (2 Tim. 4:8). Now you must fight, but then you shall rest. After the conflict, peace.

Above and before all, remember your Savior. It is He who has called you to this conflict, and He will sustain you in it. Like all good leaders, He expects nothing of you that He has not already embraced for Himself:

> Wherefore seeing we also are compassed about with so great a cloud of witnesses, let us lay aside every weight, and the sin which doth so easily beset us, and let us run with patience the race that is set before us, looking unto Jesus the author and finisher of our faith; who for the joy that was set before him endured the cross, despising the shame, and is set down at the right hand of the throne of God. For consider him that endured such contradiction of sinners against himself, lest ye be wearied and faint in your minds. Ye have not yet resisted unto blood, striving against sin. (Heb. 12:1–4)

Do they hate you? They hated Him first, and without a cause (Ps. 35:19). Do they crucify you—even metaphorically—as despised servants of God? They crucified Him, the Lord of glory (1 Cor. 2:8).

> If the world hate you, ye know that it hated me before it hated you. If ye were of the world, the world would love his own: but because ye are not of the world, but I have chosen you out of the world, therefore the world hateth you. Remember the word that I said unto you, The servant is not greater than his lord. If they have persecuted me, they will also persecute you; if they have kept my saying, they will keep yours also. But all these

things will they do unto you for my name's sake, because they know not
him that sent me. (John 15:18–21)

Keep Christ before your own eyes, and you will be able to keep Him before
the eyes of the saints. It is Jesus that the people of God need. They need to be
close to His side, that they may be strong. They need to understand themselves
as part of His body, that they may be united. They need to learn the unsearchable
riches that are in Him, those treasures of wisdom and knowledge: they need to
see the glory of God shining in the face of Jesus Christ. This is the crying need
of Christ's people: more of Christ—more of His surpassing excellence, more
of His majesty and glory, more of His perfection and power, more of His love
and compassion. Hold Christ before yourself and others in order that all the
wonders of the salvation that God has accomplished in Him might be known
and felt in ever increasing measure, and they might be able to stand in the evil
day, holding fast to Christ and held fast by Christ.

In such a battle, you are in good company—the best company. You walk with
Christ and with those who have walked with Him in past times. The preacher
Rowland Hill, considered by some to be "the second Whitefield," exhorted
himself and his fellow laborers in this way:

> Lo! round the throne, a glorious band,
> The saints in countless myriads stand,
> Of every tongue redeemed to God,
> Arrayed in garments washed in blood.
>
> Through tribulation great they came;
> They bore the cross, despised the shame;
> From all their labors now they rest,
> In God's eternal glory blest.
>
> They see their Savior face to face,
> And sing the triumphs of His grace;
> Him day and night they ceaseless praise,
> To Him the loud thanksgiving raise:
>
> "Worthy the Lamb, for sinners slain,
> Through endless years to live and reign;
> Thou hast redeemed us by Thy blood,
> And made us kings and priests to God."
>
> O may we tread the sacred road
> That saints and holy martyrs trod;
> Wage to the end the glorious strife,
> And win, like them, a crown of life.

10 THE WARNINGS OF PAUL'S MINISTRY

And this I say, lest any man should beguile you with
enticing words. For though I be absent in the flesh, yet
am I with you in the spirit, joying and beholding your
order, and the stedfastness of your faith in Christ.
— COLOSSIANS 2:4–5

This is by no means the first time the Truth War has intruded into the
church. It has happened in every major era of church history. Battles over
the truth were raging inside the Christian community even in apostolic
times, when the church was just beginning. In fact, the record of Scripture
indicates that false teachers in the church immediately became a significant
and widespread problem wherever the gospel went. Virtually all of the
major epistles in the New Testament address the problem one way or
another. The apostle Paul was constantly engaged in battle against the lies
of "false apostles [and] deceitful workers [who transformed] themselves
into apostles of Christ" (2 Corinthians 11:13). Paul said that was to
be expected. It is, after all, one of the favorite strategies of the evil one:
"No wonder! For Satan himself transforms himself into an angel of light.
Therefore it is no great thing if his ministers also transform themselves
into ministers of righteousness" (vv. 14–15).[1] — JOHN MACARTHUR

Deception is equally revolting whether we are deceiving or being deceived. Every lie is an affront to the God who has made us, because it goes against the very being of the God who delights to describe Himself as "the LORD, The LORD God, merciful and gracious, longsuffering, and abundant in goodness and truth" (Ex. 34:6); the "God of truth and without iniquity" (Deut. 32:4). When Christ came to make God known, He came full of grace and truth (John 1:14). God's Spirit is the Spirit of truth (John 14:17). Deception is contrary to everything

---

1. John MacArthur, *The Truth War* (Nashville: Thomas Nelson, 2007), 23.

God calls His people to be as speakers and doers of truth: the one who dwells with God is the one who speaks the truth in his heart (Ps. 15:2). Lying goes against the grain of everything the Lord delights in, for He desires truth in the inward parts (Ps. 51:6).

The devil—the prime adversary of God and of His people—is the master deceiver. He is a malevolent fraudster and a deadly imposter. Deception is one of the main strategies that he employs as he seeks to lead people away from the truth of God.

His character and conduct are seen throughout Scripture, even from the beginning. The serpent is described as "more subtil [literally, crafty, cunning, or sly] than any beast of the field which the LORD God had made" (Gen. 3:1), and it was through the serpent that the devil worked to deceive the woman. Commenting on the tragic events that followed, Paul writes that "Adam was not deceived, but the woman being deceived was in the transgression" (1 Tim. 2:14). Satan's deceit lay at the root of Eve's sin and Adam's subsequent fall. Again, Paul could warn the Corinthian church, "But I fear, lest by any means, as the serpent beguiled Eve through his subtilty, so your minds should be corrupted from the simplicity that is in Christ" (2 Cor. 11:3).

In Isaiah 14 the prophet describes God's judgment on the king of Babylon. The language employed may have some secondary reference to the devil.[2] In what could be a description that casts some dark light on the character of the adversary, we read of self-deception: "How art thou fallen from heaven, O Lucifer, son of the morning! how art thou cut down to the ground, which didst weaken the nations! For thou hast said in thine heart, I will ascend into heaven, I will exalt my throne above the stars of God: I will sit also upon the mount of the congregation, in the sides of the north: I will ascend above the heights of the clouds; I will be like the most High" (Isa. 14:12–14).

We have another, more definite description in John 8:44, where, in debating the Jewish leaders of His day, our Lord Jesus says, "Ye are of your father the devil, and the lusts of your father ye will do. He was a murderer from the beginning, and abode not in the truth, because there is no truth in him. When he speaketh a lie, he speaketh of his own: for he is a liar, and the father of it." This description is echoed in the book of the Revelation, where the apostle John describes the devil as the one who deceives the "whole world" (Rev. 12:9) and the "nations" (Rev. 20:3).

---

2. Wayne Grudem, *Systematic Theology* (Grand Rapids: Zondervan, 1994), 413. Ezekiel 28:12–19 has been viewed in this manner as well.

In Acts 5 we have a sad account of the deceit and dishonesty of Ananias and his wife Sapphira. Upon selling a piece of property, Ananias—with his wife's connivance—intentionally gave the appearance of having generously contributed all the proceeds of the sale to the common good of the early church, while he actually brought only a portion of the money to the apostles, keeping the balance for himself (Acts 5:2). Of course, both Ananias and Sapphira were responsible for their sin. They could not simply excuse themselves and say, "The devil made me do it." Nonetheless, the inspired record tells us that the devil had a hand in bringing about this evil, for Peter could ask, "Ananias, why hath Satan filled thine heart to lie to the Holy Ghost, and to keep back part of the price of the land?" (v. 3).

In addition to his direct influences and demonic minions, Satan enjoys the help of human dupes who either knowingly or unknowingly do his bidding, having been taken captive by him (2 Tim. 2:24–26). The Puritan Thomas Brooks said of such individuals that they seduce people and "carry them out of the right way into by-paths and blind thickets of error, blasphemy, and wickedness, where they are lost forever."[3]

The Bible describes satanically misguided and malicious people in stinging language, calling them "natural brute beasts" (2 Peter 2:12) and "wells without water, clouds that are carried with a tempest; to whom the mist of darkness is reserved for ever" (2 Peter 2:17). Elsewhere they are identified as "men of corrupt minds, reprobate concerning the faith" (2 Tim. 3:8); "deceivers [who] are entered into the world" (2 John 7); those who "serve not our Lord Jesus Christ, but their own belly; and by good words and fair speeches deceive the hearts of the simple" (Rom. 16:18); and "clouds they are without water, carried about of winds; trees whose fruit withereth, without fruit, twice dead, plucked up by the roots" (Jude 12–13). The seriousness of deception is underlined by the fact that twice the Bible warns of the most fearful judgments reserved for the liar. Our Lord Jesus describes these ministers of unrighteousness as "ravening wolves" (Matt. 7:15), warning of those who will "deceive many" (Matt. 24:5, 11) and labeling them "false Christs, and false prophets" (Matt. 24:24).

The Colossian church had such malicious deceivers at work in their midst, sowing the seeds of untruth. Because of the lie's nature, no parade announced its arrival. The message did not come with alarm bells sounding and warning whistles blowing. Rather, it came cloaked and concealed. The message was not a direct frontal attack on the truth, but a covert assault.

---

3. Thomas Brooks, *Precious Remedies against Satan's Devices* (Edinburgh: Banner of Truth, 1984), 230.

As with most successful frauds, the false teachers in Colosse traded in what appeared to be genuine. Their message seemed and even sounded biblical, but the spiritual food they offered was laced with toxins. The bottle was labeled "medicine" but contained poison. This demonic message subtly but definitely devalued the glory, majesty, supremacy, centrality, and sufficiency of Jesus our Lord as the sole provider of our salvation, pointing elsewhere for the spiritual blessings that are connected to Him alone.

The Colossian church was hearing the whisper, "Christ is not enough." Christ was good, to be sure, but He did not have in Himself all saving fullness. The Colossians were told that they needed something more in order to be full, other religious helps beyond Jesus. (Paul deals with some of these in Colossians 2:16–23.)

In contrast to the false teachers, the apostle Paul taught that Christ alone was completely sufficient for the Christian. The Christian life is not a process of adding to Christ, but a matter of appropriating what we already possess in Him.[4] In Jesus, we are complete (Col. 2:10), and Paul wrote this letter largely as the antidote to deceptive and profoundly dangerous denials of Jesus.

Paul's polemic

In these verses Paul makes his first direct attack against the errorists who were plaguing this church. What was before implied is now plainly expressed: "And this I say, lest any man should beguile you with enticing words" (Col. 2:4).

Paul's language is definite and vigorous: he has lifted Christ up before them as the repository of all wisdom and knowledge. He has done this, to put it literally, "for the [definite] purpose that no one may deceive you with persuasive words." That is, Paul has described Jesus positively in order to ensure that these believers will be fortified in their faith and not deceived into looking to anyone or anything else to give them spiritual blessings and joy. Paul is emphatic: "*all* the treasures of wisdom and knowledge" (Col. 2:3). There is not one hint of anything that we need as God's people that is to be found outside of our Savior. All that we need for life and salvation, every drop of what God Himself intends to give us, is bound up in Jesus Christ our Lord.

Paul's warning springs out of his concern for the well-being of these saints. He is providing the reason why, up to this point in the letter, he has spent so much

---

4. Warren Wiersbe uses this helpful terminology in his *Bible Exposition Commentary* (Wheaton, IL: Victor Books, 1989), 2:154.

time and energy exalting the Lord Christ and assuring them of his strong desire for them to possess strong, united, assured hearts.

Paul's warning does not follow a wild harangue or a cold silence but rides on the back of a warm greeting and earnest prayer and is carried on a wave of pastoral affection. Just as we receive warnings about hell and cries to flee from the wrath to come most readily from those whom we know have our best interests at heart, so pastoral warning is most effective in the context of warm affection. What a stranger could not say a friend can easily speak, for the relationship bears it and, indeed, opens a way for the warning or admonition. Paul can put these believers on their guard because he has demonstrated his concern in his earnest pursuit of their spiritual health (Col. 1:9–12; 1:28–2:2). He has shown it in his joy at every evidence of grace among them (Col. 1:4, 24, 27; 2:5). It is seen in his felt fellowship with them in Christ Jesus (Col. 1:24; 2:5). By these means he has opened a door into their hearts.

It is worth noting that Paul identifies these Christians as essentially healthy. They are presently "in the faith" (Col. 1:23), and they manifest good order and steadfastness in that faith (Col. 2:5). He writes to them with the wolves of error pawing at the door of the church in order that they might not let them in. He wants them to be persuaded of the sufficiency of Jesus, and not led away by counterfeits. His vigorous language is designed to put them on their guard. He uses similar vocabulary in verse 8, writing, "Beware lest any man spoil you through philosophy and vain deceit, after the tradition of men, after the rudiments of the world, and not after Christ." He is urging them to keep a watchful eye open for those who would cheat them.

In other words, though they presently stand firm, there is a danger to their souls. The assault on their faith has begun, and it will be insistent. Their faith—though now stable—will require ongoing support, encouragement, and reinforcement if they are not to be deceived with "enticing words."

This deception is essentially delusion by means of false reasoning, leading astray by means of plausible words. Literally, the sense of *beguile* in this verse is "to reason alongside of." This is how the false teachers of Colosse operated, and how false teaching usually proceeds. Incorrect notions are brought in alongside the truth concerning Christ, and lies slowly infiltrate the church.

Some who seek to deceive simply hate the truth and try to drive us from it. Others actually believe the lie, worshiping the creature rather than the Creator (Rom. 1:25; 2 Thess. 2:11), and—with absolute but fundamentally flawed sincerity—would draw the saints from the truth as it is in Jesus. However, there is a sense in which all deceit is deliberate, for it is the product of Satan, a liar and the father of it (John 8:44). His malice lies behind all lies, for he knows and hates the truth and will do all that he can to drive or draw us from it.

Enticing or persuasive words have been the devil's modus operandi from the beginning (2 Cor. 11:3)—the pattern of behavior revealing that the master criminal is again at work. Recall how he used seductive and devious speech through the serpent in the garden of Eden: "Yea, hath God said, Ye shall not eat of every tree of the garden?" (Gen. 3:1). See how the devil undermines the truth of God, misquoting the Creator and sowing disbelief in Eve's thinking about God's promises and warnings. Then, said the deceiver, once the foundations of his lie had been laid in doubt and shadows, "Ye shall not surely die" (v. 4), contradicting the very essence of God's plain speech. His words gradually entangled Eve in a web of lies, and soon she was utterly captured, with eternally devastating results. He twisted God's Word again when he tempted our Lord, claiming that God's angels would keep Christ in all His ways, bearing Him up in their hands lest He dash His foot against a stone, but simply glossing over the vital qualifying statement that such protection is for the man who has made God his refuge with genuine and humble faith in the path of duty—not the man who is testing God by leaping from temples (cf. Matt. 4:6 with Ps. 91:11–12).

False teachers operate much like their master. They will misrepresent the character of God and undermine His revelation. Like their spiritual father, they will strike at Christ the revealer of God, assaulting the very mystery that God has been pleased to reveal: "Who is a liar but he that denieth that Jesus is the Christ?" (1 John 2:22). Deceit will strike at the sufficiency of Jesus as Savior and Sanctifier, at His supremacy, centrality, and exclusivity. It will assail Him as Lord and as Christ. Where outright assault will not work, Satan and his minions will teach men to devalue, degrade, and ultimately despise Christ. The whisper will go up, "Christ is not enough!" and the result will be devastating.

That Prince of Puritans, John Owen, warned about this very approach when he commented on Matthew 16:18, asserting that Christ Himself is the rock upon which the church is built. This, he said, is why Satan always strikes at the foundation—the person and work of Jesus:

> For…the power and policy of Hell ever were, and ever will be, engaged in opposition unto the church built on this foundation—that is, the faith of it concerning his person, office, and grace, whereby it is built on him. This, as unto what is past, concerneth matter of fact, whereof, therefore, I must give a brief account; and then we shall examine what evidences we have of the same endeavour at present.

The gates of Hell, as all agree, are the power and policy of it, or the actings of Satan, both as a lion and as a serpent, by rage and by subtlety. But whereas in these things he acts not visibly in his own person, but by his agents, he hath always had two sorts of them employed in his service. By the one he executes his rage, and by the other his craft; he animates the one as a lion, the other as a serpent. In the one he acts as the dragon, in the other as the beast that had two horns like the lamb, but spake like the dragon. The first is the unbelieving world; the other, apostates and seducers of all sorts. Wherefore, this work in this kind is of a double nature;—the one, an effect of his power and rage, acted by the world in persecution—the other, of his policy and craft, acted by heretics in seduction. In both he designs to separate the church from its foundation.[5]

If he could, Satan would rip the church from her moorings. How sad and terrible that such lies should be so easily and so readily believed! Words are a powerful medium for error as well as for truth, and they were the weapons with which the false teachers assaulted the church. Paul warned the Colossians that what some men said and how they said it would be the mechanism used to lure them away from the Savior in whom they had believed. The words would be plausible, the concepts would sound right on the surface, the notions would appear familiar, the ideas would not seem so far from the truth, but the effect would be deadly.

To reason so as to prove something likely or probable is not in itself an illegitimate skill, but it can be fatal when abused. We sometimes speak of "talking someone round," persuading him from one opinion to another. The Colossians were in danger of being talked round by a plausible falsehood. Deceit will not stride up and slap the church in the face to alert her to its presence; it will sidle up, link arms, fall in step, and begin to whisper and cajole. Satan did not immediately accuse God to Eve: "He is a liar—ignore Him! Do what you want, not what God says!" Rather, he sowed those seeds of unbelief and rebellion subtly and seductively. Smooth words and flattering speech are readily employed to deceive the hearts of the unsuspecting or naïve (Rom. 16:18). Deceit deals in flattery and sophistry; it offers something allegedly deeper and purer; it says it can make plain what is hard or hidden; it plays on our weaknesses; it shifts the emphasis slightly and throws the whole system out of kilter. It is devastating not simply because it is deceit as such, but because it is enticing, attractive, persuasive. An obvious lie is easily rebuffed, but something that seems plausible is more dangerous—this is

5. John Owen, *Works* (Edinburgh: Banner of Truth, 1965), 1:35–36.

the "cunning craftiness, whereby [wicked men] lie in wait to deceive" (Eph. 4:14). A deceiver will use spiritual, religious, or even Christian terminology (without true Christian meaning) to pull the wool over your eyes, reasoning you from truth and toward error.

These enemies of the cross in Colosse were fast talkers and smooth speakers, perhaps flatterers. They sounded intelligent and insightful. Possibly they cultivated an impressive aura of otherworldliness. In rich and somber tones they presented imposing and fine-sounding arguments to these Christians. They did not begin by urging them to forget Jesus. They gently suggested that perhaps the time had come to supplement Jesus. They did not first despise Him in order to dethrone Him; rather they began by subtly devaluing and degrading Him. They turned the eye of faith from Christ by degrees.

God also warns His people in the Old Testament against the words of false teachers. In Jeremiah 23:16 we read, "Thus saith the LORD of hosts, Hearken not unto the words of the prophets that prophesy unto you: they make you vain: they speak a vision of their own heart, and not out of the mouth of the LORD."

Our Lord Jesus issued statements of precisely the same kind, warning His disciples against the hypocritical religious leaders of His day: "Take heed and beware of the leaven of the Pharisees and of the Sadducees" (Matt. 16:6). With regard to His return, Jesus again explicitly and bluntly warned of a flood of lies: "Take heed lest any man deceive you: for many shall come in my name, saying, I am Christ; and shall deceive many" (Mark 13:5–6).

Like his Savior, the apostle Paul could not neglect the danger of deceit. To sit back and do nothing was not an option. Accordingly, he sought to alert the churches that no one should deceive them. He was ready to sound the alarm when danger was at hand, naming names when necessary and appropriate:

> Take heed therefore unto yourselves, and to all the flock, over the which the Holy Ghost hath made you overseers, to feed the church of God, which he hath purchased with his own blood. For I know this, that after my departing shall grievous wolves enter in among you, not sparing the flock. Also of your own selves shall men arise, speaking perverse things, to draw away disciples after them. Therefore watch, and remember, that by the space of three years I ceased not to warn every one night and day with tears. (Acts 20:28–31)

> Beware of dogs, beware of evil workers, beware of the concision. (Phil. 3:2)

Alexander the coppersmith did me much evil: the Lord reward him according to his works: of whom be thou ware also; for he hath greatly withstood our words. (2 Tim. 4:14–15)

The apostle Peter likewise warns of the deception that comes from the mouths of false teachers. In 2 Peter 2:3 he writes, "Through covetousness shall they with feigned words make merchandise of you: whose judgment now of a long time lingereth not, and their damnation slumbereth not." Again he warns, "When they speak great swelling words of vanity, they allure through the lusts of the flesh, through much wantonness, those that were clean escaped from them who live in error" (2 Peter 2:18).

Why so many warnings? Because of so many dangers, toils, and snares through which we must go in order to reach glory. Fraud, as John Owen noted, is one of Satan's two primary weapons against the church, so we find it often employed in a variety of ways and contexts.

But we might also ask, "Why was Paul so earnest in his language to these believers against the errorists and their message? Why such straight talk and sober admonition? Is there really so much at stake?"

Absolutely! With some, to be sure, the entrance of deceivers and their lies will simply reveal the emptiness of their profession as they are drawn away. Paul warns Timothy against Hymenaeus, Alexander, and Philetus, who seem to fall into this category, carrying others with them in their descent into darkness:

This charge I commit unto thee, son Timothy, according to the prophecies which went before on thee, that thou by them mightest war a good warfare; holding faith, and a good conscience; which some having put away concerning faith have made shipwreck: of whom is Hymenaeus and Alexander; whom I have delivered unto Satan, that they may learn not to blaspheme. (1 Tim. 1:18–20)

But shun profane and vain babblings: for they will increase unto more ungodliness. And their word will eat as doth a canker: of whom is Hymenaeus and Philetus; who concerning the truth have erred, saying that the resurrection is past already; and overthrow the faith of some. (2 Tim. 2:16–18)

A fellow university student in the United Kingdom, a young man, made a bold profession of faith and was the boast of some in the church. He seemed to make rapid progress and had a vocal and energetic testimony. He began to attend "Bible studies" run by a man in the city and lapped up the teaching he received. Before long, he was—with much zeal and utter commitment—seeking to persuade all who would hear him that Jesus was not truly God, even in the face of sober warnings and earnest entreaties from faithful friends. He eventually turned his back on the truths he was hearing from the pulpit and in private and wholly embraced the lie. Let us not, then, imagine that these are ancient problems. The false teachers are still with us, still breeding error, and still dangerous to the souls of men.

But the saints are also in danger. To be sure, the Lord Jesus warns, "There shall arise false Christs, and false prophets, and shall shew great signs and wonders; insomuch that, if it were possible, they shall deceive the very elect" (Matt. 24:24), but such warnings as these are one of the means of keeping true believers to the end. The elect will not be finally deceived, but they might be considerably deadened. To lose sight, even temporarily, of Jesus as He is presented in all His saving fullness in the Word of God will have a debilitating effect on true believers. Insofar as they drift from Christ, so far will there be a corresponding decline in their spiritual vitality. Consider the example of Christmas Evans, one of the great preachers of Welsh church history. Twice during his otherwise fruitful ministry, he was temporarily deceived, once by Sandemanianism[6] and once by hyper-Calvinism.[7] Even a brief departure in degree from the truth as it is in Jesus produced in him a corresponding and profound declension of soul. He wrote of his experience with Sandemanianism in these terms:

> The Sandemanian heresy affected me so much as to drive away the spirit of prayer for the salvation of sinners. The lighter matters of the kingdom of God pressed heavier upon my mind than the weightier. The power which gave me zeal and confidence and earnestness in the pulpit for the conversion of souls to Christ was lost. My heart sank within me, and I lost the witness of a good conscience. On Sunday night, after I had been fiercely and violently condemning errors, my conscience felt ill at ease, and rebuked me because I had lost communion and fellowship with God, and made me feel that something invaluable was now lost and wanting. I would reply that I acted according to the Word. Still it rebuked me, saying that there was something of inestimable value gone.

---

6. Sandemanianism is a heresy that, among other things, perverts the notion of saving faith, making it simply an act of intellectual assent in the divine testimony concerning Christ rather than any heart apprehension and full-orbed trust in Jesus.

7. Hyper-Calvinism is a perversion of the biblical doctrine of God's sovereignty, in which it is argued that since God has chosen His elect and will most assuredly bring them in to His kingdom, there is no need to preach the gospel to the unconverted, or appeal to sinners to repent and believe in Jesus as He is freely offered in the gospel.

To a very great degree had I lost the spirit of prayer, and the spirit of preaching.[8]

God was pleased to use the witness of a man called Thomas Jones and the writings of the Particular Baptist theologian, Andrew Fuller, to turn Evans back toward the truth. Evans's experience of God's reviving his heart is also instructive:

I was weary of a cold heart towards Christ, and his sacrifice and the work of his Spirit—of a cold heart in the pulpit, in secret prayer and in the study. For fifteen years previously, I had felt my heart burning within, as if going to Emmaus with Jesus. On a day ever to be remembered by me, as I was going from Dolgellau to Machynlleth, climbing up towards Cadair Idris, I considered it to be incumbent upon me to pray, however hard I felt in my heart, and however worldly the frame of my spirit was. Having begun in the name of Jesus, I soon felt as it were, the fetters loosening and the old hardness of heart softening, and, as I thought, mountains of frost and snow dissolving and melting within me. This engendered confidence in my soul in the promise of the Holy Spirit. I felt my whole mind relieved from some great bondage: tears flowed copiously and I was constrained to cry out for the gracious visits of God, by restoring to my soul the joys of his salvation;—and that he would visit the churches in Anglesey that were under my care. I embraced in my supplications all the churches of the saints and nearly all the ministries in the Principality by their names. This struggle lasted for three hours; it rose again and again, like one wave after another, or a high flowing tide driven by a strong wind, until my nature became faint by weeping and crying. I resigned myself to Christ, body and soul, gifts and labours—all my life—every day and every hour that remained for me:—and all my cares I committed to Christ. The road was mountainous and lonely, and I was wholly alone, and suffered no interruption in my wrestling with God.

From this time, I was made to expect the goodness of God to churches and to myself. Thus the Lord delivered me and the people of Anglesey from being carried away by the flood of Sandemanianism. In the first religious meetings after this, I felt as if I had been removed from the cold and sterile regions of spiritual frost, into the verdant fields of the divine promises. The former striving with God in prayer, and the longing anxiety for the conversion of sinners, which I had experienced at Lleyn, was now restored. I had a hold of the promises of God.[9]

---

8. Quoted in Tim Shenton, *Christmas Evans: The Life and Times of the One-Eyed Preacher of Wales* (Darlington, UK: Evangelical Press, 2001), 173.

9. Ibid., 179–80.

Christmas Evans did not turn utterly away from Christ. He was restored, yes, but he had been to a degree and for a time sucked in by a lie of Satan, and it crippled him both as a Christian man and as a Christian minister. Notice what he says about the compromised ministry and curtailed zeal that he suffered during this period in which he was turned aside from the truth. As a Christian man he lost his joy and passion, and as a Christian minister he lost his power. Worse, he dishonored God in Christ and preached something less than the good news to sinners whose souls hung in the balance.

What horrors come to pass when Christians and sometimes churches are gripped by error in some form and degree, even if only temporarily! Everything about their life becomes crippled and their testimony to the saving power of God in Christ compromised to the extent that they depart from Him. God is blasphemed, Christ dishonored, and the Spirit grieved, while Satan rejoices, saints are cast down, and unsaved sinners neglected or misdirected as the frosts of heresy and error enter the soul.

Paul could not bear to see this happen. He had already told these believers that his great goal was to "present every man perfect in Christ Jesus." He desired that none should decline and none perish under his care. As a true watchman over God's people, he fervently prayed for them and faithfully sent word cautioning them about the dangers that threatened. He knew that if these Colossians embraced a "Jesus plus" gospel, they would lose all. Paul therefore digs into their hearts and warns them that the deceptive words of false teachers are far from harmless. They are paths to despondency, debility, and declension, and—worse—catalysts for apostasy.

Paul's pleasure

Such an exhortation as the one that Paul had just given might shake the Colossians and cause panic and instability at the very moment at which they need to stand fast. Paul is about to dismantle with the hammer of truth and the crowbar of warning the specific errors and particular dangers that threaten these saints (from Colossians 2:6 onwards). There is some destructive smiting and close cutting to be done. As he comes to that, he again assures these saints of his close attachment to them, giving them a joyful endorsement and vigorous encouragement.

Remember that as Paul writes these words he is sitting in a Roman prison, with Timothy close at hand and probably Epaphras—one of the concerned pastors of the Colossian congregation—nearby: "For though I be absent in the flesh, yet am I with you in the spirit" (Col. 2:5). His words suggest that he is not unwilling to be with them, rather unable. Nevertheless, he assures them that the fellowship he feels with them is not severed by mere geographical distance. Paul, it seems, is conscious of the potential dangers of prolonged physical absence from fellow saints. Some say that absence makes the heart grow fonder. Others, less rosy in their perspective, suggest that absence makes the fond heart wander. Paul fears the latter even while he cultivates the former: prolonged absence gave scope for the insinuations of enemies and the doubts of friends to take root in the heart. Fellowship can be too easily undermined by absence. All Christians should reckon with the difficulty of sustaining healthy relationships with their fellow saints because of prolonged absence; if we are missing from the assemblies of the saints (Heb. 10:25) it ought to be because we are unable, being providentially hindered, and not because we are unwilling, being careless or neglectful.

Even though he is imprisoned so many miles away, he is still with them "in the spirit" (Col. 2:5). This is not some weird and wonderful assertion of astral projection or travel or some kind of alleged psychic phenomenon like extrasensory perception. It is not mysticism, though there is something mystical here. Paul uses similar language in 1 Corinthians 5:3–5 to testify of the same reality: "For I verily, as absent in body, but present in spirit, have judged already, as though I were present, concerning him that hath so done this deed, in the name of our Lord Jesus Christ, when ye are gathered together, and my spirit, with the power of our Lord Jesus Christ, to deliver such an one unto Satan for the destruction of the flesh, that the spirit may be saved in the day of the Lord Jesus."

Although absent in the flesh, he understands their condition, enters into it with them, feels with and for them, and responds to and with them to the particular circumstances they face. How can Paul say this with such certainty?

There are several answers to that question. First, it is because of the truth of their union with Jesus Christ. Paul and the Colossians are together joined to Christ, the head of the church. He is in them all, the hope of glory. This is a living reality rather than a cute idea. We are members of one another (Rom. 12:4–5). There is an undeniable element of shared experience. Second, God's providence and calling have established a particular relationship between Paul and the Colossians: he has a specific stewardship with regard to these saints (Col. 1:25). That does not mean that we can pretend to the same degree and extent of fellow-feeling with all the saints, but—in accordance with God's call and government—there are times when God knits the hearts of people together. Again, there is an accuracy of knowledge. Paul knows some of what has been taking place. He is close to Philemon, probably a member of the church. Onesimus, the runaway slave of his friend Philemon, may be with Paul. It is likely that Epaphras is there too, a concerned overseer who has crossed land and sea in order to seek the apostle's advice. He is not ignorant of their circumstances, has insight into their particular challenges, is aware of their particular dangers, and has a sense of their present blessings. Finally, there is undeniable depth of feeling: the preceding verses of this letter demonstrate an evident intensity in Paul's heart, a deep affection giving rise to penetrating concern. Earnest desires for their well-being spring from a heart knit to theirs.

Now, this being so, we might ask why anyone should bother being part of or attending any local church. Can we not just be present in spirit, perhaps channeled through the Internet or some other medium? Such a question would reveal a dangerous attitude and a fundamentally flawed view of Christ's church. When you are an imprisoned apostle you may argue this way—and not before! We do not reason from exceptions to norms. We must embrace everything that is involved in the new covenant realities of participation in Christ's church. Listening to online sermons, reading blogs, gathering news, but never fully entering into God-ordained community, with all its commitments and comforts, is not an option for most healthy saints.[10] What this example does mean is that there are times when, although physically absent, we can genuinely enter into the life of those whom we love in Christ. For example, a pastor absent because of sickness or some other legitimate duty has the flock in his heart even when they are not under his eye. Charles Spurgeon, during his extended absences due to profound physical sickness, wrote letters and even sermons for the church to receive. Robert Murray M'Cheyne, when conducting a mission to the Jews while recuperating from a grievous illness, wrote pastoral letters to his flock that showed beyond a shadow of doubt where much of his heart's love was directed. Again, there may be times when other members of the church are absent for legitimate business reasons or because of other providential hindrances, times when they enter into the life of the church in spirit, though absent in the flesh. Furthermore, there are sister churches that we know, friends that we have, and fellow saints facing challenges, needs, joys, and trials into which we can enter. We are urged, for example, to "remember them that are in bonds, as bound with them; and them which suffer adversity, as being yourselves also in the body" (Heb. 13:3).

Paul was absent in the flesh, but in spirit he remained intimately near his Colossian brothers and sisters. We must not lose sight of the Christlikeness of

---

10. Soldiers serving on the battlefield, those confined to hospitals or nursing homes, together with others in similarly restrictive situations may legitimately have to suspend some of the elements of life in the body of Christ while under such providentially hindering cir-cumstances.

this attitude. This is the reality of the relationship of union with Christ, the head with the body. Although He is not with us in the flesh, He is always present with us by His Spirit. He has an accuracy of knowledge regarding our experiences that is rooted in His divine omniscience. There is a depth of feeling that transcends every other relationship. How sweet, and how necessary for our comfort and courage, is the fact of Christ's identification and presence with His redeemed people. We read in John's gospel, chapters 13 through 17, an extended treatment of this rich theme. Or again, He tells His church as she sets out to deal with sin that "where two or three are gathered together in my name, there am I in the midst of them" (Matt. 18:20). Again, he confronts Paul before his conversion with this staggering question: "Saul, Saul, why persecutest thou me?" (Acts 9:4). So close is the union between Christ and His people that He can say of good works done to His saints, "Verily I say unto you, Inasmuch as ye have done it unto one of the least of these my brethren, ye have done it unto me" (Matt. 25:40). Paul has already emphasized twice in this letter that Jesus is the head of the body, the church (Col. 1:18, 24). The Lord Christ is with His people always, even to the end of the age (Matt. 28:18-20). This is the privilege of all the saints.

Here, then, is the apostle in his prison. He casts a mental eye over the Colossian congregation and situation as he knows it and as it has been described to him. What does he see?

It is plain that he is looking with an eye without jaundice. Some people can see the dark cloud associated with every silver lining—they zero in on the wrinkle or pimple on an otherwise clear face. They take note of every pothole on a long, straight road. Others gaze on the world through rose-tinted spectacles, blithely and naïvely imagining that there is nothing gloomy or dangerous, and sometimes even re-interpreting reality as they go in order to keep from being disappointed. Paul is sober-minded: he sees things as they are, not as he wishes or fears them to be. He is blind neither to danger nor to sin, but he can also see grace and goodness where it truly exists. He can see faith as well as frailty, advance as well as opposition, and he encourages these saints with what is good and right.

Like one viewing a battle from a distant hill—a great spiritual conflict in which his own soul has a deep investment—he reviews an army under fierce assault but with an unbroken line and with discipline intact. He says, first, that they have "order"—good order. They are like troops drawn up in battle array, perhaps needing to be invigorated by a stout heart (cf. Col. 2:2), but holding the line nevertheless. There are enemy skirmishers out. Here and there the foe probes at the Colossian line, but as yet they are well-organized and holding firm, ready to defend or advance as required. So far this congregation has repulsed the soul-damning doctrines of the heretics, and they remain standing shoulder to shoulder, in unbroken ranks.

Furthermore, he observes the "the stedfastness of your faith in Christ." This has to do with firmness and strength. It is as if Paul commends this army unit for presenting a solid front. They are compact, unyielding, and stable. It is the same word that is used of the anklebones of the man whom Peter healed, recorded in Acts 3:7: "His feet and ankle bones received strength." That is, for the first time since birth, this man was able to stand on his feet without his ankles giving way under him. In the same way, the faith of these Colossians is not giving way under the assaults of their enemies. They are holding fast to Jesus, having a determined adherence to one object, demonstrating an unshaken faith in the unshakeable Christ.

Paul has this congregation in view as he sits imprisoned. He surveys them in his mind, and a broad smile breaks across his face even as a tear springs to his eye. They are holding! The dangers are real, the battle is being joined, but—as yet—there are no significant successes for the enemy. While they are of good order and steadfast faith in Christ Jesus, they cannot be overcome. While they stand firm, while they hold to Christ, while there is a fundamental commitment to God's truth in the face of invading error, Paul can switch his attention in this letter to the enemy forces and turn the full force of his holy rhetoric against them.

No wonder Paul could say he rejoiced! The Colossians had not wavered in their doctrinal integrity and in their commitment to Christ. We read in church history of Polycarp, bishop of Smyrna from the end of the first century and well into the second century. Toward the end of his life, a severe persecution broke out under Emperor Marcus Antoninus, and Polycarp, by now an exceedingly old man, was captured. When the Roman proconsul urged the aged saint to save his life by paying religious homage to Caesar and cursing the name of Jesus Christ, Polycarp listened politely and attentively. Then the committed disciple calmly answered, "Eighty-six years I have been his servant, yet in all this time he has not so much as once hurt me. How then may I blaspheme my King and sovereign Lord, who has thus saved [or preserved] me?"[11]

Threatened once more and pressed to recant, Polycarp nobly stood fast before being burned at the stake for his attachment to the Lord Christ. Like Polycarp who followed them, these Colossians by God's grace were holding firmly to Jesus alone who saved them, even though the enemy would have them bow to and embrace another.

---

11. *Foxe's Book of Martyrs*, ed. A. Clarke (London: Ward, Lock and Co., n.d.), 20.

Here is the ground of genuine ministerial concern and true ministerial joy. Nothing so much engages the heart of a gospel minister as the desire to see Christ's church with unbroken line and intact discipline, holding fast to Jesus Christ. To the Thessalonians Paul could write, "For now we live, if ye stand fast in the Lord" (1 Thess. 3:8). It was life itself to Paul to know that the saints stood fast. He later urged the Thessalonian church to "stand fast, and hold the traditions which ye have been taught, whether by word, or our epistle" (2 Thess. 2:15), and the Philippians were exhorted in similar fashion: "Therefore, my brethren dearly beloved and longed for, my joy and crown, so stand fast in the Lord, my dearly beloved" (Phil. 4:1).

When the battle draws near, the true pastor asks, "Are they ready?" When the battle is joined, he asks, "Do they hold?" To attain and maintain a vital, healthy relationship to Christ is such a man's abiding concern, his gospel obsession. If you hold fast to Christ with strong faith, then whatever comes, you may stand. Lack this, and the least demonstration of enemy power will shake the church. John Calvin put it this way:

> As the contrivances of men have…an appearance of wisdom, the minds of the pious ought to be preoccupied with this persuasion—that the knowledge of Christ is of itself amply sufficient. And, unquestionably, this is the key that can close the door against all base errors. For what is the reason why mankind have involved themselves in so many wicked opinions, in so many idolatries, in so many foolish speculations, but this—that, despising the simplicity of the gospel, they have ventured to aspire higher?[12]

But to whom or what will they aspire? There is nothing and no one higher than Jesus Christ: God has highly exalted Him and given Him the name which is above every name, that at the name of Jesus every knee should bow, of those in heaven, and of those on earth, and of those under the earth, and that every tongue should confess that Jesus Christ is Lord, to the glory of God the Father (Phil. 2:9–11). Christ Jesus is the Son of God's love. He is

> the image of the invisible God, the firstborn of every creature: for by him were all things created, that are in heaven, and that are in earth, visible and invisible, whether they be thrones, or dominions, or principalities, or powers: all things were created by him, and for him: and he is before all things, and by him all things consist. And he is the head of the body,

---

12. John Calvin, *Commentary on the Epistle of Paul to the Colossians* (Grand Rapids: Baker Books, 2003), 175–76.

the church: who is the beginning, the firstborn from the dead; that in all things he might have the preeminence. For it pleased the Father that in him should all fulness dwell; and, having made peace through the blood of his cross, by him to reconcile all things unto himself; by him, I say, whether they be things in earth, or things in heaven. (Col. 1:15–20)

In Him, and only in Him, the Christian is secure, saved and being saved, experiencing heavenly joy in this world, looking with holy anticipation to the blessings that are to come when he partakes of the inheritance of the saints in the light. By Him we are delivered, in Him we live, for Him we exist, and to His glory we must cheerfully consecrate our all, standing fast in Him in good order and holding fast to Him in steadfast faith.

FELLOW CHRISTIAN   Deceit is not merely an ancient problem but a perpetually modern phenomenon; it afflicts every age. How many in our day are in some degree deceived and correspondingly weak, debilitated, and declining in their souls? Why is this? It happens when we have sucked up a persuasive poison that says that Jesus is something other or less than He is in truth. We suspect His unfailing heart of love toward us; we wonder if He can or will keep us to the end; we deny that He demands holiness of us; we make "religion" a supplement to God's grace in salvation; we listen to a world that erodes our conviction in the supernatural, sapping our faith in life and our hope in death; our hearts lose sight of the reality of the risen Jesus at God's right hand in glory, reigning over all things and interceding for us; we fall away from the simplicity of faith. In short, we lose sight of Jesus as He is, the Jesus so magnificently set forth in Colossians 1.

Whether you realize it or not you are in a great spiritual warfare; the battle is hot, and life itself is at stake. The enemy of your soul has had thousands of years to perfect his art and wants to take you captive to his false ways. Even if he cannot finally kill true Christians, he longs to cripple them. He wants to see you stumble and falter; he wants to see the church weak and confused; he wants to see sinners kept from Christ. This being his great desire, he sends false teachers into the fray as one of the primary means of accomplishing his despicable ends: "Be sober, be vigilant; because your adversary the devil, as a roaring lion, walketh about, seeking whom he may devour" (1 Peter 5:8). How can you withstand him and those who work for his cause?

First and foremost, let your heart be fully and firmly attached to Jesus Christ the Lord. The antidote to error is truth. There is no room for a lie in the heart of a man who is taken up with Jesus. There should be no more room on the throne when Christ is seated upon it. There is no corner where darkness can easily dwell when the light of the Spirit is in the soul of a man. Love for the Lord Jesus as He is set before us in the Scriptures will leave no space into which the devil can breathe his lies. When he comes, as he did at the first, and challenges the truth and character of God, we shall be able to point to Jesus our Messiah and declare without doubt, "There is the assured truth of God; there is the revealed character of God; there is all the fullness of God," and send the devil fleeing back to the pit.

Second, you will be much helped in this if you find and enter into the life of a God-honoring, Christ-exalting, Spirit-filled, Bible-preaching, well-balanced, biblically ordered church.[13] Get into a place where the Word of God is faithfully, diligently, clearly, earnestly, plainly, regularly opened up and applied to the souls of men. Find a spiritual home where the rule of learning is precept upon precept, line upon line (Isa. 28:10–13), in which wise exposition and faithful application are the blessed rule and not the happy exception. If you are not hearing and receiving the Word of God into your soul, then you will be an easy target for the devil. The more that you hear and learn the Word of God in truth, the more you will be able to recognize and righteously respond to the counterfeits when they come: "I have written unto you, young men, because ye are strong, and the word of God abideth in you, and ye have overcome the wicked one" (1 John 2:14). Take care not to fall into the foolish individualism of the modern West at this point and imagine that you are an army of one: the church is a body, a unit composed of many members. You will find strength and safety in true Christ-centered, Spirit-indwelt community, not in apparently splendid but actually foolish isolation. In most instances, the soldier who marches into battle alone, no matter how well armed and armored, will very rapidly succumb to the hordes that oppose him.

Third, allied to that, do not neglect the cultivation of personal holiness, for the body is composed of individual members, and the health of each member contributes to the overall health of the body. Therefore, in company with every soldier in the armies of the Lamb, put on daily the whole armor of God. Take up and learn to employ all the appointed means of defense and offense that the Lord of heaven has provided for the church militant. God has not left us to stand relying

---

13. Read the great confessions of faith of the past with regard to the identity and character of the true church of Jesus Christ and diligently compare their teaching with the Scriptures to see from where they draw their foundation stones. In addition, use good books that will help you identify such a church. One recent one is Mark Dever's *Nine Marks of a Healthy Church* (Wheaton, IL: Crossway Books, 2004).

on our native resources against the enemy of our souls. He has provided spiritual equipment to defend against the devil's assaults. Remind yourself of Ephesians 6:10–20 and learn what you have been given and how to use it.[14] Remember that your strength for the fight comes not even from the arms and armor you are given, but from the Lord who gives both spirit for the fight and the means to stand against the foe. Therefore, be much in private prayer and study. Today we often call such worship quiet time, but it would be well with us if were less quiet and more fervent, if it partook more of the character of one of its older names, private devotion. Be much alone with God, looking to Christ in dependence on His Spirit, and searching His truth: "Wherewithal shall a young man cleanse his way? by taking heed thereto according to thy word. With my whole heart have I sought thee: O let me not wander from thy commandments. Thy word have I hid in mine heart, that I might not sin against thee" (Ps. 119:9–11).

Fourth, get to know the men who are leading the church to which you belong or might belong. In al[l ... w]e would urge you to avoid any church that is led by women simply [... He] has not appointed women to be shepherds of His flock (1 Tim. 3:1[...] [su]re also, in this regard, that the church is not led by men who are led [... in]cluding their wives. As appropriate and with graciousness, seek to kn[ow ... (pros)]pective) pastor or pastors. Ask them about their backgrounds and do[ctrinal] beliefs. Ask them about their favorite authors and preachers. Observe them with a gracious caution rather than a suspiciously critical spirit, in order that you might know what manner of men they are, not just in the pulpit but out of it—in their homes, with their wives and families and friends. With whom do they keep company in the world of books and blogs and Websites and magazines and DVDs and newspapers? Jesus says that people will be known by their fruits: be a gracious but insightful fruit inspector. Cultivate a genuinely Berean spirit. Develop the nobility of mind that characterized those believers. Do not set out to be a heresy hunter, smelling error where there is none. Rather, as you hear preaching, receive the Word with all readiness and search the Scriptures daily to find out whether the things you hear are so (Acts 17:11). Brothers and sisters, if you find that the man or men to whom you might, or—fearfully—already have, entrusted your soul under God is sowing seeds of doubt and error, then you must respond in righteousness. Our duty to someone who is straying from the truth (and to others under their influence) is to deal

---

14. There is no more thorough and helpful treatment of this passage than that of the Puritan, William Gurnall, in *The Christian in Complete Armour* (Edinburgh: Banner of Truth, 1964; also available as a modernized abridgement in three volumes).

faithfully with the erring person or people in love. In a healthy situation, there might be scope for this—opportunities for interaction and, if need be, holy confrontation or procedures for church discipline that are open to you. If those avenues are closed off or prove fruitless, then the time has come to flee as if your life depended on it. It does. So do the lives of your family and your friends. You are a sheep in the presence of wolves, and your blessedness and usefulness depend on your escape, for you cannot honor God as you should if you are enmeshed in lies. Be wise, for we are not speaking here of minor differences of opinion (even recognizing that different people will judge minor differences differently). Be gracious, for there is nothing achieved by sinful aggression. Be brave, for you may be called upon to confront that error in some way. Be humble, for you may yet be proved wrong. Be faithful, for you cannot afford to walk in error.

If, on the other hand, you find faithful men full of the Spirit of Christ, diligent in the discharge of their stewardship from God, then esteem them, love them, help them, encourage them, be open to them, and never stop praying for them. There is a real sense in which the shepherds of Christ's flock wear an insignia that marks them out as overseers. In the same way that snipers in combat identify officers by their badges and pick them off first to create disorder and confusion in the ranks, so Satan's snipers will seek to pick off those who wear the insignia of the shepherd, knowing that it is still a functioning principle that if you can strike the shepherd, the sheep will be scattered. Bless God that the Great Shepherd is beyond their reach, but be warned that the undershepherds are exposed still and daily expose themselves by the very nature of the work that they do on the front lines in Christ's great battle with sin in the flesh, in the world, and from the devil.

The devil passionately hates Christ's pastors. If he ca[n] ... he knows that more often than not others will stumble wi[th] ... pastors are marked men. For their sake and for Christ's, daily stand in the gap for them; pray that their faith may not fail them.

For your sake and for Christ's, heed the warnings they see fit to issue. These men are appointed by the Lord Jesus as overseers of His flock. One of their tasks is to identify and keep out or root out error. We do not deny the graces and gifts given to all the people of God, but this is one of the particular duties that devolve upon the elders. They have been particularly equipped by Jesus to discharge this duty. There is a fearful and sometimes deadly pride that imagines that though all others should stumble, we will not. We are the ones who can dabble with error, we are the ones who can toy with a lie, we are the ones who can lie down with scorpions and play with serpents and come away unscathed. Do not be fools, for your souls' sakes! If a faithful man of God warns you to keep from poisonous untruth, then do not tempt God by making a game of approaching it. If you would be safe, keep far from those spiritual minefields that true pastors have taped off, and do not go trespassing into such places. If you wander there, it is possible that you will, by God's grace, escape alive, but you may lose a limb or carry some other injury as a result that will make you limp all the way to heaven. Heed the truth taught and the warnings issued: let him who thinks he stands take heed lest he fall (1 Cor. 10:12).

FELLOW PASTOR

Paul knew that his meeting with the Ephesian elders recorded in Acts 20 would be the last time they saw his face, so he spoke soberly and plainly:

> Wherefore I take you to record this day, that I am pure from the blood of all men. For I have not shunned to declare unto you all the counsel of God. Take heed therefore unto yourselves, and to all the flock, over the which the Holy Ghost hath made you overseers, to feed the church of God, which he hath purchased with his own blood. For I know this, that after my departing shall grievous wolves enter in among you, not sparing the flock. Also of your own selves shall men arise, speaking perverse things, to draw away disciples after them. Therefore watch, and remember, that by the space of three years I ceased not to warn every one night and day with tears. And now, brethren, I commend you to God, and to the word of his grace, which is able to build you up, and to give you an inheritance among all them which are sanctified. (Acts 20:26–32)

God has called you to be a watchman over His flock. A ministry of warning is part of your calling as a shepherd of the congregation. An elder is an overseer, not a man oblivious to the diseases that might be infecting the people entrusted to his care. Not only are we called to live holy lives before our people and to preach God's truth to them, we are also called to defend them when trouble is at hand. We must "be able by sound doctrine both to exhort and to convince the gainsayers" (Titus 1:9).

Think again of David's testimony as he stood ready to do battle with Goliath:

> And Saul said to David, Thou art not able to go against this Philistine to fight with him: for thou art but a youth, and he a man of war from his youth. And David said unto Saul, Thy servant kept his father's sheep, and there came a lion, and a bear, and took a lamb out of the flock: and I went out after him, and smote him, and delivered it out of his mouth:

and when he arose against me, I caught him by his beard, and smote him, and slew him. Thy servant slew both the lion and the bear: and this uncircumcised Philistine shall be as one of them, seeing he hath defied the armies of the living God. (1 Sam. 17:33–36)

If David cared and risked so much for the sheep of his father's flock, how much more should you be actively engaged in protecting God's true sheep that are under your care? If for mere animals David was ready to give his life to secure theirs, and if for the sake of God's flock the Good and Great Shepherd has already laid down His life to redeem them, then what are you willing to do for never dying souls?

Consider the stewardship that has been given to you. The people for whom you care are God's sheep entrusted to you. May it never be said of them what was said of Israel of old by God Himself: "And they were scattered, because there is no shepherd: and they became meat to all the beasts of the field, when they were scattered. My sheep wandered through all the mountains, and upon every high hill: yea, my flock was scattered upon all the face of the earth, and none did search or seek after them" (Ezek. 34:5–6).

We need to be proactive and vigilant in this matter. False teachers are not a hypothetical danger—they are a present threat, and they are bombarding the saints constantly. Remember too that it is not so much the obvious charlatans and preposterous frauds that need to be warned against as those who come with persuasive words, sounding right and seeming right without being right and drawing the saints off the straight and narrow way.

What, then, must we do?

First, *we must guard our own hearts*. Before we are Christian ministers, we are Christian men, and we cannot be effective in anything unless we ourselves are firmly anchored upon Christ the Rock. As you would counsel others to walk closely with Christ, so walk closely with Him yourself. Never get to the point where you read your Bible as a minister rather than as a man, where you read it as a professional sermonizer rather than a saved sinner called to teach others also. Let Christ have first place in your heart. In all your seeking, seek Him above all.

Let the bulk of your study be in the truth as it is in Jesus. The shepherd of the flock, generally speaking, does not go looking for wolves, but he does watch for their approach. You do not need to go hunting error—it will come hunting you and your flock, and you must simply be ready to respond when it does.

Keep in close contact with other faithful shepherds, men with a track record of careful concern for their sheep. Cultivate relationships with "old hands" who have fought off the predators during their ministries. Seek out friends who are wise, faithful, honest, and courageous enough to address you should you begin to veer from the truth. Open your heart and your ear to such men as these. If you are wrestling with matters and feel yourself possibly stepping out into space, make sure you have a man to hold the rope who is willing and able to haul you in if you begin to lose your footing.

Hold fast to the old paths; they are safe for travel. Do not despise the wisdom of those who have gone before. Do not set out to be the man who reinvents the wheel, the man who boasts of doing what none have done before, treating what none have treated before, going where none have gone before. If you do that, the chances are that you may be departing from the ways that men of God have marked out over generations of faithful shepherding, ways that weave among dangers and snares and take the sheep safely to green pastures. Commit yourself to studying the great statements and confessions of historic Reformed Christianity: the ancient creeds, the Heidelberg Confession, the Canons of Dort, the Belgic Confession, the Westminster Standards, including the daughters of the Westminster Confession—the Savoy Declaration and the Second London Confession of Faith. These are tried and trusted timekeepers that master watchmakers have checked against the atomic clock of Scripture itself, and they can be relied upon to keep you walking in time with God.

Furthermore, *we must preach positive truth.* The structure of Paul's letter is no accident. He has spent the bulk of his introduction turning the multifaceted gem of Christ crucified so that the light of the Spirit falls upon Him to best advantage. Paul knows that this is the best way to prevent error from creeping into the church. Two truths should grip us as pastors: first, where the true knowledge of Christ declines, declension and debilitation follow, and room is made for superstition, ritual, mysticism, and numerous other follies; second, positive truth prevents error's grip—clear views of Christ are a shield against deceptive rhetoric and the only means to spiritual vitality, so Paul prays for and pursues strong, united, and assured hearts. And so should you and I:

> I charge thee therefore before God, and the Lord Jesus Christ, who shall judge the quick and the dead at his appearing and his kingdom; preach the word; be instant in season, out of season; reprove, rebuke, exhort with all longsuffering and doctrine. For the time will come when they will not endure sound doctrine; but after their own lusts shall they heap to themselves teachers, having itching ears; and they shall turn away their ears from the truth, and shall be turned unto fables. But watch thou in all things, endure afflictions, do the work of an evangelist, make full proof of thy ministry. (2 Tim. 4:1–5)

This is a sober charge indeed: before God and the Lord Jesus Christ and in the light of the coming judgment, "Preach the Word!" Let us so hold Christ before our people that, under God, we may say that they were given no reason to desire anything else, given no suggestion that there was satisfaction of soul to be found anywhere else, offered no possibility that salvation was to be found in any other name.

Third, *we must be aware of enemy activity*. Paul says in 2 Corinthians 2:11 that "we are not ignorant of [Satan's] devices."[15] New heretics are constantly regurgitating old errors, repainting Satan's old mantraps in gaudy colors and decking out his snares for the unsuspecting believer today. Heresies are constantly undermining God's people, where they are allowed to do so. We need to know the false teachers and their false teachings as they are brought to bear upon our own flocks. We are not called to be walking encyclopedias of heresy; we are called to defend and feed our particular flocks. We are not called upon to be wolf hunters but rather true shepherds, and that involves keeping off the wolves when they come. We must fight the wolves threatening our particular sheep, not the ones threatening someone else's flock. We must beware of jumping on bandwagons. There is no necessary value in assaulting the wolves that have been snatching sheep on the next range of hills while ignoring the pack creeping up on the lambs of your own flock. We must, then, neither be locked in our studies nor glued to our telescopes, but rather among our sheep, knowing their environment, appetites, diets, and predilections. If need be, there are books, journals, and periodicals that will help us to identify and address false teachings that we must face. There are ministries and organizations that have this as a specific focus, and they can offer some assistance to the pastor seeking to be faithful in this regard.[16]

But let us never cease to take care when handling spiritual poison. Know your enemy, by all means, but do not cultivate his acquaintance. It is an agonizing thing to see men studying for the pastoral ministry mixing bedtime cocktails out of the poisonous novelties of the present age, all too often the same toxins that have always afflicted the body of Christ, merely rebranded for the twenty-first century. It is horrible to see men who, while setting out to establish churches or

---

15. Here again we suggest Puritan treatments of such principles, among them Thomas Brooks's *Precious Remedies against Satan's Devices*, William Gurnall's *The Christian in Complete Armour*, John Downame's *The Christian Warfare*, or Richard Gilpin's *Satan's Temptations (Daemonologia Sacra)*, not to mention John Owen on temptation to and mortification of sin. Several of these have been modernized or heavily employed in more recent treatments of this topic.

16. Here we would suggest Alpha and Omega Ministries (http://aomin.org), the *Christian Research Journal* (http://www.equip.org), *World* magazine (http://www.worldmag.com), and similar generally balanced and reliable guides.

revitalize languishing saints, begin lusting after the latest theological glamour models, only to find that their way leads down to death. It is terrible to watch men with a reputation for reliability begin to veer off the right way, perhaps having the pastoral equivalent of the so-called midlife crisis, developing an itch for novelty, or suddenly succumbing, if not to some crushing temptation, then perhaps to some insidious teaching.

Fourth, *we must not shirk our responsibility.* Pastors are called to lead the people of God and keep them from danger, not to wander after them into it (although he might follow them to rescue them, if need be). Our Lord said of the true Shepherd of the sheep, that "when he putteth forth his own sheep, he goeth before them, and the sheep follow him: for they know his voice" (John 10:4). He is our model here. Pastors must be willing to stand between their people and the enemies that would attack them. We must do all that we can to see that they are not bewitched by siren voices and deluded by persuasive words. When we find that one or another has begun to be drawn out of the way, we need to be willing to go after the straying sheep and, God helping us, bring them back, however much butting and kicking we may be subjected to in the rescue mission.

Let us be clear: we are not at all advocating that the pulpit should become a platform for bombastic ranting and raving on a weekly basis against this false doctrine and that pernicious cult. Rather, as particular false teaching begins to intrude and false teachers begin to circle our particular flock, we must rise up to warn our people earnestly and faithfully.

Those warnings must come from an evident heart of love. As pastors (and as parents or true friends or evangelists), we would do well to learn this lesson from Christ and from His apostle. We must cultivate not merely the appearance of concern and affection, but its reality, expressed in what we say and what we do, in order that people may know we are earnest and not misconstrue our motives and intentions. In addressing the flock, we must not be blind to what is good and pleasant any more than we can ignore what is bad and threatening. We must not panic the sheep by harangues and broadsides. Where there is good order and steadfast faith, we can offer encouragements to stand firm and hold fast, even while we reveal the real dangers that stand against us. Such exposure of falsehood must be done in a godly manner. It is not a matter of glee and delight as we whip off the mask of yet another wolf in sheep's clothing. Neither is it a matter of vindictiveness, of gloating over another fool caught in his folly. It should never appear to be so: "And the servant of the Lord must not strive; but be gentle unto all men, apt to teach, patient, in meekness instructing those that oppose themselves; if God peradventure will give them repentance to the acknowledging of the truth; and that they may recover themselves out of the snare of the devil, who are taken captive by him at his will" (2 Tim. 2:24–26).

Nevertheless, love for God and His people demands courage to be clear and pointed, courage to excise the cancer of error wherever it has taken hold. We must love people enough to cut when cutting is required. Let no one be able to claim that he was not given plain warning when plain warning was required. Paul was ready to identify Hymenaeus, Alexander, and Philetus by name; John was ready to point out vicious Diotrephes as well as gracious Demetrius. At the same time, the apostles and their cohorts could be more general: "They went out from us, but they were not of us; for if they had been of us, they would no doubt have continued with us: but they went out, that they might be made manifest that they were not all of us" (1 John 2:19). John, like Peter and Jude and Paul, sometimes gives enough information to identify the kind of people and their type of error without needing or perhaps being able to name names. The distinctive features of false teaching, as well as the known identities of false teachers, were readily made plain.

The apostles all made it their aim to have the same testimony: "Wherefore I take you to record this day, that I am pure from the blood of all men" (Acts 20:26). Every faithful pastor must be able to say the same.

Finally, *we must pray for our people*. We cannot save them, nor in ourselves keep them safe and secure. Samuel's words to the children of Israel should be true of us regarding our congregations: "Moreover as for me, God forbid that I should sin against the LORD in ceasing to pray for you: but I will teach you the good and the right way" (1 Sam. 12:23). The saints of God whom we serve face many trials and tribulations. It is God's grace in Christ that has brought them safe thus far through dangers, toils, and snares and God's grace in Christ that will lead them and us home to glory. We may be the appointed means for defending their spiritual security, but we are God's stewards and their servants for Christ's sake. It is only as we call upon God for sufficient grace for our duties and the sovereign exercise of His saving and sanctifying power that we shall be able to discharge our calling with the same commitment and character as the apostle Paul: "Now the God of peace, that brought again from the dead our Lord Jesus, that great shepherd of the sheep, through the blood of the everlasting covenant, make you perfect in every good work to do his will, working in you that which is wellpleasing in his sight, through Jesus Christ; to whom be glory for ever and ever. Amen" (Heb. 13:20–21).

EPILOGUE

And as [this doctrine that Christ is the great Prophet and Teacher of the church] will serve us for a test of doctrines, so it serves for a test of ministers; and hence you may judge who are authorized and sent by Christ the great Prophet, to declare his will to men. Surely those whom he sends have his Spirit in their hearts, as well as his words in their mouths. And according to the measures of grace received, they faithfully endeavour to fulfil their ministry for Christ, as Christ did for his Father: "As my Father has sent me (saith Christ) so send I you," John xx.21. They take Christ for their pattern in the whole course of their ministration, and are such as sincerely endeavour to imitate the great Shepherd.[1]

—John Flavel

We have tried to paint a portrait of Paul for you. We have sketched him with a Scripture pencil from Colossians and sought to block in that sketch with the rich colors of Paul's character and attitude drawn from other portions of God's Word. We have traced his testimony, from the joy he experienced in his sufferings for the church to the joy he expressed at the faithfulness of the church. We have seen that the original on which Paul modeled himself is our Savior, Jesus Christ, and we have seen the perfect lines and profound colors of Christ the Lord often swimming before our eyes as we have considered His faithful servant.

In his letter to the church of Christ in Colosse, Paul has opened a window into his own heart. He has shown pastors what they ought to be, in terms of calling,

---

1. John Flavel, "The Fountain of Life" in *Works* (Edinburgh: Banner of Truth, 1968), 1:128.

character, commitment, and concerns. He has shown us their tools, their task, and their toil. He has written a divinely inspired manual for men of God to follow. He has painted a picture, drawn from his own life, of how pastors ought to be.

He has also shown local churches the kind of men that they ought to be praying for. That is, he has shown them how they ought to pray for the molding of the pastors they already have while also showing them for what kind of men they ought to beg the Lord as they seek out those to whom they will commit the care of their souls, under God. He has demonstrated the kind of ministry that true children of God should pursue and prize.

Thank you for taking the time to consider this portrait of Paul. We invite you to do so often, from the pages of Scripture, from the works of old masters, and—if it is helpful—from the pages of this book.

In doing so, we are like children staring up at the picture of a truly great man, a man who, for all his graces and gifts, nevertheless knew himself to be the least of the apostles, less than the least of all the saints, and the chief of sinners. We see in him a man who was formed by God's sovereign purpose and called in accordance with His sovereign grace to preach the Lord Jesus, and, in doing so, to show pastors and preachers what it means to follow in the footsteps of the crucified Christ.

Paul's portrait also has the qualities of a mirror. In it, we can see our own reflections and compare them to lines and colors of apostolic ministry. We may be boys still, but do we begin to see the man? If the mature Paul is the flower in bloom, is our life at least showing the bud? If such a man is the fruit, are the seeds being sown in us? Can you see the man that your pastor is becoming? Do you see a picture of the kind of man that you want to care for your soul?

Fellow pastor, is this, then, the man that you are—or are at least becoming? Is this what you long to be? Fellow Christian, do you, in the kindness of the risen Christ, already have such a man over you in the Lord? Is this the man you will set out to identify if you are in need of a pastor and preacher to watch over you?

Pray that only ministers modeled on Paul would serve Christ's church throughout the world. Seek from God great discernment to identify only such men for the office of the elder. Anticipate great joy when the risen and glorified Head of the church lovingly grants such gifts to His congregations. If you are a pastor of the flock, or seeking to be one, pray for grace even more than for gifts, that you might nobly and humbly fulfill the high calling that the Word of God places upon you. Seek and cultivate ever increasing measures of Paul's Christlike spirit.

Men such as these commend the gospel of God's grace. Men such as these do good to God's redeemed people. Men such as these set out to bring glory, honor, and praise to God's most precious son, Jesus Christ our living Lord, and are—by His Spirit—equipped and enabled to do so. May the Lord raise up such men to the praise of His glorious grace!

"Now unto him that is able to do exceeding abundantly above all that we ask or think, according to the power that worketh in us, unto him be glory in the church by Christ Jesus throughout all ages, world without end. Amen" (Eph. 3:20–21).

DATE DUE

The Library Store   #47-0103